Perfect Da

TENERIFE
LA GOMERA

Travel with
Insider
Tips

MARCO POLO

www.marco-polo.com

Contents

For chapters: see inside front cover

TOP 10

Not to be missed!
Our TOP 10 hits – from the absolute No. 1 to No. 10 – help you plan your tour of the most important sights.

1 PARQUE NACIONAL DEL TEIDE ➤ 122

Towering over the volcanic landscape of the national park is the Pico del Teide, the highest mountain in Spain (3,718m/12,200ft, photo). The cable car takes you up to 3,550m (11,650ft) and, if you wish, you can then climb up to the summit.

2 LA LAGUNA ➤ 74

As you stroll through the historic centre of this World Heritage Site, the cathedral, churches and cloisters are a clear reminder of Tenerife's colonial past.

3 ICOD DE LOS VINOS ➤ 92

An enormous dragon tree is this small wine town's main attraction. Just to the north, in the parish church, you can admire an imposing silver cross.

4 MASCA ➤ 94

The gorge that opens up by this picturesque mountain village in the Teno Mountains promises fit outdoor enthusiasts a spectacular experience.

5 PUERTO DE LA CRUZ ➤ 96

This popular holiday destination ranks highly for its attractive old town centre, and also for the Lago Martiánez swimming complex, designed by César Manrique, in which water activities and art flow harmoniously together.

6 LA OROTAVA ➤ 100

Even the famous German naturalist and explorer Alexander von Humboldt could not resist the charm of the historic district's streets and alleys.

7 SAN ANDRÉS ➤ 52

People from Santa Cruz love the fish restaurants here. What is more, Tenerife's most beautiful palm-fringed beach can be found on the Playa de las Teresitas.

8 MONTAÑAS DE ANAGA ➤ 77

Tenerife's hiking paradise offers a captivating mix of unspoilt laurel forests, panoramic views and remote mountain villages.

9 VALLE GRAN REY ➤ 150

A wonderful valley on La Gomera with beautifully laid terraces, palm groves and a touch of flower power.

10 PLAZA DE ESPAÑA & PLAZA DE LA CANDELARIA ➤ 54

These interlocking squares were given a makeover by London's Tate Modern architects Herzog & de Meuron; their saltwater lake is particularly impressive.

THAT TENERIFFA & LA GOMERA

Find out what makes the island tick, experience its unique flair – just like the Tinerfeños themselves.

LIGHT AND DARK

You are spoilt for choice as far as Tenerife's beaches are concerned. Of course on a volcanic island, dark sand is to be expected and is a reminder of the island's fiery birth. **Playa de la Arena** (➤ 108) on the sun-kissed west coast is one example, although the Atlantic's pounding waves can make bathing a bit of a whirl. By contrast, on the **Playa de las Teresitas** (➤ 52) inviting golden yellow beaches await you, and green patches of colour in the form of fan palms provide welcome shade. Here, too, breakwaters ensure that swimming is completely safe.

MOJO AND PAPAS ARRUGADAS

Really Canarian: Gourmets will not always find everything to their taste on Tenerife, but grilled fish served with *papas arrugadas* (wrinkled potatoes) and a green *mojo* sauce is a real highlight. The Canarian "national dish" tastes best somewhere on the waterfront, for example in **Restaurante Pancho** (➤ 114) on the Playa de la Arena. And, of course, you also eat the potato skin studded with tiny salt crystals.

THE ISLAND FROM ABOVE

Miradores is the name given to all the vantage points on Tenerife from which you can see something. There are a lot of these viewing points all over the island. The most spectacular panorama is offered on the **Pico del Teide** (➤ 126), from which you have a bird's eye view of the whole island. In just eight minutes, you can be comfortably whizzed up to 3,550m (11,650ft) in the cable car.

GUANTANAMERA

Regardless the season, Puerto de la Cruz's **Plaza del Charco** (➤ 98) in the old town is *the* place to meet. On the rectangular-shaped square surrounded by terrace restaurants, locals mingle with the tourists, children run about in the little play area, and popular evergreen music is provided every evening by the band in Café Dinámico.

FEELING

Sun-kissed: beach life on the Playa de las Teresitas by San Andrés

That Tenerife & La Gomera Feeling

In the Teide National Park you will feel like you have landed in some bizarre lunar landscape.

AT THE FOOT OF THE VOLCANO

On Tenerife, you just have to go hiking. That doesn't mean you have to rush out and climb to the summit of the Pico del Teide (3718m/12,200ft), there are plenty of satisfying tours at the base of this eye-catching volcanic cone. One attractive route gently undulates up and down to the **rock face of the Fortaleza** (► 152). June is the best time for this walk; that is when the red *echium plantagineum* (also known as **viper's bugloss)** flowers. Spectacular weather conditions also mean that you are often walking high above the trade wind's layer of cloud, and the sky is bright blue.

LUNAR LANDSCAPE

There actually is a place that bears this name on Tenerife (*Paisaje Lunar*), but you may feel like you are on the moon in practically the entire **Teide National Park** (► 122). This is not true in June, however, when during the Canarian mountain spring the bizarre volcanic crater landscape comes to life, and Teide gorse and red Teide viper's bugloss transform the region into a carpet of yellow and red blossoms.

DRINKS ON THE PROMENADE

Admittedly the name: **Café Paris** (Puerto de la Cruz, Avenida Colón s/n, daily from 9–11) is not exactly typically Canarian, but the café itself definitely is. In the morning, you can order breakfast and in the afternoon white coffee and a piece of sugary sweet and very fattening cake. Later on in the evening you can sit on the large terrace enjoying a cocktail or the Dorado beer brewed on the island and watch the hustle and bustle on the lively seaside promenade.

The Magazine

ISLAND LIFE

On first impressions you might think that Tenerife is a chunk of Britain teleported to the sunshine. English breakfasts and Sunday roasts, plus Premier League football shown in sports bars are typical of Playa des las Américas and Los Cristianos.

On a clear day you can look across from Mirador Pico del Inglés at the Anaga mountains

Every year around five million non-Spanish tourists take holidays on the island. The majority are British and the second largest group is from Germany. Twenty thousand Brits live here year-round, with double that number owning holiday or second homes.

More Than Just a Tourist Enclave

Tenerife is still very much a Canarian island with a robust culture. Universidad de la Laguna is an obvious and vigorous counterbalance to euro-vacation land. The 25,000 students arriving from all across the country represent a contemporary and energetic 21st-century Spanish influence on the island. And Santa Cruz de Tenerife is an authentic Spanish city; this is one of Spain's most exciting cityscapes, and a perfect place for that most traditional of Spanish pastimes, the evening *paseo walk*.

Island(s) of Eternal Spring

On the Canary Islands, the temperatures are mild all year round; in the summer it is nowhere near as hot as places in southern Europe for example, which explains why an increasing number of Spaniards from the mainland enjoy the summer break on the Atlantic islands. For Central Europeans the Canarian "winter" is like their spring; the average daily temperature, even during the coldest month of the year in February, rarely falls below 20 degrees Celsius. On the south coast of Tenerife, you can bathe all year round.

TENERIFE FACTS

- Tenerife is the largest of the seven islands that make up the archipelago of the Islas Canarias or Canary Islands.
- The autonomous region is made up of two provinces – Santa Cruz de Tenerife (incorporating Tenerife, La Palma, La Gomera and El Hierro) and Las Palmas (incorporating Gran Canaria, Fuerteventura and Lanzarote).
- The Canary Islands have thirteen seats in the Spanish Senate (government) plus two elected by the autonomous council. Tenerife supplies three seats.
- The Canary Islands are home to 2.1 million people, of whom 906,000 live on Tenerife.
- *Tener* is the word used by the native inhabitants (the Guanches) for either "mountain" while *ife* was the word for "white". Tenerife can thus be literally translated as "white mountain".

FESTIVE FIESTAS

Tenerife's calendar bursts with fiestas of all sorts, ranging from noisy town processions to *romerías*, festive pilgrimages from a town's central church into the country, often ending at a beautifully remote rural chapel.

The exuberant Tinerfeños love to party. Enthusiasm and exuberance mark these events, which – thanks to the mild climate – generally tend to take place in the open. Religious celebrations and saints' days are indeed the most common excuse for a fiesta.

Santa Cruz Goes Mad

Carnaval is celebrated throughout Tenerife, but nowhere with the same determined madness as in the capital, Santa Cruz. Although the festivities go on for three weeks in February, the core events and spectacular parades of scantily clad dancers last for a week. Only the craziness of Rio de Janeiro outdoes the Tenerife show, which ends six weeks before Easter.

Each year the organisers choose a theme. After the first few days of mask competitions, concerts, parades, children's events and heats for the election of the Carnival Queen *(Reina del Carnaval)*, the serious celebrations begin with the gala night for the election of the queen, usually on a Wednesday night. The following Friday the grand parade takes place and on the Wednesday after is the "burial of the sardine", when a procession takes a symbolic sardine around town for burial, marking the end of Carnaval and the countdown to the reawakening of spring. The long nights of dancing continue until the end of the following weekend. Several other traditional festivities are well worth a visit. Almost half the island is out on the streets of the island's many towns during the Easter week and the Feast of Corpus Christi. The traditional-style costumes and attire seen at the *fiestas* are usually modern creations. The only original elements of the Canarian national costumes are the wide-rimmed hats and the skirts with a petticoat.

"Only the craziness of Rio de Janeiro outdoes the Tenerife show"

Overwhelming spectacle: Selection of the carnival king in Santa Cruz de Tenerife

Traditional dress is often worn at fiestas

May

Los Realejos: Romería de San Isidro Labrador

The earliest records referring to this festive pilgrimage date back to 1676. In those days farmers from around Los Realejos, on the outskirts of Puerto de la Cruz, would gather to lead ox-driven carts through the steep streets of town. Nowadays the gaily decorated carts are hauled around on the back of trucks after a ceremony in honour of San Isidro, the patron saint of farmers.

June

La Orotava: Octava de Corpus Cristi – Fiesta de las Alfombras

The citizens of La Orotava go to huge lengths to celebrate Corpus Christi (the Thursday following the eighth Sunday after Easter). Apart from services and processions, the high point is the unveiling of remarkable carpets made from flower petals and volcanic sands. For days before the event, the town keeps busy designing the carpets and peeling petals from countless flowers to fill them in. The most spectacular of the carpets is made in the Plaza del Ayuntamiento in front of the town hall. Tonnes of different coloured sands from the Circo de las Cañadas mountain chain are used to compose a Biblical triptych in the square.

June

La Orotava: Romería de San Isidro Labrador y Santa María de la Cabeza

The Sunday after Corpus Christi, La Orotava takes to the streets for this colourful parade. As in Los Realejos, there is a centuries-old tradition among local farmers of organising a celebration for San Isidro. Today the festivities retain all the appearance of a country affair, with cow-drawn carts and farmers dressed as magicians.

July

La Laguna: Romería de San Benito Abad

This procession features seven women representing the seven islands of the archipelago. Followed by a colourful array of people, floats, carts, dancing around maypoles and general noisy chaos, they liven up the decorated streets of La Laguna for a day.

August

Garachico: Romería de San Roque

When plague struck Garachico and the surrounding area in the

17th century, the people appealed for help from the saint of plague victims, the 14th-century French St Roch, revered for having devoted himself to bringing succour to plague victims in Italy and southern France. Centuries later, the people of Garachico still converge once a year on the rural chapel of San Roque, outside Garachico, to transport an image of the saint to the Iglesia de Santa Ana in Garachico, where Mass is celebrated. Then the people of the town and farmers, accompanied by bands, carts and flocks of farm animals, engage in a procession to take San Roque back to his chapel.

Candelaria: Fiesta de Nuestra Señora de la Candelaria (Assumption)
Though the official feast day of Nuestra Señora de la Candelaria is 2 February, it has long been celebrated in August too. Pilgrims converge on foot on Candelaria and on 14 August a grand ceremony takes place in Plaza de la Basílica to commemorate the legendary apparition of the miraculous statue of the Virgin Mary to the Guanches (➤ 134). This is followed by a procession to the nearby Pozo de la Virgen (Virgin's Well), where fireworks are lit. On 15 August a big Mass is held in front of the basilica, with another noisy procession.

30 November

Puerto de la Cruz and Icod de los Vinos: Festividad de San Andrés
No one has worked out what St Andrew has to do with drinking, but on the eve of his feast day the wine cellars of Tenerife throw open their doors to ring in the year's new wines. In some towns, like Puerto de la Cruz (➤ 96) and Icod de los Vinos (➤ 92), they celebrate in a loud manner, with parades.

During the festivities at Corpus Christi in Orotava: Who is the prettiest?

The Land of the **Guanches**

In May 1493, a Spanish force of 1,000 infantry and 150 horses landed on Tenerife near present-day Santa Cruz. Led by Alonso Fernández de Lugo, their mission was to conquer the last of the seven Canary Islands.

Islanders dressed as Guanches at the Festival of the Virgin of El Socorro in Güimar, in the north east of Tenerife

The other six had been taken since 1402 for the Spanish crown after a series of battles and sieges, some of which had lasted for many years. The story of the island's conquest had so far been a predictably sad tale of trickery, massacre, enslavement and exile with the Spaniards being remarkably ineffectual on occasion in the face of the guerrilla tactics of the islanders who were only armed with spears and stones. Earlier landings on Tenerife had proven fruitless, but the Europeans had been able to hang around long enough to cast an eye over the locals, by whom they were clearly impressed. Reports described them as tall, blond and blue-eyed. They called themselves Guanches, from *guan* (man) and *che*, a word that referred to Mount Teide. The Guanches were thus the "People of Teide" (or by extension of Tenerife). Subsequently the name Guanche came to be applied to the natives of all the islands, although they were divided into many different tribes.

Who were the Guanches and where did they come from? Carbon-dating of archaeological finds suggests the islands were inhabited from at least 200BC. It appears most likely that the islanders' ancestors migrated from North Africa, a mere 100km (62mi) east. Certain language fragments still found in many place names indicate that the original Canarian inhabitants descended from the Berbers. Why the people left North Africa is not known; one possibility might have the increasing spread of the Sahara desert.

The Guanches led a primitive Stone Age existence, mostly living in caves and subsisting by a combination of hunting, herding and simple farming. The main sources of food were goats and fish. Barley was ground and toasted to form *gofio*, a basic staple still eaten today. Tools and weapons were made of wood, stone and bone. Simple dugouts were used to skirt the coast and, on occasion, to travel to the other islands. The nine separate fiefs on Tenerife were each ruled by a *mencey* (chief) and the *taoro* (council of nobles).

First Contact and Guanche Downfall

The first European contact with the Guanches probably came in the late 13th century. One missionary expedition is recorded in 1341, although earlier contacts had probably been made before by fortune-hunters looking for the Atlantic outlet of the fabled African Río de Oro, along which huge quantities of the precious metal were supposedly transported.

The feuds between the nine tribes proved to be the Guanches' undoing. It seems unlikely they had not heard of the disasters that had befallen their cousins on the other islands, and yet at least two *menceys* sided with the invaders. The Spaniards' most implacable adversary was *mencey* Bencomo, backed by three others. In spring 1494 de Lugo launched his first armed attack, an unmitigated disaster, and it was more than two years before the Guanches surrendered – weakened more by a mysterious epidemic than cowed by Spanish arms.

In the following decades some Guanches, living in the more remote parts of the island, continued low-level guerrilla resistance, but within two centuries they had been brought to heel. A few generations after the conquest they had largely assimilated with their conquerors. All that remains today are many curious place names.

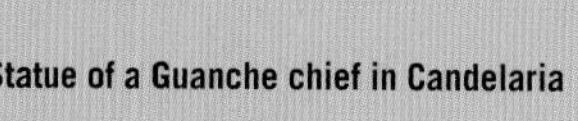

Statue of a Guanche chief in Candelaria

FREAKY FLOWERS

In spite of the wholesale felling of forests over the centuries and the rapid spread of urban and tourist development across the island, Tenerife can still claim to be extraordinarily rich in flora, with some 1,400 species of plants.

Canary bell-flower *(canarina canariensis)* in the Anaga Mountains

This is, in part, a result of the climate, for the island is said to enjoy as many as 50 distinct microclimates. No fewer than 140 species are endemic to the island, and about 200 to the archipelago. Come in late winter and early spring and you can see the native plants and trees of Tenerife at their vivacious, colourful best.

Trees

Among the trees, the dragon tree *(drago)* is emblematic. It is an odd beast. From a long smooth trunk, branches poke out at the top like fat sausages from which long, scary-looking leaves stand on end.

Another important tree is the laurel, found in parts of north-east Tenerife and in the Garajonay National Park on La Gomera (► 156). Often covered in lichen and enveloped in mist, these laurel woods are about all that remain of pre-Ice-Age forests. It is hard to imagine that millions of years ago much of the Mediterranean was covered in extensive laurel forests like these. More common than either the dragon or the laurel is the Canary pine, whose lumber goes into many of the balconies, doors and window frames in traditional island housing.

Flowers

Next to the dragon tree, the best-known floral symbol is the blood red *tajinaste rojo* (Teide Vipers Bugloss). It is found at altitudes of 2,000–2,500m (6,560–8,200ft) near Mount Teide. Its long, upright spike covered in little red flowers is instantly recognisable (mid-spring to early summer). Other flowers that flourish in the Teide National Park (► 122) include the Teide straw *(cytisus supranubius)*, with yellow flowers, and the pink Teide scabious *(pterocephalus dumetorum)*. An odd plant you may mistakenly take for a kind of cactus is the curious *cardón* (candelabra spurge). Clusters of slender, pale green, tube-like stems grow up to 3m (10ft) high and are covered in short spikes. It is most common in semi-arid locations. In the spring the bright yellow Canary Buttercup *(ranunculus cortusifolius) appears.* A winter bloomer is the lovely Canary bell-flower, with reddish-orange flowers. Many other varieties of plants and flowers grow in different parts of the island, and the laurel forest in the Anaga Mountains is a treasure trove for botanists.

***Strelitzia reginae* are commonly known as Bird of Paradise flowers**

PIRATES, PRIVATEERS AND A BAD DAY FOR LORD NELSON

On 30 April, 1657, Admiral Robert Blake appeared with a fleet of 33 warships off the coast of Santa Cruz. Spain and England were at war, and Blake was ordered to capture a bullion fleet due to anchor in the town's port.

From the earliest days of the *Conquista* of Latin America, the English had taken an interest in the fleets that poured America's mineral wealth into Spain's coffers. In 1572, Queen Elizabeth I awarded Sir Francis Drake a commission as a privateer.

A Privateer Plots Revenge

England backed Protestant Holland in its rebellion against Catholic Spain and Drake relished the chance to avenge some rough treatment he had received four years earlier from the Spaniards in the Caribbean. This he set about doing with some success, raiding bullion ships all over the Atlantic and several times threatening the Canary Islands, the Spanish ships' main port of call.

Privateer or Pirate?

As far as Madrid was concerned Drake and Blake were pirates. As Blake's fleet closed on Santa Cruz, the town opened fire. The English and Spanish versions of the outcome differ. Blake claimed to have sent the bulk of the Spanish ships to the bottom of the sea, but Madrid declared a victory, with 200 English seamen killed or wounded, and only five Spanish casualties. Santa Cruz even added a lion to its coat-of-arms as a pat on the back. In November 1706 the English were back, this time with Admiral Jennings as their leader, who, with 13 warships, attempted a landing at Santa Cruz. He was forced to withdraw and Santa Cruz got another lion.

Nelson Portrait (coloured engraving, around 1840)

(H)armless?

The young Rear Admiral Horatio Nelson was on patrol in the Mediterranean in early 1797 when he was instructed to seize Santa Cruz. With a squadron of eight vessels he arrived on 22 July. Two days later he landed his troops, but after just one night it was clear he had failed, despite the might of more than 390 cannon fired on the land batteries by his ships. The bitterness of failure was compounded by a grapeshot wound to his right arm, which surgeons were obliged to amputate.

> "The British weighed anchor and quietly slipped away"

The Spaniards were exultant but gracious. British wounded were treated and returned to their ships, although their captured ensigns (still in the Museo Militar in Santa Cruz, ➤63) were not. On 26 July, the British weighed anchor and quietly slipped away. Santa Cruz even magnanimously named a street after Admiral Nelson, who earned fame and a place in the history books after his victory at the Battle of Trafalgar in 1805.

Left: Religious service on one of Lord Nelson's ships (coloured aquatint, not dated)

Get Active!

Bored with lazing around on the beach? Tenerife has plenty of distractions if you want to get active. It's a great place to try a new sport or two and has some pretty unusual traditional pastimes that you may want to sit out!

Scuba Diving

Tenerife's position on the edge of the deep ocean trenches attracts an amazing array of species that keeps even the most avid divers happy. You can see for example parrot fish, tuna, rays, barracudas, mantas and occasionally, if you are lucky, dolphins or whales. The volcanic rock formations make Tenerife a spectacular area to dive. You can find diving centres with schools and equipment for rent in all of the larger resorts (➤ "Where to Be Entertained?" in the chapters on the individual areas.)

Windsurfing & Kitesurfing

Windsurfing is a popular sport along Tenerife's shores. The vast coastal offshore shallows at El Médano in the south-east of Tenerife offer particularly ideal conditions. The north-east trade wind blows almost all year round. Experts regularly hold their world cup events here. Beginners can do a course at one of the windsurfing or kitesurfing schools (e.g. Surf Center Playa Sur. Tel. 922/176-688; www.surfcenter.el-medano.com).

Windsurfing conditions around the islands are excellent

Good prospects: Ballesteros Buenavista Golf Course in the north-west of Tenerife

Golf

Year-round sunshine and warm temperatures are ideal conditions for golf. Tenerife has a choice of nine courses. José "Pepe" Gancedo, a successful amateur golfer – six times Spanish champion – has built a solid reputation as a course designer. Christened the "Picasso of golf course design" for his avant-garde ideas, he is architect of the Golf des Sur and the Costa Adeje courses. One of the best courses is the 18-hole Buenavista Golf course in the north-west of the island, which was designed by Spanish professional golfer Severiano Ballesterosim.

Weird Wrestling

The island's inhabitants, the Guanches, were keen warriors. To keep fit, the men sparred in bouts of strength and skill, a form of which has survived to this day. Known as *lucha canaria* (Canarian wrestling), it has a popular following. Teams of up to 12 wrestlers compete in tag-team wrestling: a cross between Greco-Roman and sumo wrestling. The key rule is that no part of the body but the soles of the feet may touch the ground. The first to break this rule loses. To find out where to see matches, contact the tourist office.

Juego del Palo

The Guanches had several variants of the *juego del palo* ("stick game") including one where, armed with heavy staffs and stones, tribal opponents attempted to smash each other's bones. A modern version you might see at *fiestas* is more a trial of skill using 2m (6.5ft) long poles.

Watch out for the WHALES

Tenerife is one of the best places in the world to go whale watching – whatever the time of year. A huge array of about 25 marine species of these huge creatures can be espied in the waters around the coast.

Pilot Whales are the most common species that you are likely to see. A large family pod has settled permanently around southern Tenerife; sightings of mothers and babies or nursery groups are a regular occurrence and particularly heart-lifting. Just as exciting are Bottlenose Dolphin encounters. These sociable creatures often dive in and out of the bow wake as boats travel along. There's a large population living year-round off Los Gigantes,

Whale-watching opportunities are available all year round

though there are also regular sightings of groups of smaller, faster, Spotted Dolphin, and Stripped Dolphin.

However, you may be lucky enough to spot something more rare. Migratory species pass through heading north in the spring to feeding grounds in polar waters, returning south in the autumn, and more than 25 species of the order *Cetacea* (the group that encompasses whales, dolphins and porpoises) have been noted in the waters around Tenerife, including Sperm Whales and Right Whales. That's almost one third of all whale and dolphin species.

Watch and Learn

Most whale-watching operations have bases along the southern coast from harbours at Los Gigantes and marinas along the Costa Adeje (► 129). Trips last around two hours and may include lunch or snacks on board. What represents an enjoyable excursion for us can be very stressful for these marine mammals. In order to stop reckless tourist boats from worrying the gentle giants as they tried to satisfy their passengers' desire for close-up shots, the Canarian government introduced rules for the tours. These stipulate that a minimum distance be maintained between the boats and the whales. The "Blue Boat" badge is meant to be a clear indication of "responsible" whale watching.

Tenerife's EXPLOSIVE HISTORY

Leaving aside fanciful ideas that the Canary Islands are all that remain of the Lost Continent of Atlantis, it appears almost certain that they are a volcanic creation, although theories about just how they were created are many.

Modern science has divided the surface of the world into a series of tectonic plates, each interlocking and tending to pull away or crush into one another. One theory suggests the Canary Islands chain was thrown up in a weak area of the Earth's crust as a result of movement between the African and American plates, possibly 20 million years ago, in the Miocene Age.

Born of the Sea like Aphrodite

All the Canary Islands are volcanic, but none quite as spectacular as Tenerife. The last major eruption was in 1798 (a smaller one occurred in 1909), when a huge gash opened up along the south-western flank of the Pico Viejo ("old peak") and spewed forth a barrage of molten magma.

Paisaje Lunar: a landscape of bizarre tuff columns in the Teide National Park

Although Mount Teide, the island's (and Spain's) highest mountain, attracts the most attention, it is just one of a series of volcanoes and fissures created along a fault line on the island millions of years ago. Mount Teide itself is a strato-volcano, a complex natural edifice that has been built up over the millennia. Strato-volcanoes are created by repeated eruptions giving off lava flows and shooting volcanic material into the air. Each eruption adds another layer and so helps build up the cone. In such volcanoes cooling magma sometimes forms a "plug" right inside the cone. In a later eruption the plug acts like a lid on a pressure cooker – when it finally blows, the explosion frequently takes much of the cone with it.

Young Mountains

Pico del Teide and its companion peaks are fairly new on the scene. It is estimated that the oldest volcanic rock formations still extant on the island go back seven million years, and include the Teno Massif in the north west (► 169) and the Anaga mountain range in the north east (► 77). Three million years ago the bulk of the activity moved to the centre, apparently creating a huge volcano. The semicircular Circo de las Cañadas mountain chain south of Mount Teide is what remains of its ancient crater, inside which Mount Teide and its companions grew during later eruptions in the past 500,000 years. This kind of massive crater, formed by the destruction of its cone, is called a caldera, and the caldera inside which Mount Teide grew is one of the biggest in the world. At 3,718m (12,195ft), Mount Teide is right up there with Vesuvius, Fujiyama and Etna.

Frozen Rivers and Remaining Volcanic Activity

Volcanoes erupt in two main ways. In the first, magma (molten material from the Earth's mantle to a maximum depth of 600km/372mi) boils up inside a single chimney, or vent. When the pressure finally forces an explosion, the magma spews up and meets the air at temperatures of anything from 700 to 1,200°C (1,292 to 2,192°F). How far it flows down the mountain side before cooling depends largely on its material make up and viscosity. Masses of more treacle-like magma flows out of the cone and flow downhill, slowing only as they cool and harden. Around the slopes of Mount Teide you will see such "frozen" rivers, some of them reaching down to the road that crosses the park.

In the second, fissured, version of a volcanic eruption, cracks open further down the mountain and the magma is forced along a subsidiary pipe from the main chimney. Mount Teide shows evidence of both types of eruption. Gases dominate volcanic eruptions. They are the first element to reach the surface and consist mainly of water vapour. Gases exiting at great speed can break up the molten rock on its way to the top and send it shooting up into the air. The resulting fragments are pyroclasts.

The weird landscape around Mount Teide is dominated by basalt. But you can also see fragments of obsidian, which look like black glass. Scoria, high in magnesium and iron, is easily recognised by its reddish tinge. It is still volcanically active, as can be testified by the fumarolas, gaseous vapour rising from points around the peak. Mount Teide could yet again reveal its uniquely devilish side.

The Teide observatory stands on the Izaña Mountain

THE WIND OF CHANGE

Music for the Future

A trip to the Canaries will never be completely climate neutral; even those who decide to take the longer journey by ship will still not arrive in Tenerife without leaving some kind of carbon print. Yet, we need to start somewhere and why not with the place we stay? In the south of Tenerife there is a pilot scheme which has drawn international interest.

Ten minutes from the international airport, on the edge of the industrial estate of Granadilla (Polígono Industrial de Granadilla, motorway exit Acceso B) is the ITER wind farm, the Technical Institute for renewable energy. In 1995, ITER entered an international architects' competition in which almost 400 architects from 38 countries took part. The goal was to design a passive house without air-conditioning and heating. Today, you can rent one of the 24 "bioclimatic" houses in the immediate vicinity of the 27 large wind turbines. The La Geria house by Spanish architect César Ruiz-Larrea won first prize. He based his idea on the method practised by

Good living in the 21st century: climate-neutral holiday home in the ITER wind farm

home owners in Lanzarote for cultivating wine. The house is in a semi-walled hollow and is thus relatively well protected from the wind and weather. This makes it possible to maintain a balanced temperature in the various rooms inside. Of all the houses, however, it is the Casa El Río by the Frenchman Morel Cedric that really stands out. In his winning design, a small water channel flows through the lounge, which is not only eye-catching, it also adds a climatic accent.

None of the 24 houses resembles the other; each is quite unique, the focus of the building material ranging from wood in one to glass or stone in the other. What they have in common is that each building recycles its service water. Solar and wind energy provides the electricity, running water comes from the site's own desalination plant, which also runs on renewable energy. The interior design is chic and trendy; designer furniture graces most of the rooms.

Measuring 89 to 114m² (960 to 1225ft²), the living area is relatively spacious and can accommodate four to six people. The revolving rotors of the wind turbines nearby create an ongoing whirr, but the majority of guests do not find the noise disturbing. It takes more time to acclimatise to the location in the approach path to the main airport on Tenerife Sur. Good soundproofing ensures that you hardly hear anything when you are inside the house at least. Many of the guests are engineers or architects, but more and more ordinary tourists are renting the houses (Casas ITER bioclimáticas, tel. 922/747-758, http://casas.iter.es; price per night for two people from approx. €100). Most of the people who stay there come from Germany.

AFTER SUNSET...

Hot days on the beaches are followed by hot nights in the resorts of Playa de las Américas and Los Cristianos.

Calm before the storm: On the Playa de las Américas night becomes day

There is plenty on offer for night owls in the resorts in South Tenerife, where many pubs, discos and karaoke bars court the holiday guests. The quality of the offer may occasionally leave something to be desired, but given the huge choice, most people should find something to their taste. The nights can be long in the north of the island as well, but relatively few foreign guests stray into the large discos in the capital of Santa Cruz. Here, the young *Tinerfeños* generally keep themselves to themselves, and enjoy dancing to Latin-American rhythms. Things also get lively in the student district of La Laguna, with its array of pubs and wine bars as well as jazz clubs.

INSIDER INFO

- At the weekends, people party until the early morning hours in the discos on Calle de Hoya in Puerto de la Cruz.
- In Playa de las Américas, the nightspots are principally concentrated around the party mile in the Centro Comercial Veronicas and Centro Comercial Starcos.
- For guests who are not quite so young, the Banana Garden in Playa de las Américas has been an established address for years and its live band creates a great atmosphere.
- On the main street by the Playa de Troya (Playa de las Américas), you will also find discos and bars for every kind of taste in music.
- Joy in Santa Cruz is the capital's long-time favourite – where the action starts around 1am and continues till dawn.

Finding Your Feet

First Two Hours

Tenerife Sur (Reina Sofía) Airport

The bigger of the two airports on Tenerife, Tenerife Sur (Reina Sofía) is in the south, 20km (12.5mi) east of Playa de las Américas.

- The airport takes almost all **international flights**, whether scheduled or charter (tel: 902/404-7 04).
- Up to **nine million** passengers pour through it every year.
- The airport **tourist information booth** (tel: 922/392-037) in the arrivals hall is open Oct–June Mon–Fri 9–9, Sat–Sun 9–5; July–Sep Mon–Fri 9–7, Sat–Sun 9–5.
- You can get **general information** on the island, as well as help with accommodation and public transport. They will point the way to buses, taxis and car-rental outlets in the airport.
- While you're here pick up a **map** of the island.

Transport from the Airport

Car Rental

- Car rental is **less expensive** compared with mainland Spain or many other European countries as the Canary Islands have special tax exemptions, which reduce the rate you pay.
- You can organise car rental **in advance** as part of your package or through most major international car-rental companies.
- To rent car you will need your **driver's licence** and must be at least 21 years old. Always have your licence, passport and car documentation with you.
- Generally you will need a **credit card** to rent a car.
- Before renting, **compare the cost of different companies**, taking into account insurance, collision damage waiver, extra passenger cover and IGIC (the local version of VAT).
- Most of the time you can get cars with **unlimited mileage** but do check the small print of the contract.
- A number of the major car-rental companies are represented at the airport near the arrivals hall. Many have offices elsewhere on Tenerife:

Avis tel: 922/392-056; www.avis.com
Europcar tel: 922/359-313; www.europcar.com
Hertz tel: 922/759-319; www.hertz.es
The largest local car-rental company is:
Cicar tel: 922/759-329; www.cicar.com

- It's useful to find out if you can rent a car in the airport and drop it off somewhere else.
- It's best to use one of the major car-rental companies as the **standard for servicing** some rental cars can be below average and there have even been reports of dangerous rental cars being allowed on the road.
- If you decide to rent a **moped** or **scooter,** you should not forget to sort out a helmet – it is obligatory to wear one.

Bus

- You can pick up public buses of **TITSA** (Transportes Interurbanos de Tenerife SA; www.titsa.com) to several destinations.
- **No 111** goes to Playa de las Américas via Los Cristianos. They run half hourly from 6:50am to 9:50pm, with three night services. They take around an hour.

- **No 111** connects to Santa Cruz de Tenerife. Departures are approximately hourly from 6:50am and the journey takes about 90 minutes, straight up the *autopista*.
- **No 343** to Puerto de la Cruz leaves several times a day and takes about one-and-a-half hours.

Taxi

- Taxis to Los Cristianos or Playa de las Américas cost about €25, but get expensive if you are trying to get to Santa Cruz de Tenerife or Puerto de la Cruz.

Tenerife Norte (Los Rodeos) Airport

The smaller Tenerife Norte (Los Rodeos) Airport in the north of the island (tel: 922/635-999) is mostly for inter-island flights and flights from mainland Spain. It is located 10km (6mi) west of Santa Cruz de Tenerife and 26km (16mi) east of Puerto de la Cruz.

Transport from the Airport

Car Rental

- See above, Tenerife Sur (Reina Sofía) Airport, for general information on car hire.

Bus

- **TITSA bus No 107** runs a service between the airport and the centre of Santa Cruz de Tenerife every two hours Monday to Friday and four services a day at the weekend, terminating at Intercambiador, the main bus station. The trip takes about 30 minutes.
- **No 108** to Icod de los Vinos runs via La Orotava every two hours and takes an hour.
- **No 102** is a little slower and goes every 30min. or so to Puerto de la Cruz.
- **Buses** are generally an inexpensive way to travel around the island.

Taxi

- You can also get a taxi to **any destination** in the north east of the island at a reasonable cost.
- Trips to Santa Cruz de Tenerife take 20 minutes and cost approximately €20–25.
- Trips to Puerto de la Cruz take 30 minutes and cost about €25.

Santa Cruz Estación Marítima (Ferry Terminal)

- The city's **ferry port** is at the north east end of town.
- Spains national ferry company, **Trasmediterránea** (tel: 902/454-645; www.trasmediterranea.es) runs ferries from Cádiz in Spain (once a week) plus a ferry service to Las Palmas de Gran Canaria (one per week), Arrecife (Lanzarote) (one per week), Puerto del Rosasio (Fuerteventura) (one per week), and Santa Cruz on La Palma (three times a week). Fred Olsen Express (tel: 902/100-107; www.fredolsen.es) operates fast ferries to Gran Canaria (Agaete).
- **Other ferry companies** operate from quays a little closer to the town centre.
- It's a 10-minute walk to the centre of town from the main terminal, the **Muelle de Ribera**, or you can get a taxi.
- Boat **tickets** are available at most travel agents or direct from ferry companies' booths in the **Muelle de Ribera** building on the waterfront.

Los Cristianos Estación Marítima (Ferry Terminal)

- This is the **main point of arrival/departure** for boats from/to La Gomera, and the westernmost islands of La Palma and El Hierro.
- There are **one or two daily ferry** connections from El Hierro and La Palma.
- The ferry terminal is a **brisk walk** from the centre of Los Cristianos, where you will find banks, a tourist office and post office.
- A short bus ride takes you further around the coast to Playa de las Américas.

La Gomera

- **Binter Canarias** (tel: 902/391-391; www.bintercanarias.com) operates daily flights between La Gomera and both airports on Tenerife and two flights per day go to Gran Canaria.
- **Fred Olsen** (tel: 902/100-107; www.fredolsen.es) runs up to five daily fast ferries (approximately €23–40) to Los Cristianos (40min), and one car ferry (80min).
- **Naviera Armas** (tel. 902/456-500; www.navieraarmas.com) provides a connection three times a day between Los Cristianos and San Sebastián on La Gomera, journey time 60 minutes (€22–44).

Island Hopping

Visiting two or three Canary Islands is ideal, in particular for people visiting the islands for the first time. Many tour operators offer holidays on more than one of the Canary Islands. For anyone who wishes to organise their own trips, there are plenty of flight and ferry connections. Gomera is not the only option for a day trip; there is also a speedboat between Santa Cruz (Tenerife) and Agaete (Gran Canaria), which only needs about an hour for the crossing. It is best to take a flight to the other islands. Combined flight and bus tours can usually be booked at the travel agencies.

Orientation

- Tenerife is the largest of the Canary Islands, covering an area of around 2,000km² (772mi²).
- It's about 130km (81-miles) long at its widest part and about 90km (56mi) north–south.
- About 300km (186mi) separate the island from the coast of Morocco.
- Other islands in the **archipelago** include Lanzarote, Fuerteventura, Gran Canaria, La Gomera and La Palma.

Tourist Information Offices

- **Santa Cruz de Tenerife**: Plaza de España s/n, 38003 Santa Cruz de Tenerife, tel: 922/239-592; Oct–Apr Mon–Fri 9–6, Sat 9–1; May–Sep Mon–Fri 9–5, Sat 9–12
- **La Laguna**: Plaza del Adelantado s/n, La Laguna, tel: 922/631-194; daily 9–5
- **La Orotava**: Calle Carrera Escultor Estévez 2, La Orotava, tel: 922/323-041; Mon–Fri 8:30–6
- **Puerto de la Cruz**: Plaza de Europa s/n, Puerto de la Cruz, tel: 922/386-000; Mon–Fri 9–8, Sat–Sun 9–5
- **Playa de las Américas**: Avenida Rafael Puig 1, Playa de las Américas, tel: 922/750-633; daily 9–5
- **San Sebastián de La Gomera**: Calle Real 4, San Sebastián, tel: 922/870-281; May–Oct Mon–Fri 8–8, Sat 9–1:30, 3:30–6, Sun 10–1; Nov–Apr Mon–Sat 9–1:30, 3:30–6, Sun 10–1

Getting Around

Although distances are not great, driving can be slow as roads are often winding and narrow. This is especially the case in mountainous areas in the north east and north west.

Buses

- **TITSA** (Transportes Interurbanos de Tenerife SA) (tel: 922/531-300; www.titsa.com) runs a fairly efficient bus service all over the island. It also provides the local bus service in the bigger towns.
- Buses are known as ***guaguas*** in Tenerife, but if you ask for the ***autobús*** people will know what you are talking about.
- The main bus station on Tenerife is the **Intercambiador** at Avenida de la Constitución at the corner with the avenida Tres de Mayo, 1.5km (1mi) south of the city centre in Santa Cruz de Tenerife.
- The other big bus stations (Estación de Guaguas) are located in La Laguna (near the motorway) as well as in the main tourist centres of Los Cristianos and Playa de las Américas.
- The **longest bus trips** (for instance Santa Cruz de Tenerife to Playa de las Américas) are still inexpensive (under €10).
- If you plan to travel around the island extensively by bus, purchase a **Bono Bus card** for around €15 or €25. This gets you more for your money, as each trip you make is discounted by 50 per cent (30 per cent if 20km/12.5mi or less). Insert the card into the bus ticket machine and the discounted fare is deducted when you tell the driver where you are going. If don't have enough money left on your card, you pay the driver the difference (at the discounted rate).
- **Seven bus routes** cover La Gomera, starting in San Sebastián and heading for Valle Gran Rey, Playa de Santiago and Hermigua. There are four or five daily runs except on Sunday when there are two or three.

Trams

- Santa Cruz de Tenerife has a tram system (tel: 922/024-800; www.metrotenerife.com) with a single line that runs to La Laguna from 6am to midnight, with services every 30 minutes throughout the night on Fridays and Saturdays.

Driving

- Drive on the **right**.
- **Speed limits** in built-up areas 50 km/h (31 mph), outside 90 km/h (55 mph) and on motorways 100 km/h (62 mph).
- The blood **alcohol** concentration (BAC) is 0.5.
- **Seat belts** must be worn by all passengers, and rear seatbelts must be worn.
- **Fines** for traffic offences can be very high and foreigners are often obliged to pay on the spot.
- **Parking** in built-up areas such as Santa Cruz de Tenerife can be difficult. Most central areas have **meter parking**, but there are also **car parks**.
- In areas marked with blue lines – ***zonas azul*** (blue zones) – you must buy a parking ticket during the designated hours, usually between 9am and 2pm and 4pm and 8pm. If you forget, or exceed your time, you will receive a fine to be paid on the spot.

- Drive particularly **carefully** in the mountains. Never stop on narrow, winding roads to admire the view unless it is safe to pull off the road completely. *Miradores* (viewpoints) are placed every few kilometres specifically for this purpose.
- Never leave anything visible in your car (rental cars attract particular attention) and preferably nothing of value even in the boot.
- **Petrol** is cheaper on Tenerife than in mainland Spain or other parts of Europe because of tax concessions for the Canary Islands. In Spanish **diesel** is *gasoleo* and **unleaded** is *sin plomo*.
- There are numerous **petrol garages** along main roads, with 24-hour opening in the larger resorts and towns.

Taxis

- **Long trips**, such as between Puerto de la Cruz in the north and Playa de las Américas in the south west, can be expensive, but there are set fares for many routes.
- Insist on the **meter** being properly set and/or establish a price with the driver before setting off.

Bicycles

- You can rent standard **bicycles** and **mountain bicycles** in some of the most visited areas.
- Bicycling is a rewarding way to get around the island, although you need to be fit to deal with some of the more **mountainous stretches**.
- Keep **water bottles** well filled as you can become quickly dehydrated in the heat.

Walking

Tenerife is one of the most popular destinations for walking holidays. The well-prepared hiking trails contribute to this popularity as does the islands mostly mild climate.

- You can go hiking on Tenerife and La Gomera all year round. Favourite areas are the **Parque Nacional del Teide** on Tenerife (➤ 122) and **Parque Nacional de Garajonay** on La Gomera (➤ 156); both parks are UNESCO World Heritage Sites.
- You can also go walking in plenty of other areas, such as the **Anaga mountains** in north-east Tenerife (➤ 77) and around **Masca** in the north west (➤ 94).
- Walking **maps** and **guidebooks** in various languages are available in bookshops in Santa Cruz de Tenerife and the tourist information offices around the island.

Boats

- Frequent **ferry** services run to La Gomera from Los Cristianos (➤ 129).
- Several **boat tours** allow you to get a seaside view of Tenerife.
- Apart from the **dolphin**- and **whale-watching trips** operating mainly out of the southern resorts, you can also join **excursions** up the coast to see the Acantilado de los Gigantes (➤ 106).

Accommodation

The Canary Islands are Europe's most popular winter sun destination. Most of the tourists come from Great Britain, followed by Germany and Scandinavia. But there are also a lot of Spaniards who come here during the summer holidays. On Tenerife numerous hotels, plus self-catering and timeshare complexes, are concentrated around a handful of intensively developed coastal strips. La Gomera has fewer places to stay, but even here the number of bed spaces is increasing to cater for its very diverse range of guests.

Finding Somewhere to Stay

- Many hotels and apartments allocate all or most of their rooms to foreign **tour operators or travel agents**, and it can be difficult for independent travellers to find anywhere to stay at certain times of year. The Christmas holidays are particularly popular, and in February, a lot of visitors come to see the carnival (► 12).
- It's usually cheaper to arrange accommodation **in advance**, with air travel, some meals and perhaps car rental or excursions included. But it's not impossible to find rooms on spec, depending on the time of year and how flexible you are about where you stay.
- The **equable climate** keeps Canarian hotels busy all year round, but the high season and highest prices generally occur between Nov and April.
- Lots of agencies in the main resorts specialise in property management for absentee owners. **Self-catering** or **timeshare** accommodation may be available to let at short notice. If possible, have a look at anything offered before committing yourself.

Types of Accommodation

Hotels

- Most tourist hotels are **modern**, disguised to a greater or lesser degree by the island's lush subtropical vegetation. The overall picture is slightly more varied. The older resort of Puerto de la Cruz has several charming hotels in **traditional Canarian buildings** with timbered balconies.
- Package tourism is a vital mainstay of the economy, but **aesthetic considerations** are more of a priority in hotel building than they were in the 1960s and 1970s. Gardens and pools are larger, architecture more diverse, and decor less stereotyped.
- The fast-expanding Costa Adeje area north of Playa de las Américas is targeting the upper end of the market and has hardly any budget accommodation. **Luxury complexes** like the extravagant Bahía del Duque (► 140) function as self-contained resorts.
- **La Gomera** has no huge resorts on the scale of Playa de las Américas. Apart from its *parador* and a single chic development on the south coast, the Jardín Tecina (► 154), accommodation is generally small and simple, suiting independent travellers who prefer more flexibility.

Self-Catering

- There's plenty of choice of **self-catering accommodation**, with around 260 complexes of apartments, bungalows or villas to rent on Tenerife, and around 130 on La Gomera.
- **Quality** is very variable.

For more information on self-catering options contact the following:

- **Paradores de España** (centralised booking, Madrid): tel: 902/547-979; www.parador.es In the UK, **Keytel International** can arrange *parador* bookings; 402 Edgware Road, London W2 1ED; tel: 020 7616 0300; www.keytel.co.uk
- **Attur** (Asociación Tinerfeña de Turismo Rural); tel: 902/21582; www.ecoturismocanarias.com
- **Viajes Aecan**, Calle San Pedro Alcantara 13, Piso 3, Santa Cruz de Tenerife; tel: 922/532-733; www.aecan.com
- **Camping Nauta**, Arona, Cañada Blanca, Las Galletas; tel: 922/785-118; www.campingnauta.com

- **Aparthotels** (apartment blocks with hotel facilities) combine the independence of a self-catering holiday with the advantage of not having to do the cooking all the time. Some have a minimum-stay requirement; most offer a regular maid service during your stay.

Character Properties

- **Unusual types of accommodation**, such as a rural idyll on an old avocado farm, a taste of *grande luxe* in Santa Cruz and a B&B in a bishop's palace in Laguna, are little used by tour operators, so book them independently via the internet.
- Both Tenerife and La Gomera have an attractive and very comfortable ***parador*** (part of Spain's state-run chain of high-class hotels, usually in historic buildings). Though not cheap, they offer a memorable stay in wonderful settings. Tenerife's *parador* stands in the spectacular crater moonscapes of the Mount Teide National Park (➤ 139).

Rural Stays

- **Country hotels** and **self-catering cottage properties** (*casas rurales*) are increasing on both Tenerife and La Gomera.
- Some of these are former ***fincas*** (farmhouses) in beautiful inland settings, which have been renovated with the help of EU funding.
- Some are used by special-interest tour operators as **walking bases**, but you'll probably need your own transport if you're travelling independently.

Budget Accommodation

- If funds are limited, there are modest rooms in a ***pensión*** or ***hostal***. These are often older-style, family-owned establishments. Standards vary a lot. Though practically non-existent in the purpose-built surroundings of Playa de las Américas, you'll find them in the older quarters of Los Cristianos and Puerto de la Cruz, or in larger towns like Santa Cruz de Tenerife and San Sebastián on La Gomera.
- **Camping** possibilities are extremely limited.
- There are **no youth hostels** on either Tenerife or La Gomera.

Accommodation Prices

Prices are for a double room per night during the high season and include sales tax.

€ under €70 **€€** €70–€120 **€€€** over €120

Food and Drink

Assuming you aren't the sort of visitor cheered by signs announcing "No Spanish food here", you'll find plenty of places happy to serve you some genuine local specialities. Canarian cuisine is basically Spanish, with a difference. Many classic mainland dishes appear on the menu (gazpacho, paella, chorizo and tapas), and there are also a whole range of typical Canarian specialities which are quite unique to the islands.

The Latin Connection

- Since the time of Christopher Columbus, the Canaries have served as an Atlantic staging post between Spain and the Americas. It's hardly surprising many dishes have a Latin American flavour. Bananas, tomatoes, potatoes, peppers, sweetcorn, avocado, papaya – all South American crop-plants successfully transplanted to Tenerife – feature largely in local cooking.
- The **hot chocolate potion** prized by Montezuma and the Aztecs appears transmuted into a sustaining breakfast dish used for dunking *churros* (sticks of sugary fried batter).
- Look out, too, for a Venezuelan speciality called ***arepas***, served in café-bars called *areperas*. These tasty little parcels of fried maize dough are stuffed with a variety of savoury fillings and offered with spicy dips. Two or three make an inexpensive bar snack.

A Taste of the Sea

- Unsurprisingly, fish is a staple ingredient of all local diets, but many species are becoming scarce due to overfishing. Look out for typical varieties like the ***vieja*** (sun fish) or the ***cherne*** (bass).
- Fish stews like ***sancocho*** or ***zarzuela*** are regular fixtures, but many good restaurants prefer to adapt their menus to whatever swims into the market that day.
- ***Papas arrugadas*** (wrinkled jacket potatoes) are a ubiquitous Canary Islands side-order, perfect with fish. Traditionally cooked in seawater, they are now boiled in brine, which reduces their water content and intensifies the flavour, leaving a white crust of salt behind.

Regional Styles

- **Soups** and **stews** are popular traditional dishes. Otherwise meat and fish are often best served *a la plancha* (grilled) or roasted. Rabbit, goat and suckling pig offer alternatives to steak, lamb and chicken.
- Restaurants described as *típico* generally serve good home-cooking, and the chance to eat outside often adds to the pleasure.
- Classic accompaniments to meat or fish dishes are the two kinds of **spicy sauce** known as *mojo. Mojo picón*, the red type, is a fiery recipe based on chilli and garlic; *mojo verde*, the green variety, is a less scorching concoction of coriander and parsley.
- ***Gofio*** (toasted cereal meal) is a Canarian curiosity, allegedly the staple dish of the Guanches. Like other such survival rations eaten in times of plenty, its virtues can be overstated.
- **Puddings** and **cakes** tend to be very sweet. *Bienmesabe* is a typical example, made with honey and almonds.
- La Gomera is renowned for its tasty goat's cheese, smoked or flavoured with natural herbs.

Drinks

- Canarian **wines** have improved enormously in the past decade or two, encouraged by more rigorous classification and regulation of the wine trade. Tenerife is the main producer, and most of its vines grow in the north of the island, especially around Tacoronte, Güímar and Icod de los Vinos. Interesting wines are produced on La Gomera too. For more information on wine, visit the **Casa del Vino la Baranda** (➤81).
- If you want to try a local spirit, look out for ***ron*** (rum), ***cobana*** (a banana-based liqueur) or ***mistela*** (a mead-like Gomeran invention made with honey or palm-syrup).
- The local **beer** is La Dorada. Ask for *a caña* (small glass) or *a jarra* (large) if you prefer draught beer.
- ***Sangría*** is on tap, though locals rarely touch it.
- **Coffee** is an art form in many different guises. Ask for *café solo* if you like it espresso-style, or *cortado* if you like a dash of milk. Locals like it made with condensed milk (*condensada*) or with a shot of alcohol – a *carajillo* or a *barraquito* are bracing pick-me-ups. *Café con hielo* is iced coffee.
- **Fresh fruit juices** are very popular; look for a *zumería* (juice bar) for exotic mixtures of papaya, avocado or mango, all locally grown.

Best...
...**Castilian food:** Los Cuatros Postes (➤65)
...**coffee and cakes:** Pastelaría El Aderno (➤115)
...**Asian cuisine:** El Baifo (➤161)
...**monastery setting:** Méson El Monasterio (➤114)
...**hotel restaurant:** El Patio (➤141)
...**terrace dining:** Restaurante Pancho (➤114)
...**traditional Canarian setting:** La Hierbita (➤65)
...**wine:** Casa del Vino la Baranda (➤81)

When to Eat

- Meal times are **generally later** than in northern Europe. Lunch starts at 2pm and dinner at around 9pm, but resort hotels and bars often compromise to suit the preferences of their clientele.
- Most restaurants offer an inexpensive ***menú del día***, generally consisting of three rather ordinary courses with bread and a drink included. But it could be more enjoyable (though not necessarily cheaper) to have *tapas* in a bar.
- **Tax** and **service** are usually covered in the prices quoted, though a small tip is generally expected. Extra charges often apply if you sit outside at a terrace table.
- **Vegetarians** may find Canarian menus don't cater very well for them. A vegetarian diet seems to baffle most islanders.

Restaurant Prices

Price per person for a three-course meal, including wine and service

€ under €20 **€€** €20–40 **€€€** over €40

Shopping

Tenerife's status as a mid-Atlantic duty-free bazaar has been eroded by EU legislation, but consumer goods continue to flood in to tempt holiday-makers with low prices.

Tax on Luxury Purchases

- **Sales tax** on luxury items (IGIC) is still remarkably low compared with most European countries, including mainland Spain. Savings passed on to the customer, however, vary greatly from one outlet to the next. Alcohol and tobacco seem especially good value (locally produced cigars are popular), along with perfume and cosmetics, jewellery, leather, confectionery, cameras and binoculars, watches, electrical and electronic goods.

Duty Free?

- Duty free does not mean tax free, but competition keeps resort prices low. Don't wait to do your shopping at the airport on your way home – the choice is limited and prices are higher than elsewhere on the island.

Where to Shop

- *Mercados* (markets) come in all shapes and sizes, from daily cornucopias of fish, flowers and fruit to weekly flea markets (*rastros*) offloading miscellaneous junk. Street traders and stallholders hawk their wares along the seafront promenades wherever tourists are to be found.
- For Canarian souvenirs, look for ***centros de artesanía*** (craft outlets), sometimes attached to workshops where the goods are actually made.
- ***Centros comerciales*** (shopping centres) and Asian-owned bazaars are in all the big resorts, though large department stores and out-of-town hypermarkets are mostly confined to Santa Cruz de Tenerife.

Caveat Emptor (Buyer Beware)

- Some stores **discourage haggling**, but prices are generally flexible – it's always worth asking for a discount.
- Most tourist-orientated shops accept **credit cards**. It's a good idea to check slips carefully before you sign, and your subsequent statements.
- Look out for signs saying ***rebajas*** (sales) or ***liquidación*** (closing-down sale) for especially low prices.
- **Pirated** and **fake goods** are widespread in the Canaries. Few are well-crafted enough to deceive sophisticated shoppers, but it's best to avoid buying music recordings and videos or designer labels from market stalls or other roadside hawkers. If something looks too good to be a true, it probably is.
- **Electronic equipment** for computers, mobile phones and the like is a risky purchase unless you have specialist technical knowledge. Some components may not be compatible with systems in the UK.
- Not everything in the Canaries is a **bargain**. Do some price and product research before you leave home.
- Don't sign up with a **timeshare tout**. If you want to invest in Canarian property, take sensible legal and financial advice.

Summer Craft Fairs

These fairs *(ferias de artesanía)*, held in Tenerife's older inland communities, can be great fun if you're hunting for typical Canarian souvenirs. Dates vary from year to year; check with the tourist office.

- **June:** Güímar, La Orotava, Los Realejos
- **July:** El Sauzal, La Laguna, Santiago del Teide
- **August:** Arona, Fasnia, Garachico, La Victoria de Acentejo, Buenavista del Norte, La Matanza
- **September:** Vilaflor, San Miguel de Abona, Guía de Isora, Tacoronte
- **October:** El Tanque

What to Buy

- **Embroidery** is a popular souvenir. The distinctive drawn-threadwork known as *calados* is often made into table- or bedlinen (placemats, pillowcases). It's an airy, openwork pattern that's on sale in markets and bazaars. Certified craft shops like **La Casa de los Balcones** are a reliable place to buy it. The main outlet in La Orotava has a working embroidery school.
- **Lace** is a speciality in the mountain village of Vilaflor. Genuine handmade products are expensive (beware of cheap machined goods – they'll look a bit too regular).
- **Leatherware** is an art form throughout Spain. You'll find bags, shoes, belts and wallets of variable quality on sale in all the resorts and markets.
- **Ceramics** based on traditional Guanche designs can be found both on Tenerife, especially at Arguayo near Los Gigantes, and at El Cercado on La Gomera. The classic style is made without a wheel and fired with a coating of red clay.
- Canarian **basketware** (*cestería*) takes a variety of forms; look out for souvenirs made from woven cane, straw, palm or banana leaves.
- Attractive bowls, dishes and spoons made from a variety of native trees make good **wooden** souvenirs, though much is made from imported olive-wood, which doesn't grow locally.
- ***Chácaras*** (castanets) make easy souvenirs to carry home, but you may see other Canarian musical instruments on sale, such as the stringed ***timple***, in some craft outlets. Recordings of **local folk music** are often on sale at markets and craft centres. The Los Sabadeños group has a particularly large following.
- Avoid buying bladed objects or souvenirs made from endangered species (such as ivory, coral, fur and tortoiseshell). These may be impounded by customs when you go home.

Home-grown Produce

- **Edible souvenirs** include prettily packaged jars or bottles of green and red *mojo* (► 41). On La Gomera, look out for ***miel de palma*** (palm syrup), and goat's cheeses preserved in oil.
- Biscuits, cakes and sweets, local wines or liqueurs made from **bananas** (*cobana*) or **honey** (*mistela* or *ronmiel*), and **cigars** made from local tobacco make other attractive souvenirs.
- Baby **dragon trees** (► 96) are on sale in many souvenir shops, though they are not frost-hardy. A genuinely worthwhile plant souvenir is a bunch of ***strelitzia***, the flamboyant flame-and-navy "bird of paradise" flowers. You can order these before your return journey, robustly packed and labelled to air-freight home.

Opening Times

- Standard shop opening times are Mon–Fri 9–1 and 4–8; Sat 9–2, but in tourist areas some outlets stay open much later, perhaps until 10pm, including Sundays. Most close during public holidays.
- **Markets** generally take place in the **mornings**, and some start quite early.

Entertainment

There is a rich choice of things to do for holidaymakers of all ages. You will discover that it is not only during the day that there is a lot on offer at the Playa de las Américas, there is a lot going on in the evenings as well.

What's On

Various multilingual newspapers are delivered free of charge to hotels. *El Día*, the daily Canarian newspaper, has useful but random snippets on what's on. Other newspapers with information on what's going on include *Island Connections* and *Tenerife News*. Also worth looking out for is the Spanish-language monthly what's-on guide, *Lagenda*, available at news stands. Tourist offices can supply information on local fiestas, markets, sports facilities or cultural events.

Nightlife

If you're based in one of the big resorts, nightlife is impossible to avoid. Lots of organised evening entertainment goes on in the larger hotels.

- The top venue for spectacular **dinner-shows** (including flamenco) is the Pirámide de Arona (Mare Nostrum Resort, Los Cristianos, ➤ 143).
- The older quarters of Santa Cruz de Tenerife and Puerto de la Cruz are lively in the evenings, though here the emphasis is more on **strolling** and **dining**. Nightspots and elegant **casinos** are more discreetly located and patronised by locals as well as foreign visitors.
- At ***Carnaval*** time, however, the entire community is festive mood.
- Outside the resorts, nightlife is extremely limited or non-existent.

Outdoor Activities

- **Hang-gliding** (*parapente*), **rock-climbing** and **parascending** are readily on tap for the determinedly adventurous. Others may be content with a good **walk** (see below), or a round of **golf** (see below).
- **Pot-holing** may be an unusual hobby, but here you can do it in one of the world's longest cave systems (the Cueva del Viento).

Spectator Sports

- Traditional Canarian trials of strength like ***lucha canaria*** (Canarian wrestling, ➤ 23) or ***juego del palo*** (stick fighting, ➤ 23) offer something different.
- Inevitably, there's also **football** (soccer).

Watersports

- A wide variety of watersports and activities – sailing, fishing, water-skiing, scuba diving, surfing, snorkelling, hiring of kayaks, pedaloes, jetskis and "banana boats" – is on offer in the holiday harbours.
- The best **diving** and **fishing** sites are near Los Gigantes, Las Galletas and south of Los Cristianos.

Golf

- Tenerife's oldest and smartest golf course is **RCG Tenerife** (Real Club de Golf) near La Laguna, which was founded in 1932 (➤ 86).
- Several newer courses are based in the south of the island, landscaped with cinder bunkers and palm trees, and with ocean views.
- The website **www.webtenerife.com** lists Tenerife's courses and facilities.
- Several **large hotels** offer golfing packages.

Finding Your Feet

Walking

- **Spectacular terrain and wildlife** make Tenerife and La Gomera attractive to walkers.
- Both islands have **stunning mountain scenery** within their national parks, and hiking can easily be arranged along well-signed routes both for independent travellers or guided groups.
- Specialist operators organise **entire holidays** based on walking (sometimes featuring bird-watching and flower-spotting). Or you can join a guided hike when you arrive. A popular excursion combines a walk from Masca with a boat trip past the cliffs of Los Gigantes.
- If you prefer to do your own thing, maps with suggested walking routes are available from tourist offices and national park visitor centres. The website www.webtenerife.com has details and maps of 25 walks around the island that you can download.

Organised Tours

- If you don't want to rent a car, it's very easy to join an organised tour to see other parts of the island, and visit big-time tourist attractions like **Loro Parque** (➤ 109), **Castillo de San Miguel** (➤ 105) or **Teide National Park** (➤ 112).
- Other routes widely advertised take you to **Masca** and the **Teno Massif**, or to **Santa Cruz de Tenerife** for shopping.

Reservations

- Many holidaymakers join **organised activities** laid on by their hotels or tour companies.
- **Travel agencies and tourist offices** fill in the gaps. Tour operator notice boards display resort-based tourist entertainment, and you'll find dozens of ideas for excursions.
- If you're looking for **culture**, go to Santa Cruz de Tenerife or La Laguna; both have theatre and classical music programmes.
- If you like exploring on your own, ask for the timetables for the public TITSA buses at the tourist information centre. The buses do not run as frequently on La Gomera; it is better to rent a car there.

Boat Trips

- **Whale-** and **dolphin-watching** trips are big business off Tenerife's west coast. More than 20 species frequent these waters, particularly pilot whales and bottle-nosed dolphins. However, there is some evidence that the number of boats is causing disturbance and even injury, so choose a properly licensed operator.
- "**Pirate cruises**", beach picnics or barbecues generally include the cost of lunch and time for a swim.
- **The best boat trip** from Tenerife is a visit to **La Gomera** – a full day's outing from Los Cristianos. You can combine this with an organised coach tour, or see the island at your own pace (you may need to arrange car rental at San Sebastián docks since some car rental agreements do not allow you to take vehicles from one island to another).

Jeep Safaris

- Advertised in the main resorts, especially around Puerto Colón in Playa de las Américas, **off-road vehicles** take you through rugged terrain to remote parts of the island.

Santa Cruz de Tenerife

Double-Decker Tour of the City

It starts at the **Plaza de España** (➤ 54). The ticket is valid all day; you can hop on and hop off as you like at 11 different stops.

Cultural Enjoyment in the Auditorio

In January, the Auditorio (➤ 61) hosts the **Festival de Música de Canarias** (www.festivaldecanarias.com), a series of classical concerts with international orchestras.

Elegant and luxurious

The spa and leisure facilities in the **Grand Hotel Mencey** (Calle José Naveiras 38; www.iberostar.com) are also open to non-resident guests.

Getting Your Bearings

Humming with activity, Santa Cruz is the urban heart of Tenerife, far removed from the tourist clichés. A major port, it is the capital of the province (which includes the islands of La Gomera, La Palma and El Hierro) and home to 220,000 people, almost a quarter of Tenerife's population. It has fine churches, interesting museums, leafy squares, an aquatic centre and, just north of town, a fine beach.

View from Hotel Contemporáneo over the Salamanca district of Santa Cruz

The Canary Islands are blessed with all sorts of tax breaks and the local version of sales tax – IGIC – is very low. As a result a good percentage of package tourists are guided through Santa Cruz for at least a morning's shopping.

One of the best parts about Santa Cruz is the chance to get lost in the bustle of a real Spanish city. There is enough to see and do to fill at least a day, and a little people-watching over a drink at a city centre *terraza* is the perfect way to while away an early afternoon. If you time your visit right you could be here for one of the most exciting festivals in the world – *Carnaval*. Since 2000, the city has undergone massive changes with a crop of contemporary buildings and communal spaces that have upped its cool factor. An enjoyable aquatic centre and a fine sandy beach just north of town add to the allure.

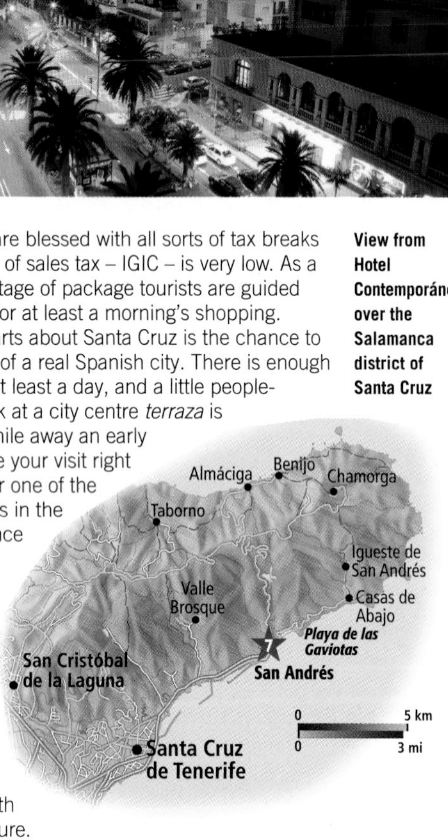

Almáciga
Benijo
Chamorga
Taborno
Igueste de San Andrés
Casas de Abajo
Valle Brosque
Playa de las Gaviotas
7
San Andrés
San Cristóbal de la Laguna
Santa Cruz de Tenerife
0 5 km
0 3 mi

TOP 10

Don't Miss

At Your Leisure

Santa Cruz de Tenerife

The Perfect Day

If you're not quite sure where to begin your travels, this itinerary recommends a practical and enjoyable day out in Santa Cruz de Tenerife, taking in some of the best places to see. For more information see the main entries (➤ 52–63).

10:00

Begin in 10 **Plaza de España** (➤ 54), where you can also pick up information at the tourist office beside the small artificial lake. Before heading into the city, wander along the waterfront for a while. Back in Plaza de España, the next logical step is to head up to 10 **Plaza de la Candelaria** (➤ 55) and the shopping streets behind it.

11:30

Head across to Plaza Isla de la Madera before ducking down into the few streets that constitute what is left of old Santa Cruz. In 11 **Plaza de la Iglesia** (➤ 56) visit the Iglesia de Nuestra Señora de la Concepción. Cross the Barranco de los Santos to the **Museo de la Naturaleza y El Hombre** (➤ 57), with its collection of Guanche mummies. Nearby is the city's big produce market, the 15 **Mercado de Nuestra Señora de Africa** (➤ 61).

1:00

Have a typically Spanish lunch at **Mesón Los Monjes** (➤ 66) on Calle Antonio Domínguez Alfonso.

2:30
After lunch, it's a quick walk across to 12 **Plaza del Príncipe de Asturias** (➤ 59) for some local art appreciation at the Museo de Bellas Artes and a quick coffee at the Kiosco del Príncipe. From here wander up Calle del Pilar to the 13 **Parque García Sanabria** (➤ 63), where the *terrazas* are great for a drink, or further on to Rambla de Santa Cruz.

3:30
If you feel the need to get out of the city, take a bus (Nos 245, 246, 247 or 910) or taxi up the coast to the inviting white sand beach of Las Teresitas (below) in 7 **San Andrés** (➤ 52). During the week it's pretty quiet. If you have time and your own car, continue on to secluded **Playa de las Gaviotas** (➤ 53).

6:00
Return to Santa Cruz for an early evening view across the whole sweep of the port as you make your way back to the centre.

8:00
Try one of the restaurants or *tascas* in the streets south of the Hotel Contemporáneo. Keep an eye open for concerts at the **Teatro Guimerá** (➤ 68) and Auditorio de Tenerife (➤ 61) or, if you're looking for bars and clubs, try the long line-up of places along **Avenida Anaga**.

San Andrés

Santa Cruz's escape route is a short drive to the north – the cheerful town of San Andrés and neighbouring white beach of Playa de las Teresitas. Head up into the hills north of the beach to discover an even more secluded beach, Playa de las Gaviotas. A little further still leads you to a typical Canarian town, Igueste, an ideal starting point for walks in the mountains.

Despite its proximity to Santa Cruz, which is barely 8km (5mi) south west, **San Andrés** has retained its fishing-village atmosphere. With one of the island's best beaches, **Playa de las Teresitas**, just 1km (0.5mi) further on, the *pueblo* (town) is the perfect place to fall back on after you tire of sand. Locals from Santa Cruz fill the restaurants with lively conversation. It makes a pleasant change to feel that the "tourists" catered for are predominantly local.

San Andrés huddles at the end of Playa de las Teresitas

The town is guarded by a semi-ruined round tower fort, known as the *castillo* (castle). Wander into the central shady square, surrounded by bars and a small 18th-century chapel of red stone and whitewash. Behind, rows of houses struggle up the hillside, looking from afar like an unsteady pyramid.

Summer, sun and sand: on the Playa de las Teresitas

The Beaches

Playa de las Teresitas is an artificial marvel. Proving that the 1970s were not all bad taste, the island's government bought 100,000m³ (130,950yd³) of Saharan sand to create a nice beach for the locals, protected by a breakwater. Palm trees stud the inland strip of this broad strand, providing welcome shade. More palms virtually hide the parking strip and handful of seafood restaurants just behind the beach.

Igueste

4km (2.5mi) north east of **Playa de las Gaviotas**, the TF11 road ends in the silent farming village of Igueste. Along with other villages scattered across the Anaga mountain range (► 77), Igueste takes you light years from the pounding tourist resorts of the south. This is the real Tenerife, and before the arrival of tourists in the 1960s, was Tenerife. The village, looking like someone has randomly cast a box of white dice about the countryside, ranges up on either side of a *barranco* (gorge), in whose often dry bed the people grow everything from bananas to avocados and potatoes.

TAKING A BREAK

There is no shortage of restaurants just back from **Playa de las Teresitas.** Or test out **Marisquería Ramon** (► 66) in San Andrés itself.

---

194 B4

INSIDER INFO

- From Igueste it is possible to hike over the ridge and down into another gorge to reach **Playa de Antequera**, about 1.5km (1mi) away. Bring decent walking boots, food and water.
- Playa de las Teresitas doesn't get too crowded, except at summer weekends, but if it's too much you can continue a few kilometres/miles over the first rise north of the beach to another much smaller one, **Playa de las Gaviotas**. This beach is formed by a small crescent of black sand, and is easily reached by car.

10 Plaza de España & Plaza de la Candelaria

These virtually interlocking squares are the most logical place to start exploring Santa Cruz de Tenerife. They are the administrative heart of Santa Cruz, right by the sea, and are worth wandering around to get a feel for the city, do a little shopping, have a snack or take a waterfront stroll.

Architectural Style

The **Plaza de España**, the central pivot of the seafront corniche has been given a makeover by the award-winning architects Herzog and de Meuron who have created a stunning lake as the core feature. Overlooking this is a sombre war memorial raised to Spanish dictator General Franco flanked by monumental bronze statues and a triumphal ancient Greek-style open arcade. In the background rises the neo-classical headquarters of the government, the Cabildo Insular.

Originally laid out after Franco's rise to power, the new-look plaza, unveiled in July 2008, stands on the site where a defensive castle, the Castillo de San Cristóbal, had stood until its demolition in 1929. For about three weeks in February revellers flood Plaza de España and the surrounding streets as they celebrate the madness of ***carnaval*** (➤ 12).

View of the Cabildo Insular, seat of the islands' government

Grand ocean liners call in to Santa Cruz

The square marks the halfway point of harbour-side Santa Cruz. To the south west are the container docks, while to the north east a mix of ferries, cruise liners and merchant vessels compete for quay space. Further north still the container docks start again.

Away from the Harbour

Heading inland, **Plaza de la Candelaria** is more like a broad pedestrian boulevard connected to Plaza de España. The square, known as Plaza Real (Royal Square) and the Plaza de la Constitución (Constitution Square) until 1787, has lost much of the charm it once had. The north-east corner is dominated by the Baroque Palacio de la Carta (now a bank), in whose interior lies a fine *patio* surrounded by timber balconies. On the same side of the square is the city casino. Watching over the centre of the square is a Baroque statue of the Virgen de la Candelaria.

The pedestrian streets that stretch inland from the square, especially **Calle Castillo**, are lined by many fashion houses and boutiques. They pull in both locals and tourists looking for a bargain.A short way off, on Plaza Isla de la Madera, is the **Teatro Guimerá** (➤ 68), built in the mid-19th century and named after Ángel Guimerá, a local dramatist. Inaugurated in 1851, the theatre is an example of the rich decoration of the era. In its heyday, it hosted performances by companies en route from Europe to tour Latin America.

Right: Sculpture in front of Teatro Guimerá

TAKING A BREAK

Try **Olympo** on Plaza de la Candelaria or **Mesón Los Monjes** (➤ 66) in a street to the north of Plaza de España.

183 D/E4

INSIDER INFO

The partnership of Jacques Herzog and Pierre de Meuron forms the heart of the **Herzog & de Meuron Architekten** architectural practice. Never afraid to innovate, they have a varied portfolio including the conversion of the old Bankside Power Station for the Tate Modern in London, the Allianz Arena in Munich and the Beijing National Stadium, more commonly known as the "Bird's Nest", which was the centrepiece stadium for the 2008 Olympics. In 2013, Herzog & de Meuron's design idea won the prestigious contract for the new museum M+ in Hong Kong.

11 Plaza de la Iglesia

The historic centre of Santa Cruz is like a tiny oasis of calm in the hustle and bustle of modern city life. Its silhouette is dominated by the most striking church, Iglesia de Nuestra Señora de la Concepción, while nearby a fine museum is another big attraction. Most of Santa Cruz has succumbed to the 20th century, frequently with little grace. However, the carefully maintained traditional houses still transport you back to the colonial town of a bygone era.

Iglesia de Nuestra Señora de la Concepción

The **church** is recognisable from many points in the city by its tall, elegant belfry, which is a mix of Portuguese Baroque and Moorish styles. There has been a church on this spot since the end of the 15th century, although the original was destroyed by fire during the 17th century.

The **façade** of the present church is another curiosity – an atrium, topped by a fine timber balcony, precedes the main doorway. Built and altered over the 17th and 18th centuries, it is just as intriguing a mix on the inside, where five naves are divided by pillars and red stone arches.

The Iglesia de Nuestra Señora de la Concepción, at the heart of old Santa Cruz

The rich *retablos* of Iglesia de Nuestra Senora de la Concepción

To the right after you enter is the **Santa Cruz de la Conquista** (Holy Cross of the Conquest) that gave the city its name. The island's conqueror, Alonso Fernández de Lugo, planted the cross when he landed in 1494. The fine choir stalls were imported from London in 1862 and the pulpit of alabaster-coloured marble originates from Genua and was consecrated in 1736.

Much of the timber ceiling and other wooden elements of the church, such as the two ***retablos***, were made from timber saved from a Spanish merchant vessel, *La Camorra*, which was sunk by English pirates in the 18th century. Among the several paintings on display is the fine ***La Adoración de los Pastores*** (*Shepherds in Adoration*) by Juan de Miranda (1723–1805).

Museo de la Naturaleza y El Hombre

Across the usually dry Barranco de Santos (Santos Gorge) stands the austere former Hospital de la Caridad (Hospital of Charity), built in 1745 to attend to the poor and sick. Today it houses the Museo de la Naturaleza y El Hombre (Museum of Natural History and Man). Entrance to the

INSIDER INFO

- In the anteroom of the sacristy in the Iglesia de Nuestra Señora de la Concepción is a fine **chapel**. It was paid for by Don Matías Carta, a prominent local citizen, whose portrait can be found in the sacristy. It was painted after his death, which explains the pallor and pose.
- The **Festival Internacional de Música de Canarias** (www.festivaldecanarias.com), staged by Tenerife together with Gran Canaria, is a highly acclaimed series of classical concerts. Renowned symphony orchestras and soloists from all around the world perform here in January and February. The venue in Santa Cruz is the **Auditorio de Tenerife**. In 2014 the festival celebrated its 30th anniversary with a guest performance by the Chicago Symphony Orchestra under Ricardo Muti.

THE DEADLY SERIOUS BUSINESS OF DEATH

The Guanches were one of the few ancient peoples to mummify their dead (or at least those important enough to merit such treatment for the journey into the next life). It appears the Guanches had a healthy respect of death and for this reason became expert in the art of embalming. This treatment was reserved mostly for dead chiefs and nobles, whose bodies were then laid out in distant burial caves. Although not as expert as the Egyptians, the Guanches must have carried out a reasonable enough job for some examples to survive to this day. Just how they learned these techniques and why they adopted them is a mystery. The embalmers themselves were treated like lepers and ostracised by the majority of society; they were regarded to be almost as abhorrent as the corpses they handled.

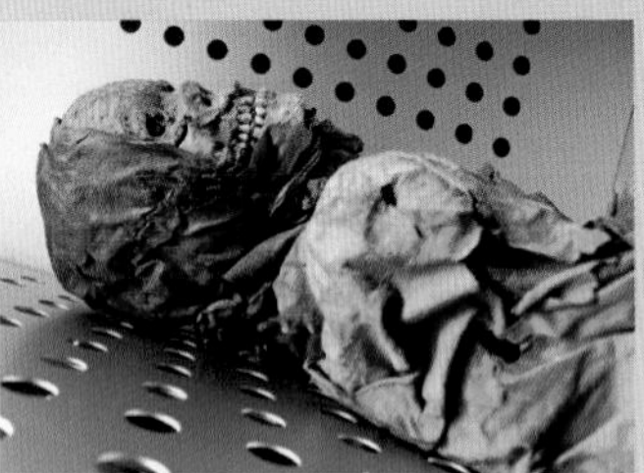

museum takes you through the quiet courtyard of the former hospital.

The collections inside are wide ranging, although the emphasis is on Guanche civilisation and culture. The most engaging items are the **Guanche mummies** and skeletons and some of the more than 1,000 skulls found by archaeologists searching for clues to the island's pre-colonial past. Some of these show evidence of trepanning (holes drilled in the skull). There is no lack of possible explanations for why the Guanches carried out trepanning, but there seems to be no one certain reason. Among the other archaeological finds are tools, pottery fragments and jewellery.

Other displays cover **flora and fauna**, especially marine life, on the islands. More interesting is the ground-floor area devoted to the **volcanic history** of Tenerife and the other islands, which has a multimedia, multiscreen exhibition.

TAKING A BREAK

Insider Tip

Try out the **Bodeguita de la Noria** in the Calle Santo Domingo which leads off from the Plaza de la Iglesia. The nice tapas bar offers small Cuban dishes. Spanish-style tapas are served in Mirador de la Noria directly opposite the parish church.

---

183 D3

Iglesia de Nuestra Señora de la Concepción
Plaza de la Iglesia s/n
Daily 9–1, 5:30–8 Free

Museo de la Naturaleza y el Hombre
Calle Fuente Morales s/n
922/535-816 Tue–Sun 9–7 €5

12 Plaza del Príncipe de Asturias

The cradle of Canary Island art is the Museo de Bellas Artes (Fine Arts Museum), which faces the leafy square of Plaza del Príncipe de Asturias in the city centre. Next door stands the Iglesia de San Francisco, an impressive Baroque church.

Museo de Bellas Artes

Down a flight of stairs you arrive in Calle José Murphy, which forms the southern boundary of the square. Here stands the city library, which also houses the Museo de Bellas Artes.

The best way to visit the museum is to head directly to the top floor. In the first room are several **sculptures**, including one of the South-American revolutionary Simón Bolívar. To the right is a display of art from the 16th to the 18th century. A great deal of it is by unknown artists, but a few paintings stand out, like a portrait of St Andrew (San Andrés) presumed to be by José Ribera (1591–1652).

Back in the first room, a series of halls straight ahead is dedicated to **Canary Islands artists** of the 19th century. The first two rooms are dedicated to landscapes and portraits by Nicolás Alfaro (1826–1905) and his student, Valentín Sanz Carta (1849–98). Both painted scenes in the islands and in continental Europe.

Detail from the façade of the Círculo de Amistad XII de Enero on Plaza del Príncipe de Asturias

Another major painter of the era was Manuel González Méndez (1843–1909), whose portraits, including a striking image of a Güímar boatman in red headgear and earrings, fill one of the rooms.

On the first floor is a statue of a *lechera canaria,* a milkmaid with canisters on her head. The rest of the floor is a mix of **19th-century Canarian painters** and a hall devoted to modern art from the islands. Among some of the more interesting artists whose work portrayed typical Tenerife themes is Alfredo Torres Edwards (1889–1943), whose striking scene of island women in traditional dress stands out.

The Iglesia de San Francisco's roof is a wooden work of art

Iglesia de San Francisco

Next door to the museum is the ochre rear wall of the Iglesia de San Francisco. The **Baroque façade** is typical of the island, a combination of dark stone and whitewash. Founded in 1680, the church is divided into three aisles separated by arches and a timber *artesonado* ceiling that resembles the upturned hull of a boat. The most important decorative elements are the Baroque **retablos**.

TAKING A BREAK

After filling up on art in the Museo de Bellas Artes, sip a coffee in the **Café del Príncipe**, right on the plaza.

---

183 D4

Museo de Bellas Artes

183 D4 Calle José Murphy 12, Plaza del Príncipe 922/244-358
Tue–Fri 10–8pm, Sat–Sun 10–3 Free

Iglesia de San Francisco

183 D4 Calle Villalba Hervás s/n Mon–Fri 9–1, 5:30–8 Free

INSIDER INFO

Also facing Plaza del Príncipe de Asturias is the **Círculo de Amistad XII de Enero**, a marvellous Second-Empire caprice built in 1904 as home to a private social club. It remains so today, which means you can only admire its extraordinary facade from the outside.

At Your Leisure

13 Castillo de San Juan & Auditorio

Virtually next door to Manrique's fanciful Parque Marítimo (right) is the medieval-style Castillo de San Juan, one of the city's old defensive forts. Built in 1679 of the local dark basalt and now closed to the public, this circular reminder of the early days of Santa Cruz's history is known as the **Castillo Negro** (Black Castle). In the old days the fort was outside the city walls and, under the watchful eye of its garrison, slave traders sold black Africans, most of whom were later transported to the Caribbean to be used as forced labour on the sugar plantations.

Just east of the fort, a new post-modern landmark of the island metropolis has emerged. The **Auditorio de Tenerife**, designed by Santiago Calatrava (born 1951) as the city's star concert hall, has the appearance of a gigantic white spinnaker on its back. Calatrava is one of Spain's most prominent architects. With a background in structural engineering he creates buildings that stretch the design envelope – working in sensual curves such as at the Ciutat de les Arts i les Ciències in Valencia or the Turning Torso building in Malmo, Sweden. However, the Auditorio is one of his most striking buildings.

Across the busy highway another remnant from the past is the tiny red-and-white **Ermita de la Virgen de la Regla**, built in 1643. It could not look more out of place, surrounded by building sites, as this entire quarter of the city is transformed into a sea of mid-level and high-rise residential housing.

182 C1/183 D1
Avenida de la Constitución s/n

14 Parque Marítimo

Designed by the Lanzarote artist César Manrique (1919–92), who is something of a legend in the Canary Islands, the Parque Marítimo is like a painting or carefully crafted garden, although people relax here as if it were just their local swimming pool. The small shallow lakes are opal blue and dotted with palms and carefully placed rock groups. There are a couple of cafeterias and restaurants and the whole thing is startlingly reminiscent of the Lago Martiánez in Puerto de la Cruz (► 90). Just to the south stretches the **Palmetum:** with about 1,600 different types of palm tree from every continent, it is expected to become the new botanic highlight of the city.

182 C1
Avenida de la Constitución s/n
Daily 10–6; summer Sat, Sun until 8
€2.50

César Manrique created a crystal-clear water paradise right by the Atlantic Ocean in Santa Cruz

Locals flock to the Mercado de Nuestra Señora de Africa, the main fresh produce market in Santa Cruz

15 Mercado de Nuestra Señora de Africa

The Market of Our Lady of Africa is a typical Spanish-produce market, spread out across interconnecting *patios*. You can find everything from fruit and nuts to ham and cheese, and much else besides. An underground level also contains a separate *pescaderia* (fish market). To mix in with the melée of locals and absorb the sights, sounds and smells is to get a taste of the real Canarian lifestyle. The market hall also integrates a colourful flower market; the *strelizia* (bird of paradise flower) and king protea, which are cultivated on the island, are available all year round.

182 C3
Plaza de Santa Cruz de la Sierra s/n
Daily 6–3

16 Tenerife Espacio de las Artes (TEA)

The multifunctional cultural complex is a further work by Herzog & de Meuron. It houses the Instituto Óscar Domínguez (dedicated to the Canarian Surrealist Óscar Domínguez, 1906–58), the photography centre of Tenerife and the Alejandro Cioranescu Island Library.

183 D3 **Avenida de San Sebastián**
922/849-057; www.teatenerife.es
Tue–Sun 10–8 **€7**

Ceramic benches and fountain bring a splash of colour to Plaza 25 de Julio

16 Plaza 25 de Julio

Better known as Plaza de los Patos (Ducks' Square), this soothing refuge is named after the date of Nelson's defeat in 1797. The bright central fountain, in *mudéjar* style (a Moorish-influenced style of architecture and decoration), is crowned by a duck and surrounded by ceramic frogs. The most attractive elements are the public benches, covered in ceramics advertising the companies that paid for them at the beginning of the 20th century.

182 C4

Halfway along Avenida de 25 de Julio

17 Parque García Sanabria

This city park is packed with a variety of tropical and sub-tropical trees and plants, a series of soothing fountains, a handful of modern sculptures left over from an urban art competition and benches for the weary. It represents a rare escape from the noise and chaos of the surrounding city. The central fountain serves also as a monument to Mayor García Sanabria, who ordered the creation of the park in 1922. The southern end livens up in the evening as people gather for a drink in the *terrazas* and children play on the swings in the small playground.

182 C5 Between Rambla de Santa Cruz and Calle Méndez Núñez

18 Museo Militar

Housed in the former fortress of the Almeida, the Museo Militar takes centre stage in what remains of a military post. You will be escorted from the gate by a soldier and, once inside, ushered to the top floor where there's a display telling the story of Nelson's abortive assault on Santa Cruz in 1797 (➤ 17). It becomes clear as you wander around the museum that this was the Canary Islands' proudest military moment. Working your way around the semicircle, first up is a display of Spanish flags and

Peace and quiet in Parque García Sanabria

ensigns, followed by an array of weapons and medals and on to an extensive section that is dedicated to the heroic defence of the city against Nelson.

Dioramas, paintings and maps all play their part in explaining the battle in detail, which is completed by such items as the instrument of British surrender and a copy of the maps drawn by Nelson himself to summarise the battle. The centrepiece is the *Tigre*, the cannon they say blew off Nelson's right arm, accompanied by a captured British flag and rifles.

The last part of the top floor is taken up with souvenirs of the Canary Islands' heroes of the Civil War and a small display on the Philippines and Cuba, which Spain lost to the US in the disastrous year of 1898 when the US sent Spain's navy to the bottom of the sea.

The ground floor is dedicated to weapons and other souvenirs from various colonial wars. The courtyard is lined with artillery pieces.

183 D/E5 Calle San Isidro 2

922/843-500 Tue–Sat 10–2 Free

Where to... Stay

Prices
Prices are for a double room per night during the high season.
€ under €70 €€ €70–120 €€€ over €120

If you're intending to stay in Santa Cruz at *Carnaval* time (mid-February), book well ahead and expect to pay over the odds for a room.

Atlántico €

It's hard to find anything much more central than this friendly, inexpensive place just a stone's throw from Plaza de España. If it's a little old-fashioned, the Atlántico makes a perfectly acceptable base for a short stay. There's no restaurant, but the lively upstairs terrace café-bar overlooking the pedestrianised shopping street outside is one of its main assets – a popular meeting place for simple snacks and drinks. The modest rate charged for the 60 rooms includes breakfast.

183 E3 Calle Castillo 12
922/246-375; www.hotelatlanticotenerife.com

Contemporáneo €€

Easy to find on the main thoroughfare through the town centre, this pleasingly designed business hotel makes a comfortable and practical choice. As the name suggests, it's a modern building with a sophisticated air. There's air-conditioning and TV in all 126 rooms. Passing traffic is noisy, but the interior is well insulated. Next to the hotel lies the cool, green Parque García Sanabria, an oasis of birdsong and *flame-trees* (➤ 63). The bar-café and restaurant provide a stylish stop. Rooms are sleek and well equipped.

Insider Tip

182 C5
Rambla de Santa Cruz 116
922/271-571; www.hotelcontemporaneo.com

NH Tenerife €€

This ultra contemporary hotel with its clean design of glass and metal is by far the coolest place in town. Though not expansive, the rooms feel spacious with a black-and-grey colour scheme and come complete with flat-screen TV and full-length window.

The garden lounge bar is an excellent place to while away the evening, though the delights of the city are just on the doorstep. There's also an excellent bistro, Nhube, on site (➤ 66), a bar, gym, Jacuzzi and sun deck. The atmosphere is definitely more of adult/business hotel than a family resort.

183 E3
Candelaria Esquina Doctor Allart
922/534-422; www.nh-hotels.com

Taburiente €€

This central hotel isn't particularly old, but an aura of old-world grandeur clings to its marble hall and classic furnishings. Impressive facilities include air-conditioning, TV, a gym, sauna, tennis and squash courts, garage parking – even a heated rooftop swimming pool. Despite this, its tariff remains surprisingly moderate. Many of the 116 rooms have attractive views over the neighbouring Parque García Sanabria (➤ 59). All rooms have safes and fridges. The restaurant offers a broad -international menu.

182 C5
Avenida Doctor José Naveiras 24A
922/276-000; www.hoteltaburiente.com

Where to...
Eat and Drink

Prices
Price per person for a three-course meal including drinks
€ under €20 **€** €20–40 **€** over €40

SANTA CRUZ DE TENERIFE

Bulan €/€€
Bulan is inside a typical old Santa Cruz house that has been injected with a vaguely Oriental chillout ambience. Diners congregate in one of the labyrinths of cosy dining areas on the ground floor for Eastern-influenced cuisine. The *pinchos Katmandu* are chicken chunks served in a peanut sauce with a splash of honey. You can just sit around the bar or head upstairs to the airy roof terrace.
183 D3
Calle Antonio Domínguez Alfonso 35
922/274-116; www.bulantenerife.com
Daily 12:30–4, 8pm–1am

Clavijo Treinta y Ocho €€€
The verdant courtyard garden off this traditional restaurant makes a wonderful location for an al fresco lunch or dinner. The menu concentrates on Spanish dishes, including excellent meats, matched by a fine list of mainland Spanish and local Canarian wines.
182 C4
Calle Viera y Clavijo 38 922/271-065
Mon–Sat 1–4, 8–midnight

El Coto de Antonio €€
Established as a smart and reliable favourite with discerning locals and business clients, this restaurant offers simple but elegantly contemporary decor. The cuisine is solid and authentic – a mix of Canarian and Basque styles. Look out for *vieja* (local sunfish) and *sancocho* (seafood stew). One of the house specialities is *pejines* (sun-cured fish marinated in alcohol and then flambéd).
182 A4
Calle del Perdón 13 922/272-105
Mon–Sat 1–4, 8–midnight

Los Cuatros Postes €€/€€€
One of the finest Castilian restaurants in town has a loyal local fan base and is always busy at lunchtimes. This is one place to come and enjoy the atmosphere of a genuine Spanish midday dining experience – but remember to make a reservation. The menu includes excellent roasted meats and locally caught fish.
183 D4
Calle Emilio Calzadilla 5 922/287-394
Mon–Sat noon–4, 8–midnight. Closed Sun

La Hierbita €€
This bar in the historic district not far from the Plaza de España first opened its doors in 1893. Typical Canarian dishes are served in the old town house, such as Almogrote from La Gomera, goat's cheese from La Palma and Puchero canaria, a hearty stew, as well as *gofio* dishes. Try the vegetarian croquettes.
183 D3 Calle Clavel 19 922/244-617; www.lahierbita.com noon–midnight

Kiosco Príncipe €
Insider Tip

This "kiosk" on a plaza that benefits from the welcome shade of large laurel trees serves a wide selection of different tapas and snacks during the day in relaxing surroundings; next door in the glazed, cast-iron pavilion, you

can dine out on a three-course Canarian meal in the evening
183 D4
Plaza del Principe de Asturias
922/247-440 9–11

El Libano €€

This is an excellent Lebanese spot hidden away in a side street, but much sought after at lunchtime by local *aficionados*. A comprehensive menu features well-known fare like kebabs and vine leaves, but strays into less familiar territory with a fine selection of vegetarian dishes.
182 A4 Calle Santiago Cuadrado 36
922/285-914 Daily 1–4, 8–midnight

Mesón Los Monjes €€

Favourably located in a street to the north of the Plaza de Espana. At lunchtime its clientele consists mostly of business people, while families make their way here for dinner. The split-level dining areas are decorated in rustic Castilian style with plain walls and lots of woodwork. Specialities include Basque and mainland Spanish recipes like *merluza con mojo* (hake with spicy sauce). Good wines.
183 D4
Paseo Milicias de Garachico 3
922/ 246-576
Mon–Sat 1:30–3:30, 8–midnight

Meson el Portón €€

Get down to this typical Canarian eatery for hearty fare. Locals opt either for the restaurant section, beneath exposed beams, at tables set with linen, or the more rough-and-tumble *tasca* next door. In a location away from the tourist

waterfront, it is a touch of the real Tenerife.
182 C5
Calle Doctor Guigou 20 922/280-764
Mon–Sat 11–11

Los Mocanes €€/€€€

The menu offers mainly Canarian dishes – fish and meat dishes, salads, tortillas. There are delicious *gofio*-based desserts.
182 A3/4 Calle Castro 21
922296-038; www.losmocanes.com
Daily noon–4 and Wed–Sat 8–11:30

Nhube €€/€€€

The cool marble floors, full-length glass walls and designer furniture in this hotel restaurant match the excellent modern fusion theme of chef Ferrán Adrià's menu. At lunch-time it is popular with the power-lunching crowd and evenings see young fashionable locals. It's a place to dine and savour in style and to see and be seen.
183 E3
Candelaria Esquina Doctor Allart
922/534-422; www.nh-hotels.com
Mon–Sat 7–11 (for buffet breakfast), 11–11 for à la carte; Sun 8–noon (for buffet breakfast), noon–11 for à la carte

El Rincón de la Piedra €€/€€€

Renowned for its charming setting – a lovely old Canarian house with fine timbers and carved woodwork – this rambling restaurant has a friendly atmosphere. It offers well-prepared Canarian specialities such as local fish, crisp, fresh salads and huge *solomillo* (steaks).
182 B4 Calle Benavides 32
922/ 249-778 Mon 7:30pm–11:30pm, Tue–Sat noon–4:30, 7:30–11:30

SAN ANDRÉS

Marisquería Ramón €€

Ramón specialises in locally caught seafood and is one of the most reputable restaurants behind Playa Las Teresitas. What better way to interrupt a lazy day on one of Tenerife's most glorious beaches than by sampling some of the chef's delicious creations? Or fortifying yourself for an excursion into the Anaga Mountains? Reflecting its location, the interior here is simple, light and bright.
194 B4 Calle Dique 23
922/549-308 Daily noon–11

Where to... Shop

Santa Cruz owes its trading success to nearly 150 years of "free port" status. Cruise passengers disembark for a spree in the shops close to the harbour, and excursion trips from the main resorts are sold as shopping expeditions. Most shops are on or around Plaza de la Candelaria and the pedestrianised Calle Castillo. The parallel Calle Béthencourt Alfonso is also good for window-shopping.

Many shops close on Sunday, public holidays and in the afternoon (1–3pm), so arrive early. Genuine local crafts bear the quality seal *Arte Tenerife*. The products are sold in their own chain of shops. These pavilion-like stores can be found in Santa Cruz and La Orotava as well as on the beach promenades in the south.

BOUTIQUES & BAZAARS

Shops selling perfume, alcohol and tobacco lure customers with "duty-free" or "tax-free" price tags in the streets near the port. Locally made *puros* (cigars) are a popular buy.

Many bazaars specialise in rugs, jewellery, porcelain, silks, watches, cameras, mobile phones and optical and electronic gadgets. You can always try for a discount on marked prices, though some stores decline to haggle.

Remember electrical products or computer components may not be compatible with what you have at home. You should also check whether the guarantee is internationally valid.

The classier fashion boutiques lie a little further from the waterfront, on and around Calle Castillo.

DEPARTMENT STORES

Santa Cruz has branches of mainland Spain's big chain department stores like **El Corte Inglés**, with a big branch one block west of the bus station, **Cortefiel**, and a local store called **Maya**. All sell food and wine, men's and women's clothing, luggage, home wares, electronics and so forth.

Huge out-of-town hypermarkets like **Continente** cater for local needs at bargain-basement prices (Autopista del Sur, Santa Maria del Mar exit, 6km/3.5mi south). Other large shopping centres are **Las Chumberas** and **Alcampo** (off the motorway to La Laguna).

CRAFTS & LOCAL PRODUCE

The large selections and fair prices of several reputable *artesanía* stores within five minutes' walk of each other make Santa Cruz a good place for gifts and souvenirs – though they lack the local interest of specialist craft-producing centres such as La Orotava (➤ 100).

The *pavillon* of *Arte Teneriffa* on Plaza de España is worth a visit for **typical crafts** such as embroidery, lace, basketwork, woodcarvings, dolls in Canarian costumes and food products like honey and spicy *mojo sauce*. Equally recommendable: **Artesanía Celsa**, Calle Castillo 8; **Casa de los Balcones**, Plaza de la Candelaria).

MARKETS

A visit to Santa Cruz's daily fresh-produce market is one of the most entertaining aspects of shopping in the capital. The vibrant stalls of the **Mercado de Nuestra Señora de Africa** (Daily 6–3) are a fascinating sight (➤ 62). There are 300 stalls brimming with a pungent cornucopia of fruit, vegetables, meat and fish, flowers, herbs and spices, cheese, live rabbits and poultry.

Where to... Go Out

Local newspapers like *Tenerife News* or *La Gaceta* tell you what's on when or check out the local tourist information office.

OVERVIEW

The central monument is the starting point for a small **tourist train** that trundles round the historic city centre (every hour from 10am). The **tourist office** is on Plaza de España (tel: 922/239-592, Oct–Apr Mon–Fri 9–6, Sat 9–1; May–Sep Mon–Fri 9–5, Sat 9–noon).

THEATRE & CONCERTS

Santa Cruz's two main venues for performing arts are the hyper-modern **Auditorio de Tenerife** (➤ 61, Avenida de la Constitución, Box office: tel: 902/317-327, general: tel: 922/568-600; www.auditoriodetenerife.com) and the classic **Teatro Guimerá** (Calle Imeldo Seris, tel: 902/364-603; www.teatroguimera.es).

FESTIVALS & EVENTS

Santa Cruz's ***Carnaval*** dwarfs all other events in the Canaries. This fantastic jamboree lasts for several weeks. Each year a different theme is chosen for the parade floats, but the bizarre Ash Wednesday procession known as the "Funeral of the Sardine" is a regular fixture. A huge, brightly decorated and highly combustible fish effigy is carried through the streets to the mock wails of costumed mourners, then set alight near the harbour with fireworks and dancing.

New Year starts with a party in the main square; as the clocks chime midnight, each reveller tries to gulp down 12 grapes as quickly as possible. The **Cabalgata de los Reyes Magos** (Epiphany, 5–6 Jan) and **Semana Santa** (Holy Week) are celebrated with colourful Spanish processions.

The **international music festival** (Jan–Mar) is a well-known draw throughout the islands. On 25 August, Santa Cruz combines the **Feast of St James** (Spain's patron saint, Santiago Apóstolo) with a good-humoured thanksgiving for the defeat of Nelson who attacked the city in July 1797 (➤ 21).

ON THE WATERFRONT

Beyond San Andrés harbour is one of the island's most beautiful beaches, **Playa de las Teresitas** (➤ 53). To the south of Plaza de España, near the Castillo de San Juan is a lido complex of swimming pools, the **Parque Marítimo** (➤ 61). For information on watersports, contact the **Club Nautico** (Avenida de Anaga, tel: 922/273-700; www.rcnt.es).

NIGHTLIFE

Santa Cruz's central plazas buzz with cafés and bars all day and night. Most nightspots are on **Avenida Anaga** (the waterfront boulevard leading north of the centre) and **Rambla de Santa Cruz**.

There are lots of bars and pubs in the old district between Plaza de España and the church. From midnight at the weekend, the **A Saudade** in the Buenos Aires *barrio* (Calle Fernando Arozena Quintero 3) is one of the most popular discos in town and is also one of the largest on the Canary Islands. Go-Go dancers, live music and plenty of Latin sound contribute to the club's success. Hotel Mencey (Calle Dr. José Naveiras 38) has a **casino** (take your passport and dress smartly); slot machines open at 4pm, gaming tables at 8pm.

La Laguna & the North East

Noches de Museo

Every last Friday in the month, the **Museo Historia y Antropología** (➤ 75) organises an expert tour through La Laguna.

Bird's Eye View of World Heritage

The Baroque bell tower of La Laguna's **Iglesia de la Concepción** (➤ 74) makes it possible (Tues–Sun 10–noon and 5–7:30).

Healthy Greens from the Island

The **Mercado del Agricultor in Tacoronte** (➤ 80) provides the best overview of what kinds of fruit and vegetables grow on the island (Sat and Sun 8–2).

Getting Your Bearings

The north-east tip of Tenerife, explored by only a small percentage of the millions of visitors to the island each year, packs a lot into a small area, from mountain walks in the Anaga range to surfing off the north coast, and from the pretty old city of La Laguna to the centre of the archipelago's wine industry. The climate here can be cool and unpredictable.

Barely 10km (6mi) inland from Santa Cruz is the city that, until well into the 18th century, was capital of the entire archipelago – La Laguna. An important university centre, La Laguna has preserved its intriguing old town centre but also has a thriving student nightlife scene.

To the north and east stretch the rugged Montañas de Anaga (Anaga Mountains), with fine walks and interesting tours (► 86). Among the sights in the mountain range are the isolated coastal village of Taganana and the cave dwellings of Chinamada. Along the north coast are several small beaches and settlements – surfers flock to this part of the island. On the road west of La Laguna you are in wine country. You can learn more in the area's wine museum near El Sauzal (► 81) and explore a couple of the little towns along the old Puerto de la Cruz road. South of La Laguna a lovely road winds inland through the Bosque de la Esperanza towards Mount Teide (► 122).

Fishing boats at Punta del Hidalgo

Walkers in the Montañas de Anaga near Chinamada

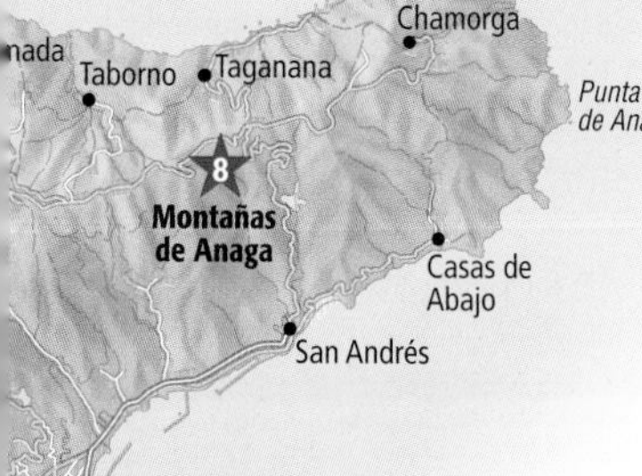

TOP 10

At Your Leisure

Canary pine line the way through the Bosque de la Esperanza

Two Perfect Days

If you're not quite sure where to begin your travels, this itinerary recommends two practical and enjoyable days out in La Laguna and the North East, taking in some of the best places to see. For more information see the main entries (► 74–82).

Day One

9:00

Start in Plaza del Adelantado in 2 **La Laguna**, from where you can indulge in a relaxed morning walking tour of the city's old centre (► 74). The most straightforward walk takes you north along Calle Obispo Rey Redondo past the cathedral and up to the **Iglesia de la Concepción**. From there move east a block and go back along **Calle San Agustín**, along which you can admire some of the city's finest colonial mansions. Set aside an hour for the **Museo de Historia y Antropología de Tenerife** in the Casa Lercaro.

12:30

If you can accustom yourself to Spanish eating times and hang on a little before lunch, drive west to 22 **Tacoronte** (► 80), Tenerife's wine capital and worth a little wander. Make for the centre of town and the **Iglesia de Santa Catalina (below)**.

2:00

After a short drive further west you reach the turn-off for **El Sauzal**. Follow the signs to the 23 **Casa del Vino La Baranda** (► 81), a wine museum in a fine old restored *hacienda*. Here you can learn about the island's wine-growing history and enjoy a tasty lunch over a delicious local tipple.

4:00

After lunch, proceed to 23 **El Sauzal** (► 81) for a quick look around, then drive back to Tacoronte before going north towards the town of Valle de Guerra. Shortly before you reach it, you can stop to visit another beautiful country house, the 24 **Casa de Carta**

(above; ➤ 82), home to the Museo de Antropología (Anthropology Museum).

5:30

Before returning to La Laguna for the evening, you could continue up the road to 25 **Bajamar** (➤ 82) and **Punta del Hidalgo** further on (➤ 82), two rocky, black-sand coastal resorts. Take an evening swim in the water pools, have a sunset drink and then drive back to La Laguna (16km/10mi) for dinner (➤ 84).

Day Two

The second day takes you around the 8 **Montañas de Anaga** (➤ 77). The options are broad, but it is worth visiting the villages of **Taganana** (➤ 77), **Taborno** (➤ 78) and **Chinamada** (➤ 78), as well as the **beaches**, where the seafood restaurants of **Playa de San Roque** make a good lunch stop. Try the suggested driving route (➤ 166).

2 La Laguna

Properly known as San Cristóbal de la Laguna, the original town was founded next to a small lake in 1496. As well as being the capital, La Laguna was the Canary Islands' military headquarters and, since 1819, has been the seat of the Nivariense diocese (*Nivaria* was the island's ancient Latin name), which covers Tenerife and the other western islands. With more than 150,000 inhabitants, it is also an important university centre. The old town, with its imposing churches, convents and mansions, is a joy to explore – and has been a UNESCO World Heritage Site since 1999.

The leafy **Plaza del Adelantado**, fronted by the Baroque (but much revamped) *ayuntamiento* (town hall) and the busy produce market, is a good place to start exploring the old town. Behind the town hall on **Calle Obispo Rey Redondo** is the sumptuous 17th-century **Casa de los Capitanes**, originally the residence of the island's military commanders and now used for temporary art exhibitions.

The ***Catedral***, with a neoclassical façade, was rebuilt in 1913 in neo-Gothic style. Among its artistic treasures are the 18th-century pulpit, as well as the ***Retablo de los Remedios***, which depicts Biblical allegories and several miracles. Its creator was Martín de Vos, a 16th-century student of one of the Great Renaissance Masters, Tintoretto.

More emblematic of the religious importance of La Laguna is the **Iglesia de la Concepción**, whose belfry is known simply as La Torre (The Tower). Although much tampered with since it was first built in the early 16th century, the church still has traces of its late Gothic origins. Inside, the faithful are protected from the elements by two fine *mudéjar* timber ceilings. Two of the Canary Islands' most important artists, Cristóbal Hernández de Quintana (1659–1725) and Juan de Miranda (1723–1805), both left paintings here. Several important religious orders established convents and monasteries in La Laguna,

The Plaza de San Francisco in La Laguna

The neo-classical façade of the Catedral obscures a neo-Gothic interior

among the most important being the **Convento de Santa Clara**, on Calle Nava y Grimón. The convent's church has an admirable timber ceiling, but it is currently closed for restoration work.

Grand Old Houses

More interesting for some will be La Laguna's graceful **Canary Island mansions**. Never rising more than three floors, they stand out above all for the extensive use of timber, especially in the ornate doors and heavily framed sash windows. Behind the façades are lovely interior *patios* (courtyards). Keep a look out for open doors into these grand old houses, as frequently you can go inside far enough to see the courtyards.

Some of the most important of these houses can be seen on **Calle San Agustín**. No 28, **Casa Salazar**, is in fact the bishop's residence, but during working hours you can usually go in to admire the *patio*. Just down the road at No 16 is the **Casa Montañés**, built in the 17th century, with fine timber work in the doors, windows and courtyards.

The pick of the crop is Casa Lercaro, between the two. It has been converted into the **Museo de Historia y Antropología de Tenerife**, which is interesting in itself, but a visit is also worthwhile just to inspect the house. The outstanding feature is the polished timber, used in everything from the ceilings to the floors. The museum displays are in Spanish, but they allow you to get a handle on the pre-Spanish history of Tenerife, its conquest and developments up to the present. On show are documents, maps and explanatory panels as well as artefacts, tools and household items ranging through the centuries.

TAKING A BREAK

Take a load off and enjoy a soothing ale at one of the terrazas on **Plaza del Adelantado**. Or splash out on a good meal at the nearby **El Principito** restaurant (Calle de Santo Domingo 26, tel: 922/633-916, moderate) which offers French and Spanish dishes, with fish specialities.

---

193 E3/4

Catedral
Plaza de la Catedral s/n Closed for refurbishment

Iglesia de la Concepción
Plaza de la Concepción s/n Daily 9–1:30, 6–8:30

Museo de Historia y Antropología de Tenerife
Calle San Agustín 22 922/825-949 Tue–Sat 9–8, Sun 10–5 €5

Museo de la Ciencia y el Cosmos
Calle Via Láctea s/n 922/315-265 Tue–Sat 9–8, Sun 10–5 €5

Real Santuario del Santísimo Cristo
Plaza de San Francisco s/n Mon–Sat 9–1, 4–9, Sun 9–9 Free

Environmentally friendly: the tram between Santa Cruz and La Laguna

INSIDER INFO

- The 16th-century **Real Santuario del Santísimo Cristo** (Royal Sanctuary of the Most Holy Christ), also known as the Santuario de San Francisco church, is home to a black Gothic wooden sculpture of Christ.
- La Laguna is linked to downtown Santa Cruz by tram (➤ 37). Modern low-loader wagons complete the 12.7km (8mi) journey in 37 min. And the good news for the night owl: At the weekend, the tram runs the whole night.

- You might want to check out the **Museo de la Ciencia y el Cosmos**, a little way out of the centre of town. An interactive science museum, it is popular with kids. The emphasis is on astronomy (including a planetarium), which is hardly surprising given the important telescope observatories on Tenerife and La Palma, whose activities are co-ordinated by the Instituto de Astrofísica de Canarias (IAC) at La Laguna University (➤ 126).

8 Montañas de Anaga

The rugged Anaga mountain range that dominates the north-east corner of Tenerife is a nature reserve and an escape for the citizens of La Laguna and Santa Cruz. The Tinerfeños are campaigning for the region to be declared a biosphere reserve. You can drive along narrow winding roads to small villages or, better still, put on your hiking boots and follow the trails that, in some cases, bring you out to impressive points along the island's wild north-east coast.

Around Taganana

The most substantial Anaga town is **Taganana**. It slithers down a steep hillside facing the ocean on the northern flank of the Anaga. About halfway down the slope is the **Iglesia de Nuestra Señora de las Nieves**, known mainly for a 16th-century Flemish triptych (quite a way from its original home), and a cheerful square. In terms of monuments there is not much else to it, but the precarious lanes lined with humble houses transport you into another world and there are fine views of the coast and the palm-laden gorge.

The village of Las Mercedes sits on the steep Anaga hillside

WALKING THE ROYAL WAY

Long before asphalt roads, the Montañas de Anaga were criss-crossed by a series of narrow trails known as *caminos reales* (royal ways). Several of these still exist and make for great walking opportunities. Among the best known is the **Vueltas de Taganana**, which snakes its way from the main TF12 highway (the trail starts at a *casa forestal* – forest ranger's hut) across the Llano de las Vueltas (Vueltas Plain) north to Taganana. It takes about 1.5 hours to reach Taganana, and you can walk back by following a driving track via a settlement west of Taganana called Las Chozas (the full duration is about three hours). You will pass through thick woods and be rewarded along the way with some really stunning views of the north coast.

Further West

Another intriguing hamlet is **Taborno**, with its scattering of houses along a ridge jutting north. The views from the top of the village out over the coast are breathtaking.

To the north is the **Roque de Taborno** (706m/2,316ft), a rocky outcrop covered in trees, which is often referred to as "Teneriffe's Matterhorn" owing to its shape.

A little harder to get to is the remarkable hamlet of **Chinamada**. About halfway down the TF145, which drops north from the TF12 towards Las Carboneras, a 5km (3-mile) walking trail to Chinamada is signposted. It takes about three hours to get there and back, with a little time thrown in to look around.

Apart from the sense of isolation, the main point of interest are the cave houses, partly built into the rock. Only a handful of people live in these semi-troglodyte dwellings, and surprisingly their interiors are much like those of any

The cave houses of Chinamada are worth the time it takes to hike to them

The sea swell on the north coast tends to be strong

modern house. The walking trail continues for about two hour north-west to **Punta del Hidalgo** (➤ 82) on the coast.

To the East

On the eastern side of the Anaga range, the road peters out in the village of **Chamorga**. It is as much the driving route around here (➤ 167) as the place itself that is of interest. Aside from a small chapel, higgledy-piggledy houses and some dragon trees, there is little to this half-abandoned farming village. However, it does offer several walking possibilities and the starting point for several trails is signposted. The most popular takes you to **Roque Bermejo**, a tiny settlement (with nearby lighthouse) on the east coast.

The coast also offers some surprises. **Surfers** come to the black-sand beaches off the north Anaga coast to catch waves – the swell here is about the best on Tenerife for surfing.

For a quieter seaside experience you could make for **Playa de Antequera**, south of the mountains and about 4km (2.5mi) east of Igueste (➤ 53) – an hour's walk. Locals often turn up by boat, easily the most relaxing method of approach. Insider Tip

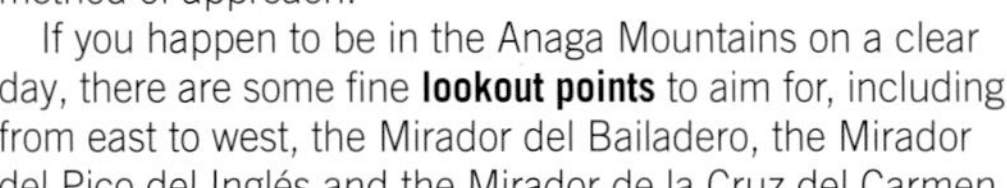

If you happen to be in the Anaga Mountains on a clear day, there are some fine **lookout points** to aim for, including, from east to west, the Mirador del Bailadero, the Mirador del Pico del Inglés and the Mirador de la Cruz del Carmen.

TAKING A BREAK

There are several simple **fish restaurants** lined up opposite Playa de San Roque. Just take your pick!

Chinamada ✚ **194 B5**
Playa de San Roque ✚ **194 B5**
Taganana ✚ **193 F5**
Taborno ✚ **193 F4/5**

INSIDER INFO

Hikers should bear several things in mind in the Anaga Mountains:

- Always carry sufficient **food and water** as in many of the small villages you cannot count on finding even a shop open.
- Wear **good hiking boots** and **be prepared** for all seasons. A hot, sunny morning can quickly turn into a squally afternoon, with mist, rain and biting winds.

At Your Leisure

The summit of Mount Teide can be seen across a sea of clouds from the Bosque de la Esperanza

20 Stunt Galería de Arte

This small gallery is a good address for contemporary art on the island with a regular exhibition programme featuring local and mainland Spanish artists supplemented with works by foreign artists.

193 E3 Calle Bencomo 7, La Laguna 922/252-528; www.stunt.es

21 Bosque de la Esperanza

The thick woods of the Bosque de la Esperanza cover a high ridge that climbs south west from La Laguna towards Mount Teide (► 122) and forms part of the island's volcanic backbone. Insider Tip The woods are wonderful for walking and along the road that runs through the middle are scattered eight fine *miradores* (lookout points).

If you are driving from La Laguna, take the TF24 road towards the unremarkable town of La Esperanza. The real treat begins as you gain altitude and enter the forest itself, filled with giant pines and other species of trees. Marked trails fall away from either side of the ridge, which the road follows through the length of the forest and beyond towards Mount Teide. Among the better lookouts to stop at are the **Mirador Pico de las Flores**, from where you can gaze north to La Laguna and beyond to the Anaga Mountains, and the **Mirador de Ortuño** (10km/6mi further), where you get the first good look at Mount Teide. The best is about 2km (1mi) on, where a lane branches right off the main road to the **Mirador de las Cumbres**. The views of Mount Teide from here are impressive, as are those of the forest. About 10km (6mi) further on you emerge from the forest into the stark landscape around Mount Teide.

192 C2 5km (3mi) south of La Laguna

22 Tacoronte

Tacoronte lies at the heart of Tenerife's wine country. It is a pleasant town and worth a stop while on an unhurried tour of the area. The name Tacoronte is believed to be a Guanche word meaning "the place where the elders meet", leading archaeologists to suggest that it was a capital for one of the Guanche tribes. After the Spanish conquest of the islands it received a community of Portuguese settlers.

The old nucleus of the town gathers around the **Iglesia del Cristo de los Dolores** (Church of the Sorrows of Christ) and the nearby **Iglesia de Santa Catalina**.

The former houses a much-venerated 17th-century image of Christ (the church is also known as the Santuario del Santísimo Cristo – Sanctuary of the Most Holy Christ). Construction on the Iglesia de Santa Catalina started in the early 16th century, but it wasn't finished until towards the end of the 18th century. Inside is a charming *artesonado* ceiling (a timber ceiling divided into squares into which wooden inserts are placed). Around the two churches gathers a web of tight lanes and several town houses.

Tacoronte can get lively, especially in the Fiestas de la Vendimia (Grape Harvest Festival) during September.

193 D3 9km (5.5mi) west of La Laguna

23 El Sauzal & Casa del Vino la Baranda

Just by the motorway exit for El Sauzal stands a 17th-century *hacienda* (farm) now used as a wine showcase and museum for Tenerife, the **Casa del Vino la Baranda**. The house, founded by a merchant originally from Andalucía in southern Spain, was the nucleus of a sprawling property that, for a few years, during the mid-19th century passed into the hands of the President of Mexico, José Joaquín de Herrera.

Originally known as the Quinta de San Simón del Sauzal, the house was taken over and restored by the Tenerife government in 1992 and converted into the attractive wine museum it is today.

After entering you pass through reception on the left and into what was the founder's family chapel, notable for the original (unrestored) *artesonado* ceiling. Down the hall are exhibition rooms and, at the end, a tasteful bar and restaurant area. Across the courtyard is the museum, a well-presented exploration of the history of Tenerife's wines and their growers. Attached to the museum is an enticing wine shop and wine-tasting room. On summer evenings you can catch classical music concerts on the *patio*.

El Sauzal itself is a pleasant place, filled with well-appointed and attractive villas, and enticing small restaurants. In the centre is the unusual **Iglesia de San Pedro**, notable for its whitewashed Moorish-looking dome. Make for the **Mirador de la Garañona**, a marvellous lookout with views out over the cliff walls.

192 C3

Palm trees and pot plants adorn El Sauzal's town hall

An unexpected skyscraper on the headland near Punta del Hidalgo

Casa del Vino la Baranda
✉ Autopista General del Norte, Km 21
☎ 922/572-535; www.tenerife.es/casa-vino
🕐 Tue 10:30–6:30, Wed–Sat 9–9, Sun 11–6
✋ Free

24 Casa de Carta (Museo de Antropología)

A detour north from Tacoronte towards the hamlet of Valle de Guerra leads you to this beautiful country home now turned into the **Museo de Antropología** (Anthropology Museum). The everyday life of the Tinerfeños and their traditional crafts are the focal themes of this well-structured exhibition, with one room dedicated to the Canarian national costume. It is also worth making time to tour the small botanical garden located in front of the former manor house.

193 D4
✉ Tacoronte–Valle de Guerra road
☎ 922/546-300 🕐 Daily 10–5 ✋ €5

25 Bajamar & Punta del Hidalgo

These two coastal towns, only 4km (2.5mi) apart, form a dated coastal resort on the north flank of the Anaga Mountains. Although due for a major facelift as it is full of unattractive apartments and soul-less hotels, the two resorts are relaxed and the landscape around them impressive. Waves pound the black volcanic rock – apart from the modest black strand at **Bajamar** (meaning "down by the sea") there is nothing in the way of beaches here – against the majestic back-ground of the Anaga Mountains.

The road ends with **Punta del Hidalgo** – the only way to continue from here is on foot. The most curious items are the ***piscinas naturales***, the "natural pools" that have been carved out of the rock. On a stormy day waves crash over the barriers and into the tranquillity of the pool, which can be slightly unnerving. Indeed, this is a windy corner, with gusts often whipping up the ocean.

It's unlikely that either resort will attract you enough to stay, but it's worth dropping by for a swim and to have a look around.

193 D4/E5
✉ Bajamar 8km (5mi) north of La Laguna
✉ Punta del Hidalgo 11km (7mi) north of La Laguna

Where to...
Stay

Prices
Prices are for a double room per night during the high season.
€ under €70 € €70–120 € over €120

PUNTA DEL HIDALGO

Aparthotel Atlantis Park €€
The two-storey apartment complex, principally booked by the more senior age group, is located just a short walk away from the natural pool in Punta del Hidalgo. All of these spacious holiday homes have a balcony and refrigerator. Apart from an outdoor pool, there is also a small heated indoor pool and a sauna. The restaurant's culinary selection includes an international selection with a wholefood focus. Anyone seeking additional activities can take part in one or other of the various educational programmes on offer; they range from beginners' Spanish to courses providing qualification as a state-approved yoga teacher.
180 C5 Calle Oceano Artico 1
922/156-411; www.atlantis-park.com

LA LAGUNA

Aguere €
This delightful B&B in the old quarter is a completely "non-package" experience. The 18th-century house was once a bishop's palace and has 22 rooms rambling around the skylit upper gallery. It was later used as school accommodation but was converted into a hotel in 1885. The 22 rooms of varying size have been refurbished and are airy and spacious. Breakfast is included in the price and is the only meal served. Take it under the swaying palms in the courtyard.
193 E3/4 Calle La Carrera 55
922/259-490; www.hotelaguere.es

Hotel Nivaria €€
This 18th-century building sits on the south side of La Laguna's charming central old town square. An elegant *patio* is one of its prime feature, and the interior, if rather sombre in parts, has an authentic Spanish atmosphere.

The 73 rooms include studios for two and apartments for up to three, furnished in modern styles. There is a restaurant and a café-bar on site, and a squash court is an unexpected plus point. Guests can also take advantage of the complimentary internet access or bicycles.
193 E4 Plaza del Adelantado 11
922/264-298; www.hotelnivaria.com

TACORONTE

El Adelantado €
A large traditional 18th-century farmhouse in ample grounds in the heart of the north can be rented per room or as a large villa. The house has two cosy sitting rooms and a room where breakfast is served. There's a terrace overlooking the private vineyard: the estate is on north-facing slopes at an altitude of more than 500m (1,600ft) and is in one of the most important wine-growing areas on the island. The owners run bonsai workshops and have gardens specialising in Canarian plants. There's a minimum stay of three nights.
193 D3 El Alentado 16, Tacoronte
922/271-135;
www.casaruraleladelantado.com

Where to...
Eat and Drink

Prices
Price per person for a three-course meal including drinks
€ under €20 € €20–40 € over €40

Some excellent family restaurants are located on the country roads around La Esperanza and the Anaga Mountains. Many restaurants have a strong local ambience, in contrast to the more touristy places found in the international resorts. A lively bar and café scene centres on La Laguna's university quarter, especially around Plaza Zurita. The area is known as El Cuadrilátero and teems with around 60 bars. Thousands of students revel in spots like the Irish-style Cerveceria 7 Islas (Calle Heraclio Sanchez) for its choice beers and, El Buho (Calle Catedral 3) and Pub Harina (Calle Dr Zamenhof 9).

LA LAGUNA

Asador Neke €/€€
This restaurant has a good reputation for well-cooked dishes using the best ingredients, many locally sourced. There's a pretty dining room and terrace with starched tablecloths that hints at attention to detail. The menu offers a good range of meats, seafood and salad dishes.
193 E3/4 Subida del Pulpito, close to the Aeropuerto del Norte 922/257-166 Mon–Sat noon–4, 8–midnight

Patio Canario €/€€
While perhaps nudging the touristy, the courtyard after which this Canarian eatery is named is a pleasant setting for tapas, cheese and meat platters, and other goodies. It is set in an 18th-century house and the *patio* in question is preceded by a friendly bar area.
193 E3/4 Calle Manuel de Ossuna 8 922/264-657 Daily noon–4:30, 8–1am

La Taberna del Oscar €€
One of the world's best tapas bars is located in a pretty pedestrian street in the historic district of this World Heritage Town. The restaurant is renowned for its sausage and ham specialities from the Spanish mainland as well as for its tasty Manchego cheese, tortillas, fried calamari, sardines, and much more. A glass of local red wine is the best accompaniment to the very attractive nibbles. But, of course, quality has its price.
193 E3/4 Calle Heradores 66 922/265-214 Mon–Sat 8–midnight, Sun 10–4:30

El Tonique €/€€
Dine in a cellar-style dining room in wood, brick and stone, with walls partly lined with a selection of its 150 varieties of wine. The mainstay of this wine bar's menu consists of imaginative, generously sized tapas, but main courses are also available. This place is popular with a lively young local crowd as well as business people.
193 E3/4 Calle Heraclio Sánchez 23 922/261-529 Mon 8pm–12:30am, Tue–Sat 1–4:30, 8–12:30; closed 15–30 Aug

TACORONTE

Los Limoneros €€€
This elegant, formal restaurant lies in a quiet, rural spot just east of the village of Los Naranjeros, providing a civilised setting for its well-heeled

clientele. It's also a restaurant frequented by the Spanish royal family when they visit Tenerife. The cooking is traditional, making much use of lamb and fish, and service is generally courteous.

193 D3
Carretera General del Norte 447B Km15.5
922/636-637 Mon–Sat 1pm–midnight

Mi Merced €/€€

This lovely interior is a typical formal Spanish café with a highly polished mahogany bar and marble floor. The food is also classical in style with both Canarian and Castilian choices as well as excellent grilled meats.

180 B4
Camino Real 280, Barranco las Lajas
922/567-236 Wed–Sat noon–5pm, 8–10:30; Sun noon–5pm. Closed Mon and Tue

EL SAUZAL

Casa del Vino La Baranda €€

The tapas-bar and restaurant attached to the wine museum (➤81) gives visitors a chance to sample some of the island's best wine produce before buying it to take away. The lovely 17th-century country house has an elegantly atmospheric setting, the Canarian dishes are well prepared and tasty, and there's an increasingly cheerful buzz as glasses are raised. There is an excellent view from the sun terrace.

192 D3 El Sauzal 922/563-886
Tue–Sat 1–4, 8–11, Sun 1–4

PUNTA DEL HIDALGO

La Caseta €

The restaurant not far from the seawater pool specialises in fresh fish and fruits de mer. It also serves paella, rabbit and grilled dishes. Its patisserie offers an enormous selection of cakes and fruit tarts.

193 E5 Avenida Marítima 1
922/156-632; www.restaurantelacaseta.es
Tue–Sun noon–11:30

Where to... Shop

SOUVENIRS

La Laguna isn't really geared towards tourist shopping. One exception, however, is the **Artesanía Los Calados** (Calle Capitán Brotons 24) which sells beautiful embroidery while **Atlantida Artesanía** (Calle San Agustín 55) sells a range of island products.

On the Plaza San Francisco, you will find the **Mercado Municipal**, a large vegetable market (Mon–Sat 7–2).

WINE

The Tacoronte region is famed for its wines and a great place to buy is the **Casa del Vino la Baranda** (➤81) at El Sauzal. Insider Tip For a small fee, you can taste wines, and get advice from the knowledgeable, multilingual staff in the impressive shop/wine museum.

Another good place is **Bodega Alvaro** (2km/1.2mi outside Tacoronte on the La Laguna road, tel: 922/ 560-359; Mon–Sat 9–5:30), Tenerife's largest wine dealer.

WALKING MAPS

If you're planning to explore the Anaga Mountains in the north east in any detail, make sure you invest in a decent map before setting off.

A selection of **walking maps and guides** is available either at La Laguna's information office on Plaza del Adelantado (➤74), or at the Mirador Cruz del Carmen visitor centre (➤99).

Where to... Go Out

LA LAGUNA

Entertainment in La Laguna caters mainly for locals and students, and virtually all performances will be in Spanish. Enquire at the **Teatro Leal** (Calle Obispo Rey Redondo 54, tel: 922/259-617) if you are interested in finding out what is on offer.

The city comes to life during its annual **jazz and international theatre festivals**. During Corpus Christi (May, June, ➤ 14), elaborate carpets of coloured sand and flowers are created in the streets, and visitors flock in from all the local islands. If you have children to amuse on a wet day, try La Laguna's **Museo de la Ciencia y el Cosmos** (Vía Láctea, tel: 922/315-265; Tue–Sat 10–5; €5), a space and science museum with hands-on activities.

HIKING

Most visitors go to the north east for exhilarating scenery and fresh air. The few roads through the Anaga Mountains can get congested in high season (watch out for stray goats on the bends). Plan walks carefully as few routes form easy round-trips, and there's no accommodation in the mountains. Though altitudes are moderate, gradients are steep and weather conditions can change quickly.

Footpaths meander all over this steeply contoured peninsula. For maps and route information, visit the Anaga Park information centre at **Cruz del Carmen** (tel: 922/633-576), where there's a panoramic *mirador* and a simple restaurant. It's a good starting point for splendid walks through primeval **laurel forest** to pretty villages like Las Carboneras or El Batán. Other interesting routes can be followed from Chamorga or round the rugged coastline from Taganana. The driveable road ends at Benijo, but paths lead to the lighthouse (Faro de Anaga).

BIRDWATCHING

Keen birdwatchers should keep an eye open for one of Tenerife's unique endemic species, **Bolle's Pigeon**. You may be lucky enough to see it perching on branches in the laurel forests of the Anaga Mountains. **Punta del Hidalgo** (➤ 82) is a good place to spot spring migrants.

Find somewhere safe to stop and listen out for **native canaries** singing along the wooded roadsides between Las Mercedes and La Laguna. The dense pine forests of **La Esperanza** may give tantalising glimpses of Tenerife's tiny acrobatic goldcrest, and also the beautiful blue chaffinch. A good place to see them is from the *mirador* at El Diablillo on the Cumbre Dorsal from Esperanza to Mount Teide.

WATERSPORTS

The coves east of the **Punta del Hidalgo** (➤ 82) and big waves whipped up by onshore winds attract **surfers**. But the currents round the northern cape can be dangerous, so you need to be more advanced than a beginner here. A safer place to **swim** is the low-key resort of **Bajamar** (➤ 82), where you can bathe in tidal rock pools surrounded by protective reefs.

GOLF

The smartest of Tenerife's courses is the **Real Club de Golf de Tenerife** near Tacoronte (tel: 922/636-607; www.realclubgolftenerife.com). Its rolling fairways enjoy the shade of old trees and offer a splendid view of Mount Teide.

The North West

Little Treats

Colonial Boulevard

In **Puerto de la Cruz** (➤ 96), wandering along the pedestrianised Calle Quintana is a bit like being on a catwalk.

Doll Museum

Just a few minutes' drive from Icod's Dragon Tree (➤ 92), young visitors in particular will love the **Museo de Muñecas** (Icod de los Vinos, Finca Artlandya, Camino el Moleiro 21; www.artlandya.com, Tue–Fri 10–6pm, €10).

Beautiful Prospects

A spectacular view of the harbour town of Garachico (➤ 105) is offered from **Mirador de Garachico** on the TF82 between Icod and El Tanque. A large panorama restaurant provides fitting accompaniment.

Getting Your Bearings

The western half of Tenerife's northern coastal strip is the area of the island richest in interest for visitors, with historical town centres, a comparatively low-key seaside resort, fishing villages, strange trees, rugged coast, banana plantations, an interactive zoo and the rugged mountain terrain around the village of Masca.

Although long dedicated to the business of tourism, Puerto de la Cruz is an interesting coastal town that has managed to preserve much of the charm of its old centre. More engaging still is the inland town of La Orotava, the prettiest old colonial city in the Canary Islands and set in one of Tenerife's most attractive valleys.

A series of beaches and villages reveals itself as you head west. Marvel at the ancient dragon tree and exotic butterflies

Right page: Barranco de Masca counts among Tenerife's scenic highlights

La Orotava is one of the most beautiful and representative places on the island

TOP 10

Don't Miss

At Your Leisure

in Icod de los Vinos, lie on the nearby beach at San Marcos, explore the fishing hamlet of Garachico, or opt to drive away from it all to Punta de Teno, which juts arrogantly into the Atlantic at the island's westernmost point.

The majesty of the coast is matched by the abruptness of its hinterland, which rears up to the east. An unequalled vantage point from which to enjoy a Tenerife sunset is the pretty mountain hamlet of Masca, along whose gorge you can also trek to the coast.

The North West

Three Perfect Days

If you're not quite sure where to begin your travels, this itinerary recommends three practical and enjoyable days out in the North West, taking in some of the best places to see. For more information see the main entries (➤ 92–110).

Day One

Morning

Plan to arrive in ★6 **La Orotava** (➤ 100) in the morning. Go on a walking tour of the town, which is full of wonderful old Canarian houses. Don't miss the Casas de los Balcones, the Museo de Artesanía Iberoamericana and the Baroque Iglesia de Nuestra Señora de la Concepción. Next head down to ★5 **Puerto de la Cruz** (➤ 96), a short drive or bus/taxi ride. It is well worth stopping on the way at the Mirador Humboldt. Here, the great naturalist Alexander vom Humboldt once enjoyed the view over the Orotava Valley during his flying visit to Tenerife in 1799.

When you get to Puerto de la Cruz, a good option is to walk down to the **Reguló** in the old fishing district (Calle Pérez Zamora, tel: 922/384-506) and eat lunch there.

Afternoon

Several choices present themselves. You could soak up some sun at **Lago Martiánez** (➤ 96) or **Playa Jardín** (➤ 96), visit the island's most popular park, 28 **Loro Parque** (above; ➤ 109), or simply explore the town on foot. You can easily combine two of these. There are plenty of dining options in Puerto de la Cruz (➤ 109–110) before returning to La Orotava for the night.

Day Two

Morning
Take the highway west towards 3 **Icod de los Vinos** (➤ 92). The top of everyone's list is the **Drago Milenario**, an old dragon tree; right). Take time for a leisurely stroll about the town centre and consider a visit to the parish church of San Marcos. Drive the few kilometres down to Icod's local beach, 32 **Playa de San Marcos** (➤ 109), where you can enjoy a swim in the protected bay and indulge in lunch at one of the waterfront restaurants.

Afternoon
From Playa de San Marcos it is 7km (4.5mi) to 26 **Garachico** (➤ 105), a charming fishing town that was once also one of Tenerife's senior ports. There is plenty to occupy an afternoon, from the natural ocean pools to the former Convento de San Francisco.

Day Three

Follow the circular driving tour (➤ 169). If you devoted the previous morning to Icod de los Vinos, you can drive straight through and, in a further variation from the suggested route, duck south to see the 27 **Acantilado de los Gigantes** cliffs (➤ 107) before backtracking to 4 **Masca** (➤ 194). From there you will head to 35 **Punta de Teno** (➤ 110) and possibly stop outside 34 **Buenavista del Norte** (➤ 110) for dinner before returning to Garachico for the night.

3 Icod de los Vinos

A wine-belt town high up above the rugged north-west coast of Tenerife, Icod de los Vinos has for years made a good part of its living from a single tree. The bizarre shape of the *drago*, the huge dragon tree, claimed to be more than 1,000 years old, keeps visitors pouring in. The grand old plant is worth the effort but there is more to Icod, such as the magnificent parish church.

If you drive into town, signs to the **Parque del Drago** will lead you to a parking area right next to the Iglesia de San Marcos. If you don't want to pay the entrance fee for the park go into the church square where you can enjoy an unimpaired view of the giant, ancient-looking tree. On a fine day, you can make out the silhouette of the Pico del Teide in the background.

The gnarled and sinewy **dragon tree** is 15m (99ft) tall and 6m (20ft) in diameter at its base. Many of the locals refer to it as the *Drago milenario*, the thousand-year-old tree. Botanists say that the Methuselah is actually only a maximum of 400 to 500 years old, a period during which it has however developed an incredibly thick trunk (dragon trees don't have rings so estimating their age is a rough science). The tree's sap is known as "dragon's blood" as it turns red on contact with the air. The "blood" traditionally was used for medicinal purposes and as a natural dye.

Around the tree spreads a well-tended **botanical garden**, in which there are several young dragon trees. The garden provides an excellent introduction to the plant world to be found on the Canaries. Besides various spurges, you will also discover extremely fragrant Canarian jasmine and magnificent white viper's bugloss, which sprout blossomed cones of up to one-and-a-half metres in the spring. There are also different kinds of laurel trees, strawberry trees that bear fruit in autumn, Canarian lavender and a large number of Canarian *Centaurea*.

INSIDER INFO

- If you have a little extra time, head for **Plaza de la Constitución**, a quick walk north of the Parque del Drago and part of the compact old town. Among its mansions is the **Casa-Museo "Los Cáceres"** (Plaza de la Constitución 1, daily 10–1, 5–8, free), a sturdy neoclassical house built early in the 19th century. Inside is a beautiful *patio* dominated by grand timber columns and an enclosed gallery. A permanent gallery features works by artist Guillermo Sureda and the *casa* hosts temporary art and photography exhibitions.
- About 200m (220 yards) along Calle San Antonio from Plaza de la Constitución, in the little square called Plazuela Cabrera Mejías, is another, **smaller dragon tree** known affectionately as the Drago Chico ("little dragon").

The ancient *drago* (dragon tree) of Icod de los Vinos has become a symbol of Tenerife over the centuries

Equal measures of patience would have been required by one Jerónimo de Espellosa y Villabriga, a Spaniard living in Cuba who, in 1668, completed, after five years, the remarkable silver cross in the **Museo de la Iglesia de San Marcos**. The museum is little more than a room in the church of the same name, and the cross is the only item of serious interest. Measuring 2.45m (8ft) in height and weighing 48.3kg (106 pounds), it is a marvel of detailed work, looking more like a complex piece of embroidery than a heavy chunk of precious metal.

TAKING A BREAK

Stop for a coffee in the snack bar at the **Parque del Drago**. Otherwise head to the bar in the bandstand in shady **Plaza de Cáceres**, which is linked to Plaza de la Iglesia.

---

189 D4/5

Parque del Drago
Plaza de la Consitucion 922/814-510 Summer 9:30–8 €5

Museo de la Iglesia de San Marcos
Plaza de la Iglesia 922/810-695 Mon–Sat 9–1:30, 4–6:30 €1

4 Masca

The dramatic location high in the Teno Massif makes the hamlet of Masca one of Tenerife's most engaging stops. Take one of the walks, including a challenging hike down to the coast. It's also a lovely place to watch a splendid sunset.

Whichever way you approach, from the north or the south, arriving in Masca (600m/1,968ft) is a theatrical process. Until the beginning of the 1960s, the only way to reach the hamlet was on a mule. Today, there is a narrow mountain road linking it to Buenavista and Santiago del Teide. Although the road is in good condition, it serpentines past some very steep precipices – and should be avoided by less confident drivers. Anyone who does decide to drive their own car to Masca should leave it on the main road above the town. Parking spaces here are limited. However, there is a regular bus service to Masca, and you can of course book an organised tour.

Surrounded by mountains, Masca consists of several little districts spread out over the mountainside. Wherever

Masca is perched prettily at the head of a steep valley

possible, terraced fields have been carved out. They are used to grow potatoes and wheat as well as small quantities of fruit and vegetables. Since the area has an ample water supply, everything flourishes. The houses are built on two levels into the slopes. Wooden steps lead up to the doors. There are no intermediate ceilings inside, meaning that there is generally only one room. The centre of the town is the small plaza by the church. You can buy souvenirs here, and the locally produced honey is excellent. Many people living here have their own beehives on the steep mountain slopes.

The path to the small ethnographic museum is signposted from the plaza.

Spectacular views: hiking through the spectacular Masca gorge

Walking the Barranco

It you want to walk down into the gorge, follow the central path past the houses and you'll see how it quickly reverts to a dirt trail. The hike there and back will take six to seven hours. Alternatively, you can arrange to meet a tour boat at 3pm to take you to Los Gigantes (➤ 107), saving you the uphill trek.

TAKING A BREAK

Chez Arlette (➤ 114) by the church has excellent views and home-made traditional dishes.

188 B4

INSIDER INFO

- If you are here in the **first week of December**, enquire about Masca's **Fiesta de la Consolación**. This is a religious feast day when villagers dress in traditional clothes and musicians break out their *timples* (like a ukelele) to liven up the atmosphere after the solemn religious procession.
- By 4pm most of the tourist buses have left Masca and peace returns to this secluded valley. Late afternoon is thus the best time for independent travellers to drive to this village hamlet, although you need to take into consideration that most of the restaurants in Masca close around 6pm and by 7pm at the latest. The drive back down to the valley in the dark demands extreme care.

5 Puerto de la Cruz

Puerto de la Cruz, once merely the port for the rich business town of La Orotava high up in the hinterland, transformed itself into Tenerife's principal tourist resort. Although some ugly high-rise hotels mar the skyline, as resorts go it's a mixed and interesting place. Explore the fishing port and the old centre, lounge about in the shallow seawater pools on the Costa de Martiánez designed by César Manrique or head for the spacious black beach of Playa Jardín.

Odd really. First they built the beach resort and then they thought about the beaches. The minuscule strips of volcanic sand and rock that constitute **Playa San Telmo** can hardly be thought of as a beach. So just to the east the Lanzarote artist César Manrique designed the pleasing **Lago Martiánez**, a leisure complex based on sky-blue, sea-water pools.

If you prefer to cavort in the ocean waves, then head west for **Playa Jardín**. This broad strand of fine volcanic sand has been turned into an attractive leisure area. The beach, as long as you don't mind the colour, is as good as any, studded with deep-black, volcanic boulders and palms. In the background is the garden part, an extensive maze of palms and other trees. A restaurant and snack bar complete the offerings.

At the eastern edge of the beach rise the forbidding walls of the **Castillo San Felipe**, an early 17th-century emplacement built to help defend the old port from unwelcome visitors. Classical and folk evening concerts are frequently staged here. Tickets available on site.

Idyllic: the fishing harbour of Puerto de la Cruz

The bells toll for all in the Baroque belfry of the Iglesia de Nuestra Señora de la Peña de Francia

Back in the centre of town, you can indulge in a little sightseeing. At the western end of Lago Martiánez, the tiny **Ermita de San Telmo** is a chapel founded in 1780 by the seamen's guild. Things have changed: this is now the place to hear Mass in German.

About 200m west, Puerto de la Cruz's main church, the **Iglesia de Nuestra Señora de la Peña de Francia** (Church of Our Lady of the Rock of France), a sturdy Baroque structure filled with gaudy *retablos,* presides over Plaza de la Iglesia.

Closer to the waterfront are two well-preserved traditional Canary Island mansions. The **Casa de Miranda**, has exquisite carved teak balconies and interior, and was built in 1730 and now serves as a restaurant of the same name.

Overlooking the little fishing port on Calle Lonjas is the **Casa de la Aduana**, once the Customs house. In this representative building, you will find, among other things, the tourist information office and a craft store.

The **Museo Arqueológico** (Archaeology Museum) is in fact a small Guanche (► 16) ceramics display. The simple bowls, plates, mugs and even a couple of *amphorae* are the main clues to how Guanche society worked. Housed in an exquisitely restored mansion, it warrants a quick visit if only as a reminder that the islands do not have a solely Spanish history.

The **Parque Taoro** just north of the old town centre can actually be described as one of the birthplaces of Tenerife's tourism. At the end of the 19th century, a large luxury hotel opened here in which predominantly well-to-do guests from England spent the winter. Later, the building housed the casino, which has now been empty for a number of years. You can walk through the garden during the day with its old tree population and look down towards the sea from the viewing points.

Out of Town

About 1.5km (1mi) from the centre of Puerto de la Cruz in the La Paz district is the **Jardín Botánico** (Botanical Garden). In 1788, King Charles III of Spain ordered the creation of this garden so that a wide collection of tropical species might be grown on Spanish soil in the appropriate climate. The good king clearly had strong views on matters floral (was it to do with his unusually prominent nose?) for he was behind the creation of the Botanical Gardens in Madrid as well. The garden has some extraordinary specimens, like the huge Moreton Bay fig and a Kigelia or sausage tree.

Right page: View from the Parque Taoro over the town's sea of houses

TAKING A BREAK

Have a drink at any of the outdoor cafés on central **Plaza del Charco**. For a fine meal in cosy surroundings, reserve a table at the 18th-century **Casa de Miranda** on **Calle Santo Domingo**.

---

190 B5

Casa de la Aduana
Calle Lonjas 922/378-103 Mon–Sat 10–8

Iglesia de Nuestra Señora de la Peña de Francia
Plaza de la Iglesia s/n
Mon–Sat 8:30–6:30, Sun mass at 8, 10 and 11 Free

Jardín Botánico
Calle Retama 2 922/383-572
Apr–Sep daily 9–7, Oct–Mar daily 9–6 €3

Lago Martiánez
Avenida de Colón s/n 922/385-955
Daily May–Sep 10–7, Oct–Apr 10–6 €3.50

Museo Arqueológico
Calle del Lomo 9/a 922/371-465; www.arqueopc.com
Tue–Sat 10–1, 5–9, Sun 10–1 €1

Parque Taoro
Carretera de Taoro All day Free

The large seawater pools along the Costa de Martiánez designed by César Manrique promise a unique experience

INSIDER INFO

- The little **ceramic figurine in Room 5** of the Museo Arqueológico, one of the only such objects found in Tenerife, is a source of constant curiosity. Does it represent a man or a god? What significance might it have had in the Stone-Age minds of the Guanches? Guesses abound but there is little certainty as to its true meaning.
- The **area around the Museo Arqueológico**, with its traditional houses and plethora of restaurants, has a homey flavour altogether. The attractive, partly car-free roads encourage you to stroll. Insider Tip

6 La Orotava

Even during the time of the Guanches, the Valle de la Orotava (Orotava Valley) was considered one of the richest areas in Tenerife. Spanish settlers were quick to move in and the valley remains a luxuriant farming oasis. The town of the same name is famous for its elaborate wooden balconies that adorn many of the town houses and for the magnificent view over the Orotava Valley, once so admired by Alexander von Humboldt.

La Orotava was founded at the beginning of the 16th century, shortly after the conquest of the island. The small settlement soon prospered and became the second most important town after La Laguna. In 1648, Felipe IV signed a degree giving La Orotava "town" status. A few years before that, today's Puerto de la Cruz had been founded as its harbour. The small harbour town belonged to La Orotava until 1813.

Although the town has spread out over the last decades, it has managed to retain the old centre with its representative silhouette. When you wander up or down the little streets, which are quite steep in parts, you will see one magnificent façade after another. These residences, each with elaborately decorated balconies, once belonged to the

The snow-capped peak of Mount Teide rears behind the island's north coast; in the foreground you can see the houses of the La Orotava municipality

GULPING DOWN YOUR GOFIO
In Guanche times the staple food was a powder called *gofio*, a toasted and finely ground cereal used to make all sorts of things. It is now most commonly made of wheat or corn, but other cereals like barley can be used. In its various versions it has the consistency of flour. Islanders swear that globs of the stuff drenched in milk make the perfect healthy breakfast and other recipes range from tortilla with a *gofio* base to biscuits of baked *gofio* and honey. *Gofio* took root in some parts of South America but mainland Spaniards never acquired the taste – so you can find it in Caracas but not Madrid!

aristocracy. The EU has put La Orotava on its list of European Cultural Heritage sites.

Traffic tends to be directed around the historic centre. Anyone driving to the town is best advised to seek a parking space in the new residential and business districts around the Plaza de la Paz or the Plaza San Sebastián and then continue on foot to the Plaza de la Constitución. This flower-bedecked square with its impressive view over the roofs of La Orotava and down to the coast is often referred to as the "balcony of La Orotava".

Casas de los Balcones

You can admire a number of elegant town houses in the Calle San Francisco. In typical Canarian style, finely turned teak wood balconies hang like galleries on the façades. They also give the houses their name: *Casas de los Balcones*. The first one, the **Casa Fonseca**, was built in 1632. On the ground floor you can buy craft products. Even if you do not want to buy anything, you should at least admire the lavishly planted inner courtyard. You can also

"Carpets" created using colourful lava ash adorn the square in front of the town hall

watch women doing the traditional hemstitch embroidery. The former residential rooms on the upper floor are now a museum and open to the public.

The neighbouring house, the **Casa de Franchi**, was built in 1670 and is equally attractive. Today, it houses a carpet museum **(Museo de las Alfombras)**. However, in this case, the floor covering is not woven, but consists of lava sand, of the kind used for the Corpus Christi "carpets": The celebrations at Corpus Christi mark the most important event in the Orotava calendar. The artistic patterns using colourful lava ash from the Caldera de las Canadas are conjured up on the paving stones in front of the town hall. Since 1847 a new artwork has been created year after year with different motifs. Work starts about four weeks before the Corpus Christi procession. The procession itself takes place in La Orotava a week after the liturgical date of Corpus Christi.

INSIDER INFO

- Next door to the Liceo de Taoro are the pleasant gardens, **Jardines Marquesado de la Quinta Roja** (Calle San Agustín, daily 9–6, free).
- Another charming little garden is the **Hijuela del Bótanico** (Calle Tomás Pérez, Mon–Fri 9–2, free), a mini-botanical collection on Calle Tomás Pérez.
- Just south of the old town centre you will find the **Centro de Visitantes in which you can obtain information about the** Nationalpark Teide. The Visitor Centre is adjoined to a botanical garden in which you can admire many endemic plants (El Mayorazgo, daily 9–6, free).
- **Casa Torrehermosa**, at Calle Tomás Zerolo 27, houses **Artenerife**, where you can inspect a wide range of crafts from across the islands (Mon–Fri 9:30–4, Sat 9–1; www.artenerife.com).
- Presiding high over Plaza de la Constitución is the **Liceo de Taoro** (tel: 922/330-119; www.liceotaoro.com, daily 9am–midnight, inexpensive), a luxury club where, for a modest fee, you can become a day member and have a drink. There are occasional art expos and cultural events too.

On the other side of the street is the **Casa del Turista**, a sleek Renaissance building dating back to 1590, originally called Casa Molina. From the terrace in the back of the building, you have a good view of the Orotava Valley. A "carpet" like the one created on the paving stones in front of the town hall for Corpus Christi is always in process here – and is made of different-coloured volcanic sand.

A few paces uphill in the triangular **Plaza San Francisco** stand the remains of a ***gofio* mill**. If you develop a hankering to see more decommissioned mills, you could continue along **Calle Doctor Domingo González García** and, in the space of about 0.5km (0.3mi), you can see half a dozen such mills in varying states of disrepair. If you want to see a mill in action, head downhill from the *Casas de los Balcones* and there is a working mill in **Calle Colegio**. The building survives from the 17th century and below you can still see the aqueduct that fed the original water-driven mill. Today it runs on electricity. If you wish to try the floury powder that has long been the main staple in the islanders' diet, this is the place to do it.

The history of the Dominican convent in the Calle Tomás Zerolo 34 spans over four centuries. At the end of the 16th century, an influential family put the premises at the disposal of the Order. The present building was erected during the course of the 17th and 18th centuries. It remained in the possession of the Dominican nuns until 1835. After comprehensive restoration, the **Museo de Artesanía Iberoamericana** was opened in some of the rooms of the former cloister. Exhibits include handcrafted articles from many Latin-American countries and also from Spain. The collection of musical instruments is also very tastefully composed; it includes for example the timple, the traditional string instrument on the Canary Island resembling a guitar or lute. Other exhibits include ceramics, textiles, basket and woodwork.

The Casas de los Balcones in Calle San Francisco are a feast for the eyes

Architectural detail from a disused *gofio* mill in La Orotava

If you follow the Calle Viera and the Calle Cólogan you will come to one of the island's most impressive churches, the **Iglesia de Nuestra Señora de la Concepción**. Building work took place in the period from 1768 to 1788. It is built on the foundations of an earlier 16th-century building, which was destroyed during an earthquake in 1705. The three-naved hall church with the large imposing dome and the two small towers is a Baroque masterpiece that includes decorative elements in the Rococo style. It was declared a national monument on 18 June 1948. Inside, besides the beautiful choir stools, the statues of La Dolorosa and Saint John (by Luján Pérez) as well as the Baroque altarpiece of the Virgen de la Concepción (17th century), you should also pay special attention to the alabaster and marble altar by the Italian artist Giuseppe Gagini. The treasury contains valuable ritual objects, which originally belonged to St Pauls Cathedral in London.

TAKING A BREAK

Insider Tip

Stop for refreshment on **Plaza de la Constitución** or for a full meal there's the **Sabor Canario** in the heart of the old town (► 113). Shoppers can browse in the attached arts and crafts store. Another attractive option is the nearby **Casa Lercaro**, yet another fine example of a rambling Canarian mansion where you can both dine and shop (► 113).

---

190 B5

Casas de los Balcones
Calle San Francisco 3 · 922/330-629; www.casa-balcones.com
Mon–Sat 8:30–6 · €2

Casa del Turista
Calle San Francisco 4 · 922/330-629
Mon–Sat 8:30–7:30, Sun 8:30–1:30 · Free

Museo de Artesanía Iberoamericana
Calle Tomás Zerolo 34 · 922/323-376
Mon 9–3, Tue–Fri 9–5, Sat 9–1. Closed Sun · €2

Iglesia de la Concepción
Plaza Casañas · Daily 9–1, 4:30–8 · Free

26 Garachico

Not to be beaten by the molten lava that flowed into, and destroyed much of, the busy port town of Garachico in 1706, its people met the challenge and rebuilt their town, which today is one of the most charming urban legacies on Tenerife.

The compact old town of Garachico is an inviting place

The small bay just west of the centre was once its main port, although nothing remains to remind us of Garachico's commercial heyday. In front of the town's esplanade are a couple of rocky inlets known as **El Caletón**, formed by the cooling lava flows of 1706 and now used as natural pools.

Castles and Convents

Standing silent watch over the inlets is the brooding **Castillo de San Miguel**, a typical defensive fort, built of the dark local volcanic rock. Inside is a collection covering the city's eventful history, although the eruption of the volcano in 1706 is the focal topic. At weekends, the saltwater pools *(Piscinas naturales)* in front of the castle are popular with sun and sea worshippers.

INSIDER INFO

- Remember to take your **swimwear** to Garachico. If the sun's out there's nothing more refreshing than a dip in the lava **rockpools** that front the town in a permanent reminder of the 1706 volcanic eruption.
- Don't leave town without at least having had a look inside the wonderful **Hotel La Quinta Roja** (Glorieta de San Francisco s/n, tel: 922/133-377; www.quintaroja.com) opposite the former Convento de San Francisco. This deep orange mansion, impressively restored and well worth splurging on as an overnight stay, has two adjoining *patios*, which are so inviting you will find it hard to resist taking a seat.

The Castillo de San Miguel, overlooking the sea, houses an eclectic collection covering the town's history

The greatest attraction is the former **Convento de San Francisco**, now home to the Casa de la Cultura (House of Culture). When you walk in to the former convent you are greeted by two beautiful courtyards. The first is simple with slender timber columns supporting the first-floor balconies. The second, which served as the main cloister, is enriched by palm trees and rose bushes. The ground floor has an odd collection whose most intriguing element is the old black-and-white photos of Garachico; they provide a fascinating look at a past world. The stuffed birds, the butterflies and the household objects are also interesting. The adjacent **church**, Iglesia de Nuestra Señora de los Ángeles, if open, is worth a look for the exquisite *mudéjar* ceiling. The church is a curiously lopsided affair, its nave flanked on one side by a aisle of equal width in which you'll see the town's *pasos* (Easter procession floats) stored. The **Iglesia de Santa Ana**, dominating the adjacent **Plaza de Arriba**, was largely rebuilt and equipped with a six-storey bell tower in the early 18th century after lava and fire finished off most of its 16th-century predecessor.

Mansions and Museums

On the same square is a noble mansion, the **Casa Palacio de los Condes de la Gomera**, on whose ground floor temporary exhibitions of local art and photography are occasionally organised. The handful of lanes around here and the pleasant **Plaza de Juan González de la Torre** all make for a rewarding stroll.

If you head east of the old centre you will find the beautifully shaded **Plaza de Santo Domingo** and the 17th-century **Convento de Santo Domingo**. It houses the hospital and the **Museo de Arte Contemporáneo** (Museum of Contemporary Art) with its small collection of modern Spanish art, which is currently shut for renovation work.

TAKING A BREAK

Try **Isla Baja** near the Castillo de San Miguel for snacks or traditional fish dishes.

---

189 D5

Tourist Information Office
Avenida República Venezuela s/n 922/133-461 Mon–Sat 10–3

Castillo de San Miguel
Tomé Cano s/n Mon–Sat 10–4 €1

Convento de San Francisco
Plazoleta de la Libertad s/n Mon–Fri 11–2, 3:30–6:30, Sat 10–3 €1

27 Acantilado de los Gigantes

Uncompromising walls of volcanic rock that drop sheer into the ocean mark the southern end of the Teno Massif's rugged coast. Known as the Acantilado de los Gigantes, they are a formidable piece of natural architecture. Directly to the south is a beach, La Canalita, and this, together with the promise of year-round sunshine, set off a tourist boom. Two interlocking resorts, Los Gigantes and Puerto de Santiago, spread south in a blaze of brilliant white apartments and hotels, restaurants and bars.

Giants' Cliff

Although you can relax on the beach and observe the staggering 500–600m (1,640–1,968ft) cliffs, a better option is to take one of the many **boat excursions** that go up close and allow you some swimming time in their shadow. There are several variations on these tours. They generally combine the cliffs with some whale- and dolphin-spotting or a trip up the coast to the little beach at the bottom of the Barranco de Masca gorge (➤95). If you are interested in walking down, but not up, the gorge, you can arrange for one of these tour boats to pick you up on the beach after trekking down from Masca and to take you back to Los Gigantes. Enquire about the *Nashira Uno* boat (tel: 922/861-918; www.maritimaacantilados.com) which operates from the yacht harbour in Los Gigantes.

In large part due to the cliffs, **Los Gigantes** is more appealing than Puerto de Santiago, which spreads several

Volcanic cliffs provide a backdrop to the harbour at Los Gigantes

The cliffs near Los Gigantes stretch into the distance

kilometres along the coast below Los Gigantes (the two resorts are supposedly separated by 1km (0.5mi) but you'd be hard pressed to identify the dividing line).

In the 1980s **Puerto de Santiago**, with its nearby pleasant black-sand beach, **Playa de la Arena**, was still a largely tourist-free fishing settlement. What has replaced it is fairly tranquil but no sense of the original village remains. Instead the usual chorus line of British and Irish pubs, full English breakfasts and endless tourist souvenirs have settled here.

The water off this stretch of coast is considered some of the clearest for **diving** and there is no shortage of dive shops that hire out gear, organise dive trips and run courses (usually PADI) for beginners and more advanced divers.

TAKING A BREAK

Restaurante Pancho (► 114) on Playa de la Arena is a popular beach restaurant and has a Canarian menu.

---

188 B3

INSIDER INFO

To get an idea of what Puerto de Santiago might once have been like, head south along the coast road to **Playa de San Juan**, a village with a small grey beach that still lives largely from fishing. A couple of side roads and paths along the next 10km (6mi) south also reveal a handful of secluded coves and rocky points.

At Your Leisure

28 Loro Parque

The Loro Parque (parrot park) is claimed to be the biggest in the world. The park's namesakes are just one of the attractions in this hybrid setting, where alligators, monkeys, tigers, giant turtles, pelicans, flamingos and other animals live side by side. The Orca Show with the "killer whales" is absolutely sensational; it takes place several times a day in an arena with space for 2,000 people.

Join the **Behind the Scenes tour**, during which you will see where the dolphins train, where the gorillas sleep and where new fish and sea horses are kept in quarantine.

A free **mini-train** picks up visitors from Avenida Venezuela, close to Lago Martiánez in Puerto de la Cruz, every 20 minutes.

Loro Parque also has the distinction of having the world's largest collection of porcelain parrots, many produced in the 18th century in the famous porcelain factory at Meissen in Germany. The Loro Parque Foundation, the charitable arm of Loro Parque, funds worldwide projects related to parrot protection and population preservation.

190 A4
1.5km (1mi) west of Puerto de la Cruz
922/373-841; www.loroparque.com
Daily 8:30–6:45 €33

29 Cueva del Viento

In Icod de los Vinos, in the El Amparo district, you can learn more about the island's volcanic heritage. Europe's longest lava tube (18km/11mi) runs through here. The tour includes a short trip into the interior of the lava tube formed about 27,000 years ago by an eruption of the Pico Viejo. Wear stout shoes and take a warm top with you; it is only 10 to 12° C inside. The extensive labyrinth is home to a wide variety of insects, beetles and other small creatures – a habitat of complete darkness. So far 190 species have been identified; the fossils of extinct animal species have also been discovered.

190 B5
Icod de los Vinos, El Amparo district
www.cuevadelviento.net
Guided tours Tue–Sat 10, 11, 1 and 2; Reservations: tel: 922/815-339 €16

30 Pueblo Chico

Pueblo Chico is just that: a "little village". Indeed this is a trip into the Canary Islands in miniature, with scale models of everything from the town of La Laguna to a Guanche village scene. A good one for the kids, it is just off the TF5 motorway between La Orotava and Puerto de la Cruz.

190 B5 Camino Cruz de los Martillos 62
922/334-060; www.pueblochico.com
Daily May–Sep 9–7, Oct–Apr 9–6 €12.50

31 San Juan de la Rambla

San Juan seems a quiet village. At its tiny historic core, made up of Plaza de San Juan and adjoining Plaza Rosario Oramas, are a pleasing little church and typically 18th-century Canarian mansions. The old town sits on a ledge just north of the TF5 highway and then slips down to the rugged coast. A newer area stands further up the hill.

189 E5
11km (7mi) west of Puerto de la Cruz

32 Playa de San Marcos

A black-sand crescent beach set deep in a protected bay and surrounded by forbidding rock walls rising abruptly away from the shore, the Playa de San Marcos is just 2.5km (1.5mi) north of Icod de los Vinos (► 96). The parking areas that snake uphill back from the beach are indication enough of its popularity. The beach is backed by a handful of restaurants, with balconies overlooking the sand.

189 D5

2.5km (1.5mi) north of Icod de los Vinos

33 Arguayo

Seemingly left to its own devices on a side road running parallel to the north–south TF820 highway, Arguayo is a detour for those with time on their hands in the Puerto de Santiago area. At the steep northern end of the village is the **Centro Alfarero**, a small ceramics museum and workshop.

188 C3 Centro Alfarero, Carretera General 37 922/863-465 Tue–Sat 10–1, 4–7, Sun 10–2 Free

34 Buenavista del Norte

Living in one of the island's most remote communities, the people of Buenavista del Norte are renowned for their self-sufficiency and still make a living from the land. Tourism does not play a big role here yet, with the exception of the much lauded 18-hole golf course and hotel on the road to Punta de Teno. The town archives of this settlement set up in 1498 contain Portuguese documents dating back to 1512.

The historic town centres on the 16th-century **Iglesia de Los Remedios** while traditional stone farmhouses (many now abandoned) dot the surrounding hills. Don't forget to make a stop at **Pasteleria El Aderno** on Calle La Alhóndiga (► 114) to buy some of the island's best cakes and pastries.

188 B5

75km (46mi) west of Santa Cruz de Tenerife

35 Punta de Teno

Punta de Teno is one of the oldest parts of the island. Millions of years ago what the Guanches thought of as a devil coughed up its molten anger in this direction. Now stark, rocky cliffs fold back in on themselves towards the south from this westernmost tip of Tenerife. The scenery has an untamed, wild feel unmatched elsewhere on the island. From in front of the Punta de Teno lighthouse you can make out the coastline of La Palma and La Gomera on a clear day. Walkers can make a long half-day of it by following the signs to hike inland and up to the heights of the Teno Massif. It is best to do this walk equipped with good hiking maps, which are available at tourist offices, and to allow about four hours for the trip there and back.

188 A4 18km (11mi) west of Garachico

A number of impressive shows take place every day in the Loro Parque

Where to...
Stay

Prices
Prices are for a double room per night during the high season.
€ under €70 **€** €70–120 **€** over €120

LA OROTAVA

Hotel Alhambra €€
A magical Moorish fantasy has been carved out of an 18th-century villa on the edge of the old town. Five spacious doubles and two suites are on offer, and extras include a garden, pool, gym, sauna and glass ceiling patio.
190 B5
Calle Nicandro Gonzáles Borges 19
922/320-434; www.alhambra-teneriffa.com

Victoria €€
This 17th-century mansion has been thoughtfully restored in a style befitting its age and dignity. The rooms are decently furnished, and the rooftop terrace has lovely views towards the distant sea. During the Corpus Christi festivities in June (► 10), La Orotava is besieged with visitors and advance booking is advisable. It has an attractive restaurant.
190 B5
Calle Hermano Apolinar 8
922/ 331-683; www.hotelruralvictoria.com

PUERTO DE LA CRUZ

Botánico €€€
Just across the road from the Jardín Botánico (► 98), this hotel displays a green-fingered touch in its grounds – a lush and shady sanctuary of fountains, fish-pools and billowing vegetation. The interior is just as well kept, with classic furnishings and spacious public areas. A host of luxurious accoutrements keeps its clientele happy, from sports facilities to spa and beauty salons, and three highly regarded restaurants. A pianist plays in the cocktail lounge, and shuttle buses minimise the 2km (1.2-mile) journey to the centre of Puerto de la Cruz. Rooms are predictably elegant and comfortable.
190 B5
Avenida Richard J Yeoward 1, Urb. El Botánico
922/381-400; www.hotelbotanico.com

Marquesa €€
Right in the pedestrianised heart of Puerto's old town, this beautifully restored building faces the church square. A maze of bright, simple rooms occupies the modern extensions at the rear. There's a tiny splash-pool on the roof terrace with a great view of Mount Teide.
190 B5
Calle Quintana 11
922/383-151; www.hotelmarquesa.com

Monopol €€
The Monopol is decorated in traditional Canarian style with ornate wooden balconies and a delightful jungle-like atrium where huge cheese-plants scramble towards the ceiling between the wicker sofas. Owned by the same family for generations, the staff are friendly, and personal touches, like the flower petals strewn daily on the entrance steps, add to its charm. Rooms vary in size, shape and style, and have neat, modern bathrooms. A small pool and

jacuzzi on a rear sun terrace offer hot and cold dips.
190 B5
Calle Quintana 15
922/ 384-611; www.monopoltf.com

Hotel Tigaiga €€

Although it wouldn't win any prizes for its late 1950s boxy design, the family-owned Tigaiga gets great reviews for its excellent service and good value for money. A robust eco-management policy has resulted in a number of awards from internationally recognised bodies, including the European Union EMAS scheme. Lush palms and 5000m² (50,000ft²) of tropical gardens (the founder was an amateur botanist) soften the exterior and there's a good sized free-form pool. There are lovely sea views from around the grounds. Rooms have a bright cheery feel, and each has a balcony.
190 B5
Parque Taora 28
922/383-500; www.tigaiga.com

GARACHICO

Insider Tip

Casério Los Partidos €€

This charming little place is in Tenerife's hilly north-west corner, with views of Mount Teide. Each of the rooms has an open fireplace and immaculate bathroom. Terraces and courtyards bright with flowers and fountains spill around the building. This isolated retreat is a long way from the congested coastal resorts, and it appeals primarily to walkers and visitors who value peace and quiet. A car is essential if you plan to do any exploring.
189 D5 Los Partidos, San José de los Llanos, El Tanque
922/693-090; www.caserio-lospartidos.com

San Roque €€€

This imaginative little hotel is a lovingly restored 17th-century house with an aristocratic pedigree. Modern sculpture and statuary grace the inner courtyard while sleek sofas and Bauhaus chairs invite casual indolence, along with a photogenic mosaic swimming pool. The rooms revel in cool furnishings and state-of-the-art bathrooms and there's good food prepared by its resident owners.
189 D5
Calle Esteban de Ponte 32
922/133-435; www.hotelsanroque.com

ACANTILADO DE LOS GIGANTES

Hotel Luabay Costa Los Gigantes €€

This upper-middle range, family-run hotel has a favourable position on the hill slopes. Most of the rooms enjoy a view of the neighbouring island La Gomera. This is an all-suites property that operates on full-board. There's a great range of activities on site from a kids' club and free WiFi in reception, to an enormous pool and a full-service spa, so it's the perfect place for recharging the batteries.
188 B3 Calle Juan Manuel Capdevielle 8, Playa de la Arena
922/862-772; www.believehotels.com

El Sombrero Apartments €

The crisp, clean, but basic three-storey apartments at El Sombrero are set around a small pool. This is a no-frills property but impeccably kept and popular with families who want to do their own thing. The units are simply furnished with traditional Canarian furniture mixed with chintzy touches. Each has a good sized balcony. Some have views across the resort down to the sea, around a 15-minute walk away. The apartments are situated at the top of Los Gigantes, so if you're not fit you'll certainly need a taxi back from the beach.
188 B3
Avenida Maritima 28
922/861-353; www.el-sombrero.com

Where to...
Eat and Drink

Prices
Price per person for a three-course meal including drinks
€ under €20 €€ €20–40 €€€ over €40

LA OROTAVA

Casa Lercaro €/€€

This is another rambling mansion reborn as a restaurant and shop for island artisan products. Much of the pleasure of eating here is the 17th-century setting. You can dine in one of several indoor and outdoor courtyard enclaves. Food is hearty and comforting Spanish fare. After eating wander around the house and its gardens.

190 B5 Calle Colegio 7
922/326-204; www.casalercaro.com
Daily noon–4:30, 7–10

Restaurant Lucas Maes €€€

One of a new breed of fusion restaurants, this one is presided over by its dynamic young chef Lucas Maes. Housed in a historic mansion the dining room has received a contemporary make-over and there's a terrace for al fresco lunches and dinners. The menu oozes luxury dishes such as lobster with truffle oil, but everything is served with a light touch and a play of flavours and textures.

190 B5
Calle Barranco de Arena 53
922/321-159 Tue–Sat 1–3:30, 7–11; closed Sun and Mon

Sabor Canario €€ Insider Tip

The former Museo del Pueblo Guanche in the historic heart of La Orotava is a showcase for Canarian crafts. Attached to it is a lovely restaurant serving local dishes – try *conejo en salmorejo* (braised rabbit) or *ropa vieja* (literally "old clothes", a classic Canarian stew). The *patio* tables in its plant-filled courtyard are enticing.

190 B5 Calle Carrera 17
922/323-793; www.saborcanario.com
Mon–Sat noon–4:30, 7:30–10

PUERTO DE LA CRUZ

La Gañanía €€€

This noble restaurant has won many awards for its imaginative cuisine and has even been graced with a visit by the former Spanish king Juan Carlos I. The chef takes inspiration for his creations from traditional Canarian dishes and focuses on fresh seasonal products. Even the bread is made on site – so you know you are eating true restaurant cuisine. Delicious desserts round off the menu. The hilltop setting in a pretty rustic dining room is delightful.

190 B5 Camino Durazno 71
922/ 371-000 Wed–Sun 1–4, 7–11; closed Mon and Tue

La Magnolia €€€

One of Puerto de la Cruz's top restaurants in the La Paz district, offering superb Catalan and international cooking in an elegant, modern setting. The speciality is fish; enormous portions appear from an open kitchen, often dressed in pungent garlic sauces. Be sure to reserve a table in advance.

190 B5
Avenida Marqués de Villanueva del Prado s/n
922/385-614; www.magnolia elpayes.com
Wed–Mon 1–4, 7–midnight

Mesón El Monasterio €€

This unusual restaurant, a former 17th-century cloister, is in the La Montañeta district of Los Realejos, a neighbouring area of Puerto de la Cruz. Farm animals and poultry wander freely around the grounds. A maze of rustic dining rooms and terrace tables provide space for Canarian roast and chargrilled specials and a huge range of wines. The staff are friendly and helpful.

190 B5
La Montañeta, Los Realejos
922/340-707 Daily 10am–11pm

ACANTILADO DE LOS GIGANTES

Restaurante Pancho €€

One of the island's best chefs has built up the reputation of this place over several years. On its spacious terrace tables shaded by lush foliage overlook Playa de la Arena's lovely beach. An imaginative Canarian menu features rice and fish dishes as well as paella. The wine cellar with its perfectly tempered wine promises perfection.

188 B3
Playa de la Arena, Puerto de Santiago
922/861-323
Thu–Tue 1–4, 7–11; closed Jun

GARACHICO

Restaurante La Perla €

Garachico is a simple place and the same can be said of its cooking, but at La Perla you'll get lashings of the stuff. Tables sport red-and-white gingham and the menu is evenly divided between fish and meat.

189 D5 Calle de 18 Julio
922/830-286 Tue–Sun 1–4, 7–10:30

MASCA

Insider Tip

Chez Arlette €

The attractive location with spectacular valley views makes this simple place one of the most popular in Masca. Despite the many visitors, the rustic style persists on its shaded terrace decked with wooden furnishings and a mass of plant life. The menu is varied and inexpensive and you can wash everything down with home-made lemonade or local wine.

188 B4 La Piedra, Masca
922/ 863-459 Sun–Fri 11–7

Where to... Shop

Puerto de la Cruz is the main shopping centre in this region. Shopping hours are long; many outlets stay open until quite late in the evening. Inland, La Orotava offers some of the best of the island's crafts.

CRAFTS

Distinctive Canarian ***bordados*** (hand embroidery), ***calados*** (drawn threadwork) and **lace** can be found in many shops. In Puerto de la Cruz and La Orotava, some craft shops are tourist attractions in their own right because of their settings in restored old timbered houses. Some have museums or restaurants on site. The best-known is the **Casa de los Balcones** (branches at Calle San Francisco 3, La Orotava or Paseo de San Telmo, Puerto de la Cruz). Also worth seeing for their architecture as well as their wares are **Casa del Turista** (Calle San Francisco 4, La Orotava), **Casa Torrehermosa** (Calle Tomás Zerolo, La Orotava), **Pueblo Guanche** (Calle Carrera 7, La Orotava) and **Casa de la Aduana** (Calle Las Lonjas s/n, Puerto de la Cruz).

Arguayo is known for its **pottery**, shaped by hand to Guanche designs without a potter's wheel. The rugged results are on display at the **Centro Alfarero** (Tue–Sat 10–1, 4–7, Sun 10–2), easily spotted on the main road through the village.

Summer **craft fairs** (*ferias de artesanía*) are held between May and October in many older towns, including Los Realejos, La Oratava, Santiago del Teide, El Tanque, Buenavista del Norte, Garachico and San Juan de la Rambla.

HOME-GROWN PRODUCE

Icod de los Vinos is renowned as a **wine-producing** area. Visitors to the ancient **Parque del Drago** (➤92) will almost certainly be invited to taste (and preferably buy) some locally made *malvasia* (malmsey) in the *bodegas* and souvenir shops.

The **Bar Restaurant Chinyero** (Avenida de la Iglesia 2B, Santiago del Teide, tel: 922/864-040; www.barrest-chinyero.com) at Santiago del Teide serves good Canarian wines with *tapas*.

Garachico's **Centro de Artesanía el Limonero** (Avenida Tomé Cano s/n) has a variety of wine and cheese for sale. At Buenavista del Norte, **Pastelería El Aderno** (Calle La Alhóndiga, 8, tel: 922/127-368; www.eladerno. com) is a prize-winning cake shop making traditional island specialities.

MARKETS

Puerto de la Cruz's daily produce market is held in a modern building on Avenida de Blas Pérez González, while souvenir sellers set out their wares to attract tourists along the seafront and in the old town.

Every Monday, African traders congregate on the main road at Alcalá with the usual souvenirs. Farmer's markets are held at **Playa de San Juan** (Wed morning) and **Garachico** (first Sun of each month), selling wines, cheese, tomatoes and bananas.

La Orotava's Mercadillo del Agricultor (Sat 8–1) is certainly worth a visit. The large market hall is located on the northern outskirts of La Orotava near the main road to the national park.

Where to... Go Out

NIGHTLIFE

In **Puerto de la Cruz**, night owls should head for the streets behind the **Lido** (e.g. Calle Hoya), where they will find **Joy** and other clubs with constantly changing names.

In the small bar **Las Tejas Verdes** (Calle Puerto Viejo 28), a trio plays authentic Spanish folk music every evening from 9pm. Many hotels and cafés offer live music, such as the **Hotel Puerto de la Cruz** (tel: 922/384-011) or the **Café Paris** (tel: 922/384-000).

Los Gigantes is mostly quiet at night apart from a few music bars like **Highland Paddy's** (Avenida Marítima, Playa de la Arena).

CASINO

Puerto de la Cruz Casino sits in the heart of Lido Martiánez (Avenida de Colón, tel: 922/380-550) surrounded by the stunning pools. It offers American roulette, black jack and one-armed bandits. Take photo ID to gain entry.

DAYTIME DIVERSIONS

Abaco (Urb El Durazno, Calle Casa Grande, tel: 922/370-107; www.abacotenerife.com; daily 10:30–1:30, 8pm–2:30am) is a well-restored 18th-century Canarian house. Here you'll see daytime **folklore displays** and shows (10am–1:30pm). The house is transformed into a cocktail lounge and live music venue in the evenings (Mon–Fri 9pm–2:30am, Sat 3:30pm–3am, Sun 3:30pm–2:30am).

Puerto's best family day out, however, is a visit to **Loro Parque** (► 109).

GARDENS

The upside of northern Tenerife's damp, cloudy climate is its local vegetation. Puerto de la Cruz's famous **Jardín Botánico** (► 98) is essential viewing for anyone keen on plants.

Less well-known garden attractions in Puerto de la Cruz include the **Sitio Litre** (La Paz, tel: 922/382-417; daily 9:30–5; €4.75), a fine orchid collection in an 18th-century colonial mansion, and the charming **Risco Bello Aquatic Gardens** (Parque Taoro, daily 9:30–5; €4).

ON THE WATERFRONT

Swimming & Watersports

Two of the best beaches are Puerto de la Cruz's **Playa Jardín** (► 96), and **Playa de la Arena** (► 108), near Los Gigantes. **Lago Martiánez** in Puerto de la Cruz (► 96) is a splendid lido with palms and sculptures.

Los Gigantes has two less elaborate lidos, El Laguilo und Oasis. At low tide when the weather is calm, you can swim in the sea basins of Garachico or La Caleta near Los Silos. You can also swim safely in calm weather in the low-tide lava rockpools of **Garachico**.

The clear waters beneath the Acantilado de los Gigantes provide one of the best locations for watersports. **Sailing**, **scuba-diving** and **sport fishing** are especially popular. For information, go to the tourist office in Playa de la Arena (Avenida Marítima 36–37, tel: 922/860-348; Mon–Fri 9:30–3:30, Sat 9:30–12:30) or the Los Gigantes marina (Puerto Deportivo, tel: 922/868-002). For diving courses try the **Diving Centre at Los Gigantes marina** (tel: 922/860-431; www.diving tenerife. co.uk); in Puerto de la Cruz try **Dive Centre Atlantik** at Hotel Maritim (tel: 922/362-801; www.scubacanarias.com).

Boat Trips

Try the launch ***Nashira Uno*** (Los Gigantes marina, tel: 922/ 861-918). Even if you don't spot dolphins or whales, sailing under the Acantilado de los Gigantes is an amazing experience. One or two unusual boats go from here – ***Flipper Uno*** (tel: 922/867-049; www.flipperuno.com), is a replica of an 18th-century galleon.

MOUNTAIN HIKES

The volcanic Teno Massif is a great place for tough walks with splendid views. The mountain-gorge village of **Masca** (► 94), perched on vertiginous, ancient rocks, is a popular starting point. The upper slopes of the **Orotava Valley** (► 100) offer other excellent walks; the most interesting trails lead around La Caldera and the strange columnar basalt formations of Los Órganos. For more details on routes and guided walks check the information centre at Buenavista.

Gregorio is an escorted walks operator, offering a large number of scenic routes for walkers of all ages and fitness levels (Hotel Tigaiga, Parque Taoro 28, Puerto de la Cruz, tel: 922/383-500; www.gregorio-teneriffa.de). Insider Tip

Another well-known trekking specialist worth contacting is **Gaiatours** (Calle San Agustín 66, Los Realejos, tel: 922/355-272; www.gaiatours.es).

The South

Little Treats

Without a Potter's Wheel

In **Candelaria** (➤ 134), a small museum shows how the Guanches used to make pottery (Centro Alfarero, Calle La Palma, Tue–Fri 8:30–2 und 4–7, Sat mornings only, free).

Night Market

Los Abrigos (➤ 142) not only offers good fish restaurants, it has a night market every Tuesday (6pm–10pm) that sells a lot of fun knick-knacks.

On the Red Mountain

From the southern end of the beach in El Médano (➤ 137), you can climb up the **Montaña Roja**. Despite its modest height of 127m (416ft), the view from the top is brilliant.

The South

Getting Your Bearings

After the subtropical lushness of the island's north, the southern and central regions of the island offer a fascinating geological and climatic contrast. Visiting Teide – only a short drive from the shimmering heat of the holiday destinations in the south – is practically obligatory when staying on the island.

Here you'll find the tallest mountain in Spain, the majestic volcanic temple of Mount Teide (3,718m/12,195ft). Surrounding it are other impressive peaks and a weird landscape. The rain-starved south coast, from the Costa Adeje to Santa Cruz, is remarkably barren. Until the 1960s few people lived in what was considered the unfortunate side of this otherwise blessed isle.

Not so today. As northern Europeans discovered the joys of Atlantic bathing in the year-round sun, the spread of resort development began, wholly engulfing the small fishing villages, like Los Cristianos, that once dozed in mostly penniless isolation. Now Playa de las Américas and the adjoining beaches form an uninterrupted pleasure dome, full of apartments, bars, English breakfasts, watersports and other diversions. A couple of days of sun and fun can make a nice counterweight to the exploration of Tenerife's cultural and natural wonders further north.

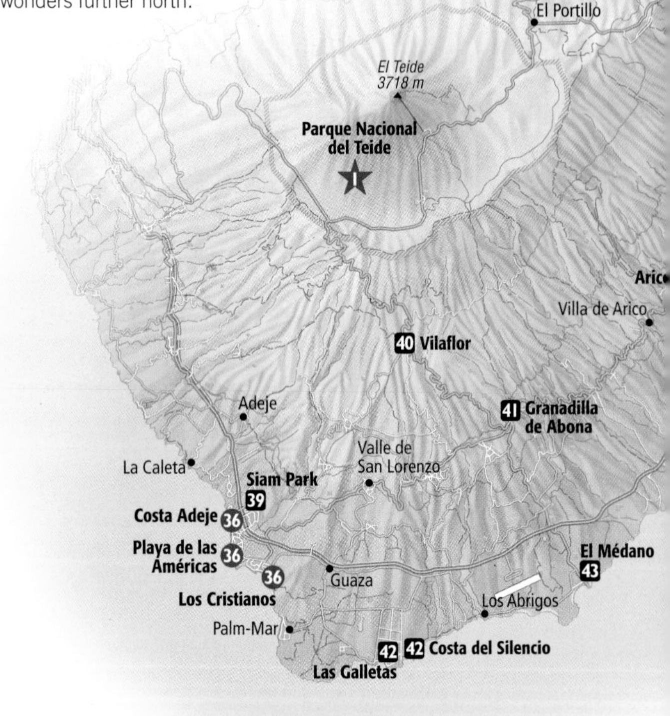

TOP 10

Don't Miss

At Your Leisure

Above: The small resort of El Médano offers beach fun for wind and kite surfers.

Below: The Caldera de las Cañadas below the Pico del Teide

The South

Three Perfect Days

If you're not quite sure where to begin your travels, this itinerary recommends three practical and enjoyable days out in the South, taking in some of the best places to see. For more information see the main entries (➤ 122–138).

Day One

Morning

After taking the approach roads through the Bosque de la Esperanza or up from La Orotava, call in at the **Centro de Visitantes** (Visitor Centre) at the border of the ★1 **Parque Nacional del Teide** (➤ 122).

If coming from the south, stop in at the **Parador de las Cañadas del Teide** (where you can stay the night) to drop your bags off. Drive to the base of Mount Teide, where you take the *teleférico* (cable car) up to the top (➤ 126). Back at the base, you can head off for lunch at one of five restaurants near the El Portillo Centro de Visitantes or at the parador.

Afternoon

With the couple of hours of daylight remaining, explore the **Roques de García** (➤ 127) and perhaps also wander as far as the great plain of **Llano de Ucanca,** after which you can retire to the Parador for the night.

Day Two

Morning

After breakfast and a morning stroll around the Parador, drive through the **Llano de Ucanca** and then the pine forests to **40 Vilaflor** (➤ 136), where you could make a stop. The 12km (7.5mi) stretch of the TF21 road between Vilaflor and Granadilla de Abona is narrow, rough and endlessly winding and drops through pine stands and farming terraces, some in use and others long abandoned. Looking south, you can make out several small volcanoes. You could take half an hour to pop into 41 **Granadilla de Abona** (➤ 137).

Afternoon

By lunchtime you can be in 36 **Los Cristianos** (➤ 130), where you will find plenty of hotels (book ahead). Have lunch at **Don Armando** (➤ 141) and devote the rest of the afternoon to relaxing on the beach.

Evening

If you're in the mood for a late night there are plenty of options, especially in neighbouring 36 **Playa de las Américas** (left; ➤ 130).

Day Three

Morning

Make an early start and stroll from the Visitor Centre in El Portillo to **Fortaleza** (➤ 152). Later on you can follow it with a midday dip back at the resort. If you are able to contain your hunger, head north up the motorway to 44 **Porís de Abona** (➤ 138), where you can enjoy lunch, for example in Casablanca, and a swim.

Afternoon

Go inland for the winding old Santa Cruz road, stop at 45 **Arico** (➤ 138) and the 46 **Mirador de Don Martín** (➤ 138). Visit the 37 **Pirámides de Güímar** (➤ 132) and then go to 38 **Candelaria** (➤ 134) to see the **Basílica de Nuestra Señora de Candelaria**, dedicated to the island's holy patron, Our Lady of Candelaria.

Parque Nacional del Teide

Majestic Pico del Teide, Spain's highest peak, is lord of Tenerife. The mountain was long held in awe by the island's Guanche inhabitants and still inspires today. It's essential to visit this mountain and the bizarre volcanic landscapes surrounding it. Explore it during a volcanological discovery tour through one of Spain's most important national parks.

Hikers should follow the marked trails in the national park

About 500,000 years old, Mount Teide is an active strato-volcano that has grown in successive eruptions (➤ 26) to 3,718m (12,195ft). All around it are lower volcanic peaks and huge mantles of long frozen lava flows. The arid lunar landscape is so unique that plans to have the area made a national park began in 1934. The Civil War put the idea on hold, but 20 years later this the largest and oldest in the Canaries; since 2007 the 189km² (73mi²) area is a UNESCO World Heritage Site. The area is sub-divided into varying classifications, from no-go zones to areas where limited activity is permitted. Check the **weather** before setting out. Cloud cover may be sporadic and

INSIDER INFO

The top of Mount Teide is high mountain territory. In winter the temperatures can drop below freezing and, even in summer, especially if there's a strong wind, it can be very cold. Also, conditions change rapidly, so a warm morning can quickly turn to a freezing afternoon.

- Always take a warm jacket, long trousers and hiking boots, as well as sunglasses, sunblock and a hat.
- Owing to the height of the mountain, the **oxygen levels** on the summit are lower than farther down. Senior citizens and people with health problems should thus seriously consider whether such an excursion is a good idea or not in their particular case.

frequently only reaches an altitude of around 1,600m (5,248ft), which is below the level of the park. In winter, north winds *(alisios)* pick up sea moisture on the way and hit the lower slopes of the volcano. If your luck is truly out the mountain itself may be covered and in winter freezing conditions, snow and ice occasionally lead to access being closed.

Park Approaches

Four roads, all of them well maintained, lead from the island's extremities to the Parque Nacional del Teide. From the north you have the choice of taking the forest trail through the **Bosque de la Esperanza** (➤ 80) or winding up the northern flank of the range from La Orotava. At the **Mirador Ayosa**, a lookout point at 2,078m (6,816ft), you leave the forest and emerge in the bare uplands of the park. From here you pass by the white science-fiction domes of the **Observatorio del Teide** before reaching the El Portillo road junction and the **Centro de Visitantes** (Visitor Centre). The route from La Orotava also arrives at this junction.

From the south, a particularly windy road heads north west from Granadilla de Abona to **Vilaflor** (➤ 136), from where it climbs through thick Canary pine forest before reaching the park limits at about 2,200m (7,216ft). From here the road drops into the **Llano de Ucanca** plain and meets the fourth road, which meanders across in less dramatic fashion from the village of **Chío** in the west.

Visitor Centres

In the **El Portillo Centro de Visitantes** you can take a quick look at the displays explaining volcanoes and the park's surprisingly hardy and varied flora and fauna such as the

As Diverse as a Continent

There is hardly any other island for which the term "miniature continent" is as appropriate as it is for Tenerife. The small area offers tremendous scenic contrasts: the verdant green north, desert-like, dry south, wide-spread forests, long beaches and the mountainous region around Teide.

❶ **Macizo de Teno** The Teno mountain range has a wild and primordial character. With the exception of the Barranco de Masca, few trails have been developed for hikers.
❷ **Pico del Teide** At a height of 3718m (12,200ft), the Teide is the highest mountain in Spain. During the ascent, you pass through almost every vegetation zone there is.
❸ **Valle de la Orotava** Humboldt praised the beauty of the Orotava Valley. These days, the broad valley is densely populated. Banana plantations vie for space with the sea of houses.
❹ **Las Montañas de Anaga** The Anaga Mountains are among the geologically oldest parts of the island. The slopes drop down steeply to the coast. They are often obscured by the trade-wind clouds, which explains the lush vegetation.
❺ **Caldera de las Cañadas** Towering over the northern edge of the imposing crater basin is the Pico del Teide. To the south, east and west around 500m (1,640ft)-high rock faces border the Caldera.
❻ **Bosque de la Esperanza** Powerful Canarian pines and Eucalyptus trees flourish in the Esperanza Forest.
❼ **Valle de Güímar** Broad, fertile valleys, such as the Valle de Güímar, fringe the mountains.
❽ **Barranco del Infierno** The mountain range is interspersed with deep and narrow gorges, called *barrancos*. With the exception of the Barranco del Infierno, through which a narrow stream flows, they do not channel water.

Parque Nacional del Teide

Enjoy the stunning view of the Pico del Teide from the Roques de García

emblematic *tajinaste rojo* plant, bats, lizards and various raptors that survive in this volcanic landscape. The 15-minute video on volcanoes is worth a look. They also have a small bookstore.

The Mount Teide cable car is a big help if you want to get to the top

Pico del Teide

If you do nothing else in the national park, zip up to the top of the mountain (almost) in the **Teleférico** (cable-car). It takes eight minutes to whisk you 1,199m (3,933ft) up to 3,550m (11,660ft), only a little way short of the peak.

On a beautiful sunny day you will be able to see across the entire archipelago. As you gaze out over the horizon it's as if you are standing on the roof of the world. On a bad day you might see nothing but the famous "sea of clouds".

Two short walks (Nos 11 and 12) lead you to the **Mirador de la Fortaleza**, which looks north, and the **Mirador de Pico**

INSIDER INFO

- In **alpine spring** (at the end of May/beginning of June), the otherwise bleak volcanic landscape suddenly displays unexpected splendour. On the over 2,000m (6,560ft)-high Caldera de las Cañados, you will see viper's bugloss, gorse and Teide Wallflower in full bloom. **Beehives** *(colmenas)* are set up in various parts of the park, continuing a long island tradition that is considered beneficial to the park's flora. The hives are signposted and clearly it is not a good idea to get too close!
- The **Observatorio Astrofísico de Izaña** (no public access) is the lesser known of the Canary Islands' astrophysical research centres (the other one is at the Roque de los Muchachos on La Palma). Run by the Instituto de Astrofísica de Canarias (IAC), the Izaña centre (2,400m/7,872ft) is dedicated to solar research and Big Bang studies. Some of the most sophisticated telescopes in Europe's astronomical arsenal search the crystal-clear skies above the islands for clues to the Beginning of it All.

Viejo, oriented south west. From the latter you can clearly see the yawning mouth of the Pico Viejo crater. Each path is less than 1km (half a mile) long.

A third walk (No 10) leads to the peak, but you may only make this 700m (2,296ft) climb (a 180m/590ft altitude gain) with the relevant permit.

If you want to hike to the top you need a permit from: www.reservasparquesnacionales.es. The permit allows you to the top of the peak (trail No 10) but not into the crater itself.

Walks in the Park

Apart from the two short strolls to the *miradores* (lookout points) around the top of the mountain and the restricted access climb to the peak (see above), a network of nine marked walking paths spreads across the park. They range from a couple of fairly simple two-hour strolls to the tougher eight-hour hike that takes you from the top station of the Teleférico to Pico Viejo and then down to the TF38 road. This latter hike involves an altitude variation of 1,500m (4,920ft).

The most popular of the short walks is a simple **3.5km (2mi) circuit** from the *parador* across the road to the **Roques de García** (walk No 3). These oddly shaped rock formations have been sculpted by the effects of erosion cutting weak stone from the tougher core of what were once volcanic dikes.

The **Roque Chinchado**, which has become something of a symbol for the park and shouldn't be missed, has been eaten away at the base and looks ready to topple over.

A fairly easy half-day walk (No 4; a full day if you have to retrace your steps to reach your transport or the *parador*) is the 16km (10-mile) **Siete Cañadas** hike, which arcs south then south west from the visitor centre to the *parador*. *Cañadas* are barren plains where temporary lakes form if it

Anyone can take the short stroll to the Roques de García – also simply called Los Roques

rains. This hike stretches through a series of such plains along the inside wall of the Circo de las Cañadas, the enormous semi-circular wall of the ancient crater.

A **more demanding hike** (walk No 7) is the climb from the road to the summit (remember you need a permit to reach the peak itself). The first half of this 8.5km (5.5-mile) hike has a fairly gentle climb, during which you pass ***huevos del Teide*** (Teide eggs), a spattering of volcanic bombs from past eruptions.

The latter half of the walk is much more challenging (remember that you gain 1,400m/4,592ft in altitude). Most hikers choose to stay a night in the Refugio de Altavista mountain refuge (about two-thirds of the way up and very basic, take your sleeping bag), although you could conceivably do the walk and return with the *teleférico* in the same day (or even take the cable car up and walk down). Call the refuge (tel: 922/010-440) in advance to be sure of a place. It opens from May to November.

Hardy hikers will be tempted to tackle the long march up to the peak via the Altavista refuge

TAKING A BREAK

You have several eating and drinking options. Five restaurants, all within 2.5km (1.5mi) of each other, operate around the **El Portillo Centro de Visitantes**. Otherwise, the **Parador** (► 139) has a restaurant and cafeteria.

---

189 E3

Centros de Visitantes
Daily 9–4

Teleférico del Teide
922/010-445; www.telefericoteide.com
Daily 9–4 (when weather conditions are suitable) €25

36 Los Cristianos, Playa de las Américas & Costa Adeje

Millions of years ago volcanoes emerged and spewed forth rivers of molten lava that slithered down to the coast. Now a kind of man-made lava of apartments and hotels is reversing the tide, gradually spreading inland from the coast and up the frontline volcanoes.

A 12km (7.5mi)-long beach promenade stretches north from Loso Cristianos. It passes the Puerto de Colón marina from Playa de las Américas

The rise from a small fishing town to a major tourist centre began in the 1970s and then accelerated. Today, in Los Cristianos, in Playa de las Americas and on the Costa Adeje, you will find a broad range of very different leisure activities. Almost all of the larger hotels have a swimming pool and tennis courts. You can go waterskiing, hire paddle-boats or take part in an organised boat trip. Especially popular are the dolphin and whale photo safaris, pirate trips, deep sea fishing as well as trips to the neighbouring island of La Gomera.

In Los Cristianos things are generally somewhat quiet in the evening, but there is always something going on in the neighbouring town of Playa de las Américas

View from the Gran Hotel Anthelia on the hotel skyline of Costa Adeje

A Place to Find the Sun

In **Los Cristianos** there is an old centre, which is what distinguishes it from other tourist centres. Although there are is no really noteworthy architecture here, the small pedestrian zone with its shops and restaurants exudes its own special flair. Sitting in one of the cafés, you soon forget the time because there is always something to look at: the arrival or departure of the ferry to Gomera, the fisherman returning to his home with his catch, the elegant yachts and, of course, the people strolling by.

Playa de las Américas, which has fused with Los Cristianos, is an endless array of hotels and apartments, interrupted by supermarkets, restaurants, bars and clubs. The daytime attraction is the line of virtually identical beaches, protected from ocean surf by sea walls, that

The Monkey Park Tenerife promises to be a paradise for primates

runs the length of the resort. A focal point of sorts is the swish **Puerto de Colón** yacht harbour.

Costa Adeje takes up where Playa de las Américas leaves off. Its northernmost end, around **La Caleta** (much of it still under construction), is the classiest effort in the area. Brightly coloured luxury hotels with verdant gardens form a pleasing backdrop to the coast's nicest beaches, especially **Playa del Duque**.

Plenty to Do

Apart from the boat trips and other water-based activities (diving and deep-sea fishing, a yellow submarine and even a pirate ship), various land-based activities have been developed. They include the **Las Águilas Jungle Park,** where you can watch free-flying eagles and condors (► 144); **Monkey Park Tenerife** (primates, lions, crocodiles and other critters); and **Siam Park** (► 136) with lots of water slides and a wave pool. All are located inland from the resorts which provide free shuttle buses. Hotels and tourist information centres can provide you with information about the various excursions.

TAKING A BREAK

If you want to take a break from the general tourist fare, sneak around to the unassuming **Rincón del Marinero** (Insider Tip) restaurant, opposite the Casa del Mar building behind the port in Los Cristianos (tel: 922/793-553, daily noon–11). The seafood is fresh and well prepared.

186 B2

WHALE WATCHING – A WHALE OF A TIME FOR THE WHALE?

A popular, all-year-round tourist attraction off Tenerife's coast is whale watching. You can spot sperm whales and also pilot whales. Environmentalists, however, warn against the risks of overly disturbing these mammals. Regulations stipulate that boats should not approach the animals any nearer than 60m (200ft), not surround them – and stop the engine at a distance of 500m (1,640ft). For those who would like to know more: The Swiss organisation **Ocean Care** (www.oceancare.org) is committed to **protecting the whales and dolphins** around the Canary Islands.

37 Pirámides de Güímar

Few tourists would stop off in the Güímar municipality, some 25km (15.5mi) south west of Santa Cruz, were it not for its mysterious pyramids, dismissed by some scientists as nothing more than a "pile of stones". The late Norwegian ethnographer, Thor Heyerdahl, however, came to the conclusion that they are an indubitable legacy of the Guanches – a group of modest step pyramids, built as temples for worshipping the sun. His findings are supported by the fact that Güímar was the seat of a Guanche king, a so-called Mencey, in the period before the Spanish conquest. In the surrounding area, there are numerous caves, which were used by the Guanches either as living quarters or to bury their dead.

The Pirámides de Güímar, of varying sizes, are like grand platforms. Stairways built into the side allowed worshippers to reach the flat stage at the top of the pyramids in order to pray. Evidence refuting long-held claims that the pyramids were simply elaborate terraces created by farmers, much like the others you see all over this part of the island, is considerable. While farming terraces are cobbled together with loose rocks, these have been carefully fashioned from volcanic stone specially transported here for that purpose. The corners and edges have been worked to fit precise rectangular plans.

Celestial Links

Were the pyramids used for sun worship?

The main complex of pyramids was built in such a way that the platforms are orientated toward sunset of the summer

AT SEA IN A PAPYRUS BOAT
In the 1930s **Thor Heyerdahl**, 1914–2002, finished his zoology and geography studies in Norway and set off for a year to study wildlife in the Pacific islands. During this time he came to believe that centuries ago South American tribesmen might have reached Polynesia. The only way they could have done so was in balsa boats, so Heyerdahl had one built and in 1947 sailed it with a crew of five from Callio (Peru) to Raroia in Polynesia. The 8,000km (4,960-mile) trip took 101 days. It was just the beginning. In 1969 and 1970 he had two boats built of papyrus reeds, the Ra I and Ra II (right), which he sailed from Safi (Morocco) to the Caribbean. Thus he showed that it was at least possible that Egyptian mariners had done the same.

solstice. Heyerdahl, who proved that ancient mariners may have crossed the Atlantic to the Americas centuries before Christopher Columbus, challenged received wisdom by suggesting there is a link between the pyramidal structures of Egypt and South America.

You can learn how and why Heyerdahl came to these conclusions by visiting the **museum and educational centre** in the **Casa Chacona**. Using pre-Colombian art and other evidence, Heyerdahl asked if foreigners, perhaps from North Africa, came to South America and communicated the ideas behind pyramid building, sun-worship and mummification. If Heyerdahl was right, there is indeed no reason why they might not have called in to the Canary Islands too. A **video** in the auditorium provides further evidence.

TAKING A BREAK

You can get a sandwich and drinks in the **café** at the **Pirámides de Güímar** complex. Or, there are a couple of restaurant/bars a few metres to the left.

---

192 C1 **Calle Chacona s/n**
922/514-510; www.piramidesdeguimar.net **Daily 9:30–6** **€11**

INSIDER INFO

Set to one side of the complex is a **full size model** of the ***Ra II***, one of the several reed vessels Thor Heyerdahl built and sailed across the Atlantic. Small-scale models of other modern ocean-going reed boats are also on display.

38 Candelaria

Less than 20km (12.5mi) south of Santa Cruz, the unsophisticated coastal town of Candelaria is far more important for what it represents than for what there is to see. If you are here on 2 February or 15 August, you will witness one of Tenerife's most important fiestas and a pilgrimage of international fame – the Fiesta de Nuestra Señora de la Candelaria, the patron saint of the archipelago.

The grand **Basílica de Nuestra Señora de Candelaria** was completed in 1958. It houses the most revered statue of the Canary Island the **Virgen de Candelaria**. At the end of the 14th century before the Spanish conquest, shepherds are said to have found a statue of the Madonna washed up on the shore to the south of the town that is now known as Candelaria. When they tried to throw stones at the effigy, their arms were paralysed. In awe of its power, the Guanches carried the statue to their king, the Mencey of Güímar. The statue was moved to a cave of honour and from then on worshipped for its miraculous powers. After the Spanish conquest, the Spaniards set up a Dominican cloister next to the cave, which soon became the most important place of pilgrimage on the island. Pope Clemens VIII declared the Virgen de Candelaria the patron saint of the Canary Islands in 1599.

The balcony on top of the Basilica's belfry is a curious architectural detail

The Theft of the Statue

Another strange legend surrounds the theft of the statue. Subjects of the ruler of Lanzarote stole the statue and took it to a cloister on the eastern Canary island. This was a deed that obviously displeased the Madonna who turned her face to the wall. When the statue was turned round during the day, it simply looked away again and the same wondrous spectacle repeated itself the following morning. Since the chapel was closed every evening, it was concluded that something miraculous was occurring.

The Virgin Mary of Candelaria attracts pilgrims from far and wide

It was decided to return the statue to Candelaria, where there were no more "twists" in the story.

However, the cloister was almost totally destroyed during a storm tide in 1826, and the statue was washed back out to sea. The Madonna now venerated in the Basilica is the work of Fernando Estévez and was sculpted in 1827. There is a marble memorial near the church that commemorates the events relating to the Virgen de Candelaria.

More to See

Aside from the Basilica, sights in Candelaria include a parish church and the charming 17th-century **Iglesia de Santa Ana**. Along the waterfront esplanade before the Plaza de la Basílica, in which pilgrims gather on the feast day, stands an intriguing series of nine outsize statues. The Canarian artist José Abad based his images of the Guanche kings on the poems describing the characters of the island rulers; these poems were composed at the end of the 16th century by Antonio de Viana.

TAKING A BREAK

A good spot to stop for a traditional Canarian lunch is **El Archete** near the Basilica (► 142).

---

193 D1

Basílica de Nuestra Señora de Candelaria
Plaza de la Basílica · May–Oct 9:30–6, Nov–April 10–5 · Free

INSIDER INFO

- Before rushing off up or down the coast, you might want to dedicate a little time to a wander around the warren of lanes that constitute what there is of the **old town**, up the hill behind the church.
- The high territory west of Candelaria but within its municipal boundaries is a protected **wildlife area** notable for its pines and other trees.
- From the main entrance to the basilica, steps lead up the Calle La Palma and into Calle Isla de La Gomera, to a **pottery works**. Here, ceramic articles are made without a potter's wheel – the method used by the Guanches. There is a little museum next to it and a sales room with replicas of Guanche pottery (Tue–Fri 8:30–2 and 4–7, Sat 8:30–2, admission free).

At Your Leisure

Sanded down by the weather: the bizarre tuff pillars at Vilaflor

39 Siam Park

Touting itself as the biggest and most spectacular water park in Europe, Siam Park has certainly made a big splash in the press. There are water rides including the spectacular Dragon raft ride and the Giant with its centrifugal pool. The 18.5ha (7.5 acre) park also offers lush gardens and animal encounters with playful sea lions. Styled like a tropical Asian jungle garden, it's a great place to let off steam in the pools. Alternatively you can learn to surf on the artificial waves at the Wave Palace where waves can be programmed to reach 3m in height, or simply laze around enjoying the shady foliage.

There is a range of restaurants and cafés on site and a floating Thai-style market where you can shop for souvenirs.

186 B2
Off exit 29 TF1, Playa de las Américas
922/750-032; www.siampark.net
May–Oct 10–6, Nov–April 10–5
€32 (also combined ticket with Loro Parque)

40 Vilaflor

At 1,160m (3,805ft), the tranquil town of Vilaflor claims to be the highest town in Spain. Its position marks the point at which the farm terraces that spread south towards the coast begin in earnest. Further up pine stands take over on the way to Mount Teide. On a fine day the views up and down from Vilaflor are good, but the town itself offers interesting sights.

At the southern end, on Calle de Santa Catalina, is the **Hotel El Sombrerito**. You can't miss the yellow paint and green timberwork and balcony. A collection of farm implements inside passes for the town's museum, but it's a cosy place to have lunch or stay.

The top of the town is dominated by the single-nave **Iglesia de San Pedro,** built in the shape of a Latin cross. A few steps from this 17th-century church are a former convent and church dedicated to Vilaflor's most famous son, Hermano Pedro (Brother Peter, 1626–67, real name Hernando Pedro de San José Betancourt) who started life as a shepherd in the hills around the town. During his adult life in Tenerife, he went to live in a cave (**Cueva del Hermano Pedro,** ➤ 137, an object of pilgrimage near El Médano at the end of Tenerife Sur Airport's eastern runway), before

INSIDER INFO

On a narrow coast road 7km (4.5mi) west of El Médano is the fishing village of **Los Abrigos**, important to the visitor for the fresh seafood served in its simple waterfront restaurants. Insider Tip

setting off for Guatemala, where he founded the Order of Bethlehem. The father was beatified in 1980 and canonised by Pope John Paul II in 2002. He is the first Canarian to be made a saint.

The **"Lunar Landscape"** *(paisaje lunar)* aptly describes a series of tuff pillars. Their bizarre formation is quite unique on the Canary Islands. Their bizarre, polished, cone-like shape is the result of thousands of years of erosion. You can only reach the lunar landscape on foot; the site itself is not open to the public. The point of departure is the church of Vilaflor (1,400m/4,600ft).

186 C3 ✉ 21km (13mi) south of the parador, Parque Nacional del Teide

41 Granadilla de Abona

A typically sleepy interior town, Granadilla is worth a quick detour if you're driving past. Head for the town centre and the **Iglesia de San Antonio de Padua**, with a grey Baroque facade and 19th-century bell-tower. Stretching away from the church is the charming little Calle de la Iglesia. Another street that the town council has started to recover from decay is **Calle del Arquitecto Marrero**. To find it, follow Calle del Pino down from the church and it's on your right. The outstanding building here is also a charming *casa rural* (► 36) called the Traspatio, a two-hundred-year-old town house in which there are three pretty apartments for rent (www.casaruraleltras patio.com, tel: 922/630-596).

186 D3

✉ 23km (14mi) north-east of Los Cristianos

42 Las Galletas & Costa del Silencio

What little evidence there may once have been of a fishing village at Las Galletas has long been buried in the swathes of holiday apartments and hotels, with the occasional tourist restaurant thrown in. The sprawl is spreading and makes for a dusty, grey mess with a pebble beach. Next around the coast to the west are the slightly more thoughtfully planned holiday resorts of the "Silent Coast". At least there are some trees here.

186 C1

✉ 13km (8mi) south east of Los Cristianos

43 El Médano

The wind howls long and hard off this south-eastern point, making the beaches on either side of it great for windsurfing. The beaches are the best natural strands on the island and are comparatively wild and empty, but the town has less to recommend it. Apartment blocks have all but obliterated the original hamlet and stretch back inland, surrounded by the barren land that is a hallmark of the south.

Off the road that connects the town with the TF1 motorway a side

The conditions for windsurfing attract fans from all around the world

road is signposted west to the **Cueva del Hermano Pedro**.

187 E2

22km (13.5mi) east of Los Cristianos

43 Porís de Abona

It would appear that the secret of this once fairly unassuming fishing village is now out. Around the inlet where locals moor their little boats, residential projects are beginning to fill the arid emptiness. Still, the two main reasons for visiting remain valid for the moment. Porís de Abona has more than its share of straightforward seafood restaurants, making it a good lunch stop en route to somewhere else. Should you decide to hang about longer, head 1km (0.5mi) around the bay to **Punta de Abona** for the best beach. Another kilometre or so down the coast is a **lighthouse** where the locals go fishing. A 1.5km (1mi) stroll brings you to another small and secluded strand of beach, the **Caleta Maria Luisa**.

191 D1/2

34km (21mi) north east of Los Cristianos

A simple Baroque church dominates the townscape of the village of Arico

45 Arico

A 7km (4.5-mile) drive inland from Porís de Abona, Arico is divided into several parts, of which the most attractive is **Arico Nuevo**, which in spite of its name (New Arico) is the oldest part of town. A narrow street unfolds downhill from the main inland highway, the TF28, lined with charming houses, uniformly whitewashed, with dark green doors and window frames. Halfway along, the street opens up into a peaceful little square, **Plaza de la Luz**, where you'll find the cheerful parish church.

190 C2

6km (3.5mi) west of Porís de Abona

46 Mirador de Don Martín

After a seemingly endless string of hairpin bends in country that just imperceptibly begins to get green, you arrive at the Mirador de Don Martín, one of the best lookout points along the inland highway between Los Cristianos and Santa Cruz. From here you can see north as far as Santa Cruz and across the ocean to the island of Gran Canaria.

193 D1

5km (3mi) south of Güímar

Where to... Stay

Prices
Prices are for a double room per night during the high season.
€ under €70 € €70–120 € over €120

PARQUE NACIONAL DEL TEIDE

Parador de las Cañadas del Teide €€€
Tenerife's only *parador* occupies a stunning national-park location at the foot of Mount Teide (► 122). Refurbished and upgraded, the hotel merges unobtrusively into the surrounding sandy plains, and picture windows overlook a startling array of weirdly eroded rocks and lava gardens. As darkness falls, this isolated setting is incredibly quiet. Inside, the hotel is comfortably cheerful, with exposed stone and open fires. Rooms are spacious and well equipped. There is a restaurant with traditional food.
189 E3
38300 La Orotava
922/386-415; www.parador.es

LOS CRISTIANOS & PLAYA DE LAS AMÉRICAS

Aparthotel Panorama €
One of the smaller aparthotel complexes in this part of the island, the 174 units are set in two- and three-storey buildings around the pool. Kitchenettes are basic but the studios and apartments are clean and spacious. A laundry and internet café are on site. The nearest beach is 300m away.
86 B2 **Avenida Gran Bretaña**
922/791-611; www.hovima-hotels.com

Jardín Caleta €
A bright modern 5- to 6-storey aparthotel complex that seems to have lots of happy clients. There are almost 250 units in all surrounding a children's playground, swimming pool, TV room and two bars. There's even a tennis court for budding Andy Murrays and a driving range for budding Tiger Woods. The units are spacious and well furnished for the 3-star standard.
186 B2
Avenida Las Gaviotas 32, La Caleta
922/710-976; www.hovima-hotels.com

Jardín Tropical €€€ Insider Tip
On spacious grounds behind the sea promenade, the imaginatively designed hotel is a small world of its own. The architecture is a Moorish fantasy of tiles and turrets, domes and arches, while the furnishings and public areas are casual but stylish. Outside, the gardens billow with colourful vegetation. All the rooms are just as charming, in carved wood and wicker. Pools set by the water's edge supplement those in the hotel grounds. There are several exceptional restaurants, and health and fitness treatments to tempt everyone.
186 B2
Calle Gran Bretaña s/n, Playa de las Américas
922/746-000; www.jardin-tropical.com

Parque Santiago €/€€
This huge complex – the size of a small village – is a family-friendly aparthotel property with good on-site facilities, including an ample choice of casual and fine dining restaurants, a fitness centre,

childrens' adventure park and internet café. The whitewashed accommodation blocks are set in three "parques" around several good-sized pools within the 6.7ha (16 acres) site, giving the feel of different local districts. Apartments have kitchenettes giving you the flexibility of self-catering of you want it.

186 B2

Avenida Litoral, Playa de las Américas

922/746-103; www.parquesantiago.com

Sir Anthony €€€

Describing a gentle crescent just back from the waterfront, the 72 rooms that make up this luxury hotel, are pleasantly unobtrusive. The spacious accommodation is bright, with marble bathrooms and, best of all, a private terrace – ideal for breakfast with ocean views. Immediately fronting the rooms are the pool and gardens, and a quick stroll away is Playa del Camisón.

186 B2 Avenida de las Américas

922/757-545; www.marenostrumresort.com

COSTA ADEJE

Colón Guanahaní €€/€€€

One of the most attractive hotels in the Fañabe district of Costa Adeje, this well-equipped establishment has a quiet and relaxing style, even though it is on a fairly busy road. Its buildings extend round large freeform seawater pools and tiled sundecks shaded by palms. The spacious rooms all have balconies.

186 B2 Calle Bruselas, Playa de Fañabe

922/712-046; www.adrianhoteles.com

Gran Hotel Bahía del Duque €€€

This luxury complex consisting of 20 individual buildings with many restaurants offers a pleasant stay. There's direct access to an immaculate beach with an adventurous selection of watersports.

186A 2

Calle Alcalde Walter Paetzmann s/n

922/746-900; www.bahia-duque.com

Sheraton La Caleta Resort & Spa €€€

This magnificent property set in beautifully landscaped grounds is one of the best hotels on Tenerife. The luxury resort's refined extras include a pool landscape, a children's club and a Japanese restaurant. Rooms are spacious and well furnished. The spa is the pièce de resistance covering 1,800m² (20,000ft²) with massage suites, and a fully equipped gym and fitness suite.

186 B2 Calle La Enramada 9, Adeje

922/162-000; www.starwoodhotels.com

GÜÍMAR

Hotel Rural Finca Salamanca €€/€€€

This charming restored farmhouse in lush gardens attracts visitors who enjoy hiking. It is set in a peaceful location – 5ha (12 acres) of avocado, mango and citrus groves surround the hotel – and has exceptionally stylish decor. The airy raftered restaurant has Canarian specialities and local wine.

192 C1 Carretera Güimar, El Puertito Km 1.5 922/514-5 30; www.hotel-fincasalamanca.com

VILAFLOR

El Nogal €€/€€€

The main attraction of this place is its location near Vilaflor. Spectacular views stretch to Los Cristianos and the Atlantic. A low-key, cream-washed building, once part of an 18th-century estate, has been sympathetically restored to create a charming hotel. Each of its 29 rooms is different and prettily decorated in traditional Canarian style. The neat gardens surround a pool terrace and the hotel has a new spa complex.

186 C3 Camino Real s/n,La Escalona

922/726-050; www.hotelnogal.com

Where to...
Eat and Drink

Prices
Price per person for a three-course meal including drinks
€ under €20 **€** €20–40 **€** over €40

LOS CRISTIANOS & PLAYA DE LAS AMÉRICAS

Don Armando €
Amid the tourist watering holes, this Spanish-looking place adds a very welcome touch of regional authenticity. Beyond the typical bar where Spanish voices can be heard, a spacious terrace restaurant offers grandstand views of the seafront. The all-day menu has several classic tapas dishes.
186 B2 Calle San Telmo, Los Cristianos
922/796-145
Mon–Sat 11:30–4:30, 8–11:30

El Patio €€€
The hotel Jardín Tropical (► 139) has several lovely restaurants and this elegant place produces some of the best cooking on the island. Ambitious menus blend Canarian and Spanish cuisine with international flair: a gastronomic version includes seven different dishes to sample, and there's an impressive cellar. The shady terrace dining room is charmingly decorated in blue and white tiles with billowing plants and fountains.
186 B2 Hotel Jardín Tropical, Calle Gran Bretaña s/n, Playa de las Américas
922/746-000 or 922/746-061
Tue–Sat 7pm–midnight

Las Rocas €€€
Terraces stretch over the waves at this romantic, chic restaurant attached to one of the resort's top hotel, the Jardín Tropical (► 139). Fish and seafood predominate. Rice dishes are another speciality, and there's an extensive list of Canarian wines. Try *langostinos al ajillo* (king prawns with garlic) or local tuna and *cherne* (sea bass). Beyond the rocks that give this place its name, views stretch towards La Gomera. Sunsets are tremendous so it's a good idea to bag a waterfront table if you can.
186 B2 Hotel Jardín Tropical, Calle Gran Bretaña s/n, Playa de las Américas
922/746-064 Daily 1–4, 7–11

La Tasca de mi Abuelo €

A small family-run place with rustic wooden tables and terracotta tiled floors serves an excellent range of tapas and other Spanish dishes. It's always packed with local Canarians. The air-dried ham is sliced as you watch – delicious!
186 B2 CC San Marino, Local 13, Los Cristianos 922/794-466
Tue–Sat noon–4, 8–11, Sun noon–4pm

COSTA ADEJE

El Molino Blanco €€
Although geared mainly towards foreign visitors, the rustic setting and welcoming atmosphere here promise an enjoyable visit. Old wine barrels have been pressed into service as light fixtures, and tables stretch from its attractive dining areas on to large garden terraces with abundant climbing plants and citrus trees. Both the wine list and menu are wide ranging; Specialities: paella, Canarian style "Carne Fiesta".
186 B2
Avenida de Austria 5, San Eugenio Alto
922/796-282; www.molino-blanco.com
Wed–Mon 1pm–midnight

Otelo I €€

Perched by the Barranco del Infierno, Adeje's famous gorge (➤ 124), Otelo does a brisk trade in providing drinks and sustenance to walkers. It serves bar snacks and a variety of popular local dishes like rabbit and *pollo al ajillo* (chicken in either garlic or a spicy *mojo* sauce). Those who don't want to walk can enjoy the gorgeous view of the countryside from the terrace.

186 B2 Calle Los Molinos 44, Barranco del Infierno, Adeje 922/780 374 Wed–Mon 11am–midnight

CANDELARIA

El Archete €€€

Probably Candelaria's best eating place, El Archete is not far from the main square (➤ 134). The atmosphere is refined and civilised, complementing its creative repertoire of interesting Canarian dishes. Specialities include *papas negras rellenas de cherne con salsa de caviar* (black potatoes stuffed with sea bass in caviare sauce).

193 D1 Calle Santa Ana 10 922/500-354; www.elarchete.amawebs.com Mon–Sat 10–5, 7:45–11:30, Sun 1–5

VILAFLOR

El Sombrerito €

This quaint guesthouse in the centre of Vilaflor is better known to the regulars as Casa Chicho. The innkeeper serves good plain Canarian dishes for a fair price. Tourists staying in the simple rather spartan rooms tend to be hikers; they appreciate the proximity of El Sombrerito to the National Park and the Lunar Landscape (Paisaje Lunar).

186 C3 Calle Santa Catalina 15 922/709-052 Daily 9–9

GRANADILLA DE ABONA

El Jable €€

Accomplished cooking of hearty Canarian fare puts this established bar/restaurant into the top league in this area. The interior walls here are made of local volcanic stone and dark wood, and adorned with wicker lampshades and bright modern paintings. It provides the perfect setting for fresh fish and meat, fine cheese and wine. Outstanding dishes include *queso a la plancha con mojo-cilantro* (baked smoked goat's cheese with coriander sauce). The restaurant occasionally hosts art exhibitions and organises wine tasting.

187 D3
Calle Bentejui 9, San Isidro
922/390-698
Mon 7:30pm–11pm, Tue–Sat 1–4, 7:30–11; closed 15–30 Jun

EL MÉDANO

Perlas del Mar €€

Opinions differ over which is the best of the fish restaurants lining the water's edge at Los Abrigos, but this one has perhaps the best location. Select your fish from the counter and specify how you want it cooked – steamed, grilled or fried. The staff are happy to help. The tables on the terrace make a fine spot to watch the sun set over the waves.

187 E2 Calle La Marina, Los Abrigos 922/170-014 Mon–Sat noon–11; closed 15–30 Sep

Los Roques €€/€€€

Los Roques is a great modern restaurant with a wonderful terrace, set directly on the coast in Los Abrigos. A fusion menu features dishes such as calamari cooked over charcoal, sea bass Thai style, and rabbit in a mustard sauce. The chef tries to source as many ingredients as possible from the islands. The salad and vegetables are grown on the owner's farm. There's a good choice of local bottles on the wine list.

187 E2 Calle la Marina 16, Los Abrigos
922/749-401; www.restaurantlosroques.com
Tue–Sat 7pm–11pm

Where to... Shop

SHOPPING CENTRES

Centros comerciales provide a source on tourist entertainment in the resorts of the south coast. The centres in Fañabe and El Duque cater very much to the well-to-do clientele of the nearby luxury hotels.

MARKETS

Flea-markets colonise a large patch of the Torviscas seafront on Thursday and Saturday mornings, and at Los Cristianos near the Hotel Arona Gran on Sunday.

The search for a **bargain** is an irresistible challenge. Artists and **street traders** use the promenades as a permanent window display. Avoid anything made of ivory, an illegal import.

CRAFTS

Head for the older country towns and villages, where **farmer's markets** and **craft fairs** *(ferias de artesanía)* make good hunting grounds. Vilaflor, Fasnia, San Miguel de Abona and Güímar all hold summer fairs. On the main routes leading up to the Teide National Park, you'll pass several large **craft centres**. There's a good one on the main road at Guía de Isora, north of Costa Adeje.

Besides the usual range of embroidery, pottery and wickerwork, look for folk music recordings, local wine and flower perfumes. In the National Park itself (► 122), you will find original souvenirs.

Where to... Go Out

NIGHTLIFE

The most frenetic discos, easily detectable by their decibel levels, cluster around the commercial strip known as **Las Veronicas** near Troya beaches. **The Starco** complex on the inland side of the main seafront promenade and **The Patch** towards Los Cristianos throb to a similar beat after dark.

Ephemeral as dragonflies, reputations can easily fade and die within a season. Yet still all the rage with their mainly English and Irish guests are the **Linekers Bar** (Centro Comercial Starco, tel: 922/798-948; www.linekerstenerife.com) and **Tibu Tenerife** (Amerikas Shopping Center, tel: 922/796-586; www.tibutenerife.com). Anyone who enjoys food with their live music can try **Banana Garden** (Avenida Rafael Puig, tel: 922/790-365; www.bananagarden.com) and **Harleys American Diner** (Avenida de España 3, tel: 922/712-290; www.harleys tenerife.com).

Towards Los Cristianos, the bizarre pseudo-classical **Pirámide de Arona** (Avenida de las Américas s/n, tel: 922/757-549; www.marenostrum resort.com) puts on the most ambitious gala perfomances in the south of Tenerife, including cabaret acts and tasters of flamenco, opera and ballet, or roll the dice at **Casino de las Américas** (tel: 922/793-758) in Hotel Gran Tinerfe. A popular evening excursion advertised in hotels and travel agencies is **Castillo de San Miguel** (San Miguel Aldea Blanca, tel: 922/ 700-276; www.castillo sanmiguel.com), a mock-medieval dinner show of jousting and jollity off the Autopista del Sur. It's good fun and includes some virtuoso feats of horsemanship.

BOAT TRIPS

Many boat trips involve **whale- or dolphin-watching** off the west coast, or a mix of beach parties and leisure cruises. Most trips depart from Puerto Colón (Playa de las Américas) or Los Cristianos, and include snorkelling or scuba diving. **Tropical Delfin** (Pier 12, Puerto Colón, tel: 922/750-085; www.tenerifedolphin.com; daily at 10:15am) is a very conservation-minded whale-watching vessel. Several times a week the modern catamaran ***Lady Shelly*** sets sail from Los Cristianos harbour for trips along the coast to the cliffs Los Gigantes. It is usually possible to get a meal on board (tel: 922/757-549; www.marenostrumresort.com). **Glass-bottom** and **submarine boats** have underwater magic, though most marine life stays some way off the churned up waters of these resorts. By far the most popular boat excursion from the southern resorts is to **La Gomera**. Hydrofoils and ferries leave regularly from Los Cristianos.

ATTRACTIONS

The waterslides of the popular **Aqualand** (Avenida de Austria, San Eugenio Alto 15, Costa Adeje; daily 10–6, tel: 922/715-266; www.aqualand.es: €22.50) provide an unexpected oasis at San Eugenio. Children just love it! One of the area's most popular visitor attractions is **Las Aguilas Jungle Park** (Carretera Los Cristianos-Arona, Km 3, tel: 922/729-010; www.aguilasjunglepark.com; daily 10–5:30, flying shows at noon and 4pm; €24), a bird park where eagles and falcons display aeronautical feats.

OUTDOOR PURSUITS

Many resort hotels have impressive leisure facilities that non-residents can pay to use. **Bicycle hire** is available in all the major resorts.

Watersports

Puerto Colón and Los Cristianos harbour are the best starting points for **deep-sea fishing**, yacht charter, sea-scooters and pedaloes. Watersports are advertised on local beaches, including **jetskiing** and **parascending**. **Scuba diving** centres operate in all the main resorts; the clear, rock-lined waters of the Costa del Silencio are a rewarding location. If **windsurfing** is your thing, head for El Médano. Sailboard hire and tuition are available on the main beaches; try Playa Sur (tel: 922/176-688; www.surfcenter.elmedano.com).

Golf

Golf del Sur (Urb. Golf del Sur, San Miguel de Abona, tel: 922/738-170; www.golfdelsur.net) has exotic palms and cacti amid bunkers of black sand. **Amarilla Golf** (Urb. Amarilla Golf, San Miguel de Abona, tel: 922/730-319; www.amarillagolf.es) has a superb oceanside setting and a pitch-and-putt course and practice driving range. The **Golf Costa Adeje** (Finca Los Olivos s/n, Adeje, tel: 922/710-000; www.golfcostaadeje.com) looks over the sea towards La Gomera. It has 27 holes.

Hiking & Flower Spotting

If you want to learn more about nature in the south, head for Adeje's **Barranco del Infierno**, a cactus-filled ravine ending in a waterfall. (Please note that the gorge is sometimes closed due to the risk of rock fall. Enquire at the local tourist office as to whether it is open).

Make for **Siete Cañadas** (► 127) in early summer to see the flamboyant *tajinaste rojo* in full bloom, its red-hot-poker spires rearing 2m (6.5ft) above the cinderbeds of Mount Teide's crater. Many typical plants of these volcanic lands can be seen growing in protected conditions at the **El Portillo Visitor Centre** (► 125), or around **Los Roques** (► 125) and the *parador* (► 127).

La Gomera

Little Treats

Sky Walk

On the **Mirador de Abrante** (➤ 146) you stand on a glass-enclosed sky walk high above the north coast. A small path from the National Park's Visitor Centre leads to the viewing point.

Rustic Repose

In the **La Vista** restaurant (➤ 154) in the little hamlet of El Cedro, you should try the watercress soup, served in the traditional way in a wooden bowl.

Fiery Rocks

"Los Roques" (the rocks) is the name of the volcanic funnels on the southern edge of the **Garajonay National Park** (➤ 156), the most well-known being the Roque Agando.

Getting Your Bearings

Just 30 minutes by ferry off the south-west coast of Tenerife, La Gomera is known to its 23,000 inhabitants as La Isla Redonda (The Round Island). Measuring 25km (15mi) by 23km (14mi), it is the second smallest in the archipelago. About 10 per cent of the island's centre is taken up by the Parque Nacional de Garajonay, a UNESCO World Heritage Site, an extraordinary mix of frequently mist-enveloped laurel forest and other vegetation, culminating in the 1487m (4879ft)-high Garajonay peak.

La Gomera attracts two kinds of tourism: fast one-day tours from Tenerife and a smaller, nature-loving crowd who stay for several days. Walking is becoming increasingly popular and trails abound.

A web of *barrancos* (gorges) spreads from Garajonay to the coast. Much of the island, especially the north and west, is terraced for agriculture (bananas remain the predominant crop).

Every day, ferries cross from Tenerife's harbour Los Cristianos to the capital of San Sebastián on the east coast of La Gomera. Two roads head west, one sweeping north through a series of picturesque villages, some with tiny beaches. It then swings south west into the pretty Valle Gran Rey, a fertile valley of farm terraces that ends in a cluster of beachside villages. The other road proceeds through the Parque Nacional de Garajonay and also links up with the Valle Gran Rey. A couple of roads zigzag south to the Playa de Santiago, which hosts dive schools and a handful of beaches.

On the beach near Vueltas in the Valle Gran Rey

Modest houses squat in among the palms and farming terraces along the Valle Gran Rey

A stone parish church marks the centre of Vallehermoso in the north of the island

TOP 10

Don't Miss

At Your Leisure

La Gomera

Three Perfect Days

If you're not quite sure where to begin your travels, this itinerary recommends three practical and enjoyable days out in La Gomera, taking in some of the best places to see. For more information see the main entries (➤ 150–158).

Day One

Morning

Get the first **ferry** from Los Cristianos in southern Tenerife for the 30-minute ride across to the modest capital, 47 **San Sebastián de la Gomera** (➤ 153). After organising car hire, head off on a brief stroll around the colonial town where you can see what is supposedly the house where Columbus lodged prior to setting off on his first voyage of discovery. Sit down for a light lunch at one of the cafés – for example in Ambigú on the Plaza de las Américas.

Afternoon

Set off on a driving tour of the 48 **north of the island** (➤ 154). Stop at **Hermigua** (➤ 154), where you can take a walk to El Cedro. The pretty drive continues to the coast and then west, where things get a little wilder. **Vallehermoso** (➤ 155) is a handy spot to stop for a drink and, if you stay on, a base for walks. As the road swings south take the turn to **Alojera** (➤ 155) before returning to the main road and descending the ★9 **Valle Gran Rey** (➤ 150), an ideal spot to spend a couple of nights.

Day Two

Morning

Join a boat trip to **Los Órganos** (➤ 150), the bizarre cliffs in the north of the island. Or alternatively, take a break from travelling and relax on the beach.

Afternoon
After lunching in one of the restaurants at Vueltas, or La Puntilla in Valle Gran Rey (➤ 150), head up to **Chipude** (➤ 152) to undertake a rewarding walk back south through gorges and past country chapels to the beach at **La Calera**.

Day Three

Morning
Drive east into the ㊾ **Parque Nacional de Garajonay** (above; ➤ 156), where you can make a quick ascent of the Alto de Garajonay and see an unspoilt laurel forest, or take a longer walk to El Cedro. Enjoy a lunchtime picnic in La Laguna Grande (➤ 1571).

Afternoon
Drive south to 51 **La Dama** and **Playa de La Rajita** (➤ 158) for a look at the Atlantic, or go on a southern circuit via **Alajeró** to 53 **Playa de Santiago** (➤ 158), where you could swim and eat before heading north to the San Sebastián road to return to the capital in time for the last boat back to Los Cristianos. If you have more time, **diving** (right) is an option in Playa de Santiago. Or visit the palm groves of 52 **Benchijigua** (➤ 158).

9 Valle Gran Rey

Tourism on Gomera began in Valle Gran Rey in the 1970s. Many hippies came to live here. Although the increasing number of tourists has come with a price – the wild, natural character of the valley has long since disappeared – Valle Gran Rey remains breathtakingly beautiful and attracts many individual travellers.

The "Valley of the Great King", named after a Guanche ruler, Orone, opens out into a delta as it reaches the coastal settlements of La Calera, La Playa and Vueltas. As you approach the valley from the north, stop at the lookout at Arure (Mirador El Santo). From here there are views across the west of the island and over the ocean to the westernmost islands of the archipelago, La Palma (to the north) and El Hierro.

Above and right page: View of the elongated terraces of Valle Gran Rey dotted with palms and white-washed houses

THE WHISTLING GOMEROS

It is not only the laurel forest that is under the special protection of UNESCO; in 2012 – the same year that, in August, wildfires destroyed 18% of the national park – the entire island was declared a Biosphere Reserve. The *el silbo gomero* (Gomeran whistle), with which the inhabitants used to communicate over long distances is also considered a cultural asset that needs protection. Confronted by the difficult terrain of their island, the Guanches found it easier to whistle messages across the gorges to their neighbours than to walk over to them. Simply put, *el silbo gomero* involves vowels and consonants being communicated like a kind of Morse code with various short or long whistles. Placing their fingers in their mouths and cupping their hands, practised *Silbaderos* are able to conduct simple dialogues over distances of up to 6km (3.5mi). In order to avoid this bird-sounding language from dying out, it is now being taught at Gomeran primary schools.

Giant Steps

The road winds down steeply past hamlets, farms and palm stands as you drop into the *barranco* (gorge). The impressive gorge walls, up to 800m (2,624ft) high, protect the valley from ocean winds, helping to make it the most agriculturally prosperous area on the island.

The fine black sand of **La Playa** makes it the most pleasant beach, although several smaller ones are dotted along the coast on either side of it. A trail leads north to **Playa del Inglés**, while trails to the south of Vueltas go to **Playa de Argaga** and **Playa de las Arenas**.

Of these hamlets, the most intriguing is **La Calera**, with hilly lanes studded with small lodgings, restaurants and bars.

Activities and Excursions

Apart from the beach, the main aquatic activities include **boat trips**. For example, many of the tour operators located around the harbour of Vueltas offer – quite expensive – excursions to the cliffs of **Los Órganos** (➤ 162). They generally leave at 10:30am and include lunch. Weather permitting, you may see dolphins and whales along the way.

Away from the coast, the big attraction is **walking**. The hiking trails are relatively well marked, but make sure you take a trail map with you. You can obtain one free of charge in the tourist office at La Playa.

A popular option is to catch the San Sebastián bus to the inland town of **Chipude**, below the southern flank of the Parque Nacional de Garajonay. From there are numerous walking options. A good three-hour round trip takes you on a return journey from Chipude to the grand rocky outcrop known as **La Fortaleza** ("the fort"). From Chipude you could also follow minor ravines south west past a couple of *ermitas* (little country chapels) and then down the Valle Gran Rey to **La Calera**, a delightful walk of about 3.5 hours.

Playa Calera is one of several modest beaches at Valle Gran Rey

TAKING A BREAK

Mango (tel: 922/805-362) offers a wonderful spot on the short beach promenade of La Playa.

184 B3

INSIDER INFO

- Just 4km (2.5mi) north of Vallehermoso is the dramatic cliff face known as **Los Órganos**. To see this stunning natural wonder you need to arrive by sea. Trips are organised by a couple of companies in Valle Gran Rey (➤ 156).
- **Oceano** in Vueltas (tel: 922/805-717; www.oceano-gomera.com) conducts **marine research** and they like to share their knowledge. You can go on four-hour **boat trips**, during which whales may also be spotted.

47 San Sebastián

A scattering of sights, beautiful traditional houses and the occasional market make the obligatory arrival in San Sebastián a pleasant first stop on La Gomera.

Wander through the streets of San Sebastián to get a feel of the town

The **Torre del Conde** (Count's Tower) was the first building erected by the Spaniards in San Sebastián, in 1447. La Gomera's first lady, Beatriz de Bobadilla, holed up here during the islanders' revolt in 1488 and Christopher Columbus stayed in the **Casa de Colón** (Calle Real 56) before setting out on his voyage of discovery. Today it is a charming colonial house with a courtyard and a smattering of Peruvian artefacts that are just about worth a visit. About 100m closer to the port, the **Iglesia de la Virgen de la Asunción** has a mural depicting the defeat of English pirates on the island in 1743.

Three caravels under the command of Columbus called in at San Sebastián en route from Spain to take on provisions in mid-August 1492. Columbus was determined to find a western route to the Indies and prove, along the way, that the Earth was round. Legend says he enjoyed a dalliance with Beatriz de Bobadilla, one-time lover of King Ferdinand of Spain and now widowed after the death of her nasty husband, who was killed during the 1488 Uprising.

TAKING A BREAK

Tasca La Salamandra (Calle República de Chile 5, tel: 922/ 141-386), a small restaurant in the old town is a perfect choice for a break. 

---

185 F2

San Sebastián Tourist Information

Calle Real 4 · 922/870-281 · Mon–Sat 9–1:30, 3:30–6, Sun 10–1

48 Hermigua, Agulo, Tamargada & Vallehermoso

Setting out across the north of the island is a real pleasure. The treat is in the travel itself as much as the destination, passing as it does through continually changing countryside and farmland, interspersed with pretty villages begging to be visited.

The fruit of vine grows around Hermigua

Although La Gomera, the second smallest island after El Hierro, is also of volcanic origin, this is barely visible in the landscape compared with the other western Canary islands. The last volcanic activity must have been a long while back, probably a million years ago.

From Village to Village

As you head out of San Sebastián along the GM1, you will find yourself quickly submerged in rural La Gomera. On the way to the north coast, you can drive down a narrow side road that ends at El Cedro and then walk from the La Vista restaurant (that has a camping site) to see the waterfall. The first village of any substance is **Hermigua**, where you can stop to stretch your legs and get a drink and a snack or visit the **Museo Etnográfico de La Gomera** (Tue–Fri 10–7, Sat, Sun 10–2; free). The 16th-century **Iglesia de Santo Domingo de Guzmán** is well worth seeing. It once belonged to a Dominican monastery that was given up in 1857.

To the north, the nicest beach is **Playa de la Caleta**, which can be reached from the old dock *(pescante)* on a little

INSIDER INFO

- The **Parque Nacional de Garajonay's** visitor centre is on the GMQ road between Agulo and Tamargada (follow signs for Las Rosas).
- In the **botanical garden** around the Juego de Bolas Visitor Centre, you can obtain information about the local flora.
- If you like secluded coves, walk two hours south west from San Sebastián to the hamlet of **El Cabrito**. The palm-backed black beach is pretty. Bring food and water.

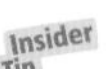

narrow, windy tarred road. The main road meanders past the coastal village of **Agulo** before twisting inland to **Tamargada** and **Vallehermoso**. The landmark of Vallehermoso is the 646m (2,120ft) high **Roque Cano**, a former volcanic plug, through which lava was funnelled to the top of the volcano, which have become exposed due to erosion. Tamargada is an attractive rural hamlet, Vallehermoso, somewhat larger, makes a handy base for walkers with accommodation and a couple of places to get something to eat.

The road continues south through high ground and the occasional village. Dirt roads lead to the isolated hamlets of **Tazo** and **Arguamul**. A 1km (0.5 mi) walk away from Aguamul is **Playa del Remo** which offers a chance to see something quieter. Further south, a side road makes for a spectacular drive downhill to **Alojera**, which has a tiny beach.

TAKING A BREAK

In the north, **Café Pedro** in Hermigua (► 161) makes a convenient place to stop during your exploration of the north.

Vallehermoso 184 C4
Tamargada 184 C4
Agulo 185 D4
Hermigua 185 D4

Across the town of Agulo is Mount Teide in its "sea of clouds"

49 Parque Nacional de Garajonay

To enter this national park, which covers about 10 per cent of the centre of the island, is to travel millions of years into the past. The *laurisilva* (laurel forest) that is protected here is among the most ancient forests on the planet and one of the few to escape the devastation caused by the last Ice Age. It is topped by the Garajonay peak (1,487m/4,877ft), from where there are views of Tenerife's Mount Teide and beyond.

UNESCO World Heritage Site

Often enveloped in swirling mists that defy the sand-and-sun impression most people have of the Canary Islands, the lichen- and moss-covered trees in the Parque Nacional de Garajonay, apart from the laurels, constitute hundreds of species. The mist produced by the clash of moist trade winds with warmer breezes from the Sahara causes as much, and sometimes more, precipitation than rain on the island. The ancient tree canopy is so thick that little or no sun penetrates, which explains the lack of other vegetation on the forest floor. In all, wandering about in here can be an eerie experience. The whole area was designated a UNESCO World Heritage Site in 1986.

Walking Country

The GM2 road from San Sebastián runs through the middle of the park and passes close to the **Alto de Garajonay**

The *laurisilva* on La Gomera is one of Earth's most ancient forests

Ups and downs in the Parque Nacional de Garajonay

(Garajonay peak, 1,487m/4,877ft). You can get the No 1 bus from San Sebastian and get off at the Pajarito stop, leaving you with about an hour's hike to the top of the peak. It is a fairly easy and popular walk. If you come by taxi or hire car, you can stop at the parking site for hikers El Contadero, from where a 1.5km (1-mile) trail leads to the Alto. On a clear day the views from the top can be magnificent. Apart from the obvious Mount Teide, you can also make out La Palma and El Hierro to the west and sometimes Gran Canaria.

Insider Tip

Plenty of other **walks** through the park are possible. You can get more information on them from the park's information centre, strangely located north of the park near Agulo. There is another small information booth at **La Laguna Grande** (➤ below, Taking a Break).

From the El Contadero pass a fine walk heads north through the thick **Bosque del Cedro** (cedar wood), although there are few cedars to be seen. The walk is well marked and signposted. You can stop in **El Cedro**, about two hours' walk away. From here you can visit the nearby **Boca del Chorro waterfall** (best in winter).

TAKING A BREAK

You could opt for a picnic at **La Laguna Grande**, a clearing about 3km (2mi) north west along the road from the Alto de Garajonay. It has a playground, barbecue grills and a café.

---

184 C3

Centro de Visitantes (Visitors' Centre)
185 D4 At Juego de Bolas near Agulo off the north coast road
922/800-993 Daily 9:30–4:30

INSIDER INFO

- When walking remember that within the boundaries of the national park you **may not camp nor light fires**.
- Don't leave any litter behind.
- Bring **warm and weatherproof gear** as it can be surprisingly cold and you could easily be caught in brief spells of rain.

At Your Leisure

Verdant vegetation envelops the complex of the Tecina Jardin hotel in Playa de Santiago

50 Parque Natural de Majona

Over one third of the area of La Gomera is under some kind of protection order. Parque Natural de Majona covers swathes of the island north west of San Sebastián. This is Canarian heath and pasture-land, which has been shaped by man, and where you can still see traditional shepherding taking place.

185 E3

51 La Dama & Playa de La Rajita

The narrow serpentine road to La Dama from the south flank of the Garajonay National Park passes through hamlets like El Cercado and Chipude before curving steeply down to the south coast. Apart from the banana plantations, La Dama offers the spectacular sight of sheer cliffs plunging deep into the Atlantic. A steep trail leads down to the black beach of Playa de la Rajita.

184 B2

About 27km (16.5mi) south of Valle Gran Rey

52 Benchijigua

Benchijigua is a sleepy little location at the head of a green ravine in the southern highlands. Neglected orange and fig trees stand around the long-deserted houses. Many hikers on their way from Roque Agando to the south coast enjoy a short break here in the shade of the date palms.

185 D3

About 20km (12.5mi) west of San Sebastián

53 Playa de Santiago

Playa de Santiago lies on arid land in the island's south east. The fishing town is trying to reinvent itself as a tourist centre with luxury hotels and the nearby airport. The dark sandy beach is one of the best places to bathe on the island. The main holiday resorts are Valle Gran Rey on the south-west coast and Playa de Santiago in the sunbathed south. Playa de Santiago is also a launch pad for diving excursions.

185 D1 **About 25km (15.5mi) south west of San Sebastián**

Where to...
Stay

Prices
Prices are for a double room per night during the high season.
€ under €70 € €70–120 € over €120

La Gomera's more enterprising and independently minded visitors have a choice of simple but stylish small hotels and *casas rurales* scattered throughout the island. The two largest holiday resorts are Valle Gran Rey on the south-west coast and Playa de Santiago in the sunbathed south.

SAN SEBASTIÁN

Parador de la Gomera €€€
San Sebastián's *parador* stands high above the port up a steeply winding road. The building is a convincing modern copy of a 16th-century convent. Low-rise wings in local stone and dark wood surround the shady courtyards and the furnishings are typically Castilian. Canarian specialities like *vieja* (parrotfish) with *mojo* feature on the menu in the stately dining room. The subtropical clifftop garden command views over the town and the local coast, with Mount Teide visible on Tenerife.
185 F2 Calle Orilla del Llano 1
922/871-100; www.paradores.com

VALLEHERMOSO

Tamahuche €
Just outside Vallehermoso's centre, this small hotel makes for a tranquil getaway. The 10 spacious bedrooms all have two generous single beds side by side in rooms of pleasing simplicity. Dark timber floors match the wooden furniture and some of the top floors have an exposed timber ceiling. Straightforward whitewash brings out the contrast and walls of exposed local stone add warmth to public areas like the dining room.
184 C4 Calle La Hoya 20
922/801-176; www.hoteltamahuche.com

HERMIGUA

Hotel Villa de Hermigua €
A simple hotel on the transit road with nine double rooms on several levels around a small sunny courtyard. There's a sunroom and TV room. Rooms are prettily decorated in local style and there's a characterful rustic breakfast room filled with antique nick-knacks. From the courtyard you can take in the beautiful panorama of the surrounding hills.
185 D4 Carretera General 117, Hermigua 922/880-777; www.hotelrural-villahermigua.com

Ibo Alfaro €€
This delightful rural hostelry is especially popular with hikers. It's a stylish little place on a quiet track above the main street. Insider Tip The cream-painted building dates from the 19th century. It was skilfully renovated in typical Canarian style using natural stone and timber. Breakfast is served on a sun terrace with lovely views.
185 D4 38820 Hermigua
922/880-168; www.hotel-gomera.com

VALLE GRAN REY

Jardín del Conde €€
Three low-rise, pastel-coloured blocks surround a large, freeform pool terrace on Valle Gran Rey's

seafront road. Behind the hotel loom dramatic terraced hills. This attractive apartment complex is tidily kept and brightly landscaped with plenty of greenery and flowering plants. Individual apartments (all with one bedroom and a balcony or terrrace overlooking the pool gardens) are light and simple in streamlined, colourful, contemporary style with kitchens. You can hire a satellite TV. A useful and separately managed mini market and bar stocking all the usual necessities are located near the basement entrance.

184 B3 ✉ Avenida Marítima s/n
☎ 922/ 806-008; www.jardindelconde.com

PLAYA DE SANTIAGO

Jardín Tecina €€€

This modern complex comprises low-rise, local-style units in an extensive village-like setting on the cliffs. High above the pebble beach of Playa de Santiago, the four-star resort is a self-contained world and thus ensures a comfortable and relaxing holiday break. The accommodation is set in an extravagant park complex with palms and subtropical, ornamental flora from all over the world, including colourful bougainvillea. There is a wide choice of sports activities available; these include an 18-hole golf course as well as a golf school at which beginners can take lessons. A diverse programme of entertainment and excursions is also provided. You can relax at one of the five pools, and the gastronomic delights of the various restaurants also leave nothing to be desired. A lift transports you to a beach club on the seafront, where watersports are on offer.

185 D1 ✉ Playa de Santiago
☎ 922/145-850; www.jardin-tecina.com

Where to... Eat and Drink

Prices
Price per person for a three-course meal including drinks
€ under €20 € €20–40 € over €40

SAN SEBASTIÁN

Parador de la Gomera €€/€€€

Plaza de las Américas is the focal point of the island's capital. The street cafés are an ideal place to round off the day. A good place to eat is the Hotel Parador. Non-residents are welcome.

185 E3 ✉ Calle Orilla del Llano 1
☎ 922/871-100 ⌚ 11:30–3:30, 7:30–11:30

LAS ROSAS

Las Rosas €€

Panoramic views are a major attraction of this roadside restaurant on the edge of a ravine. It's a popular stop off for groups, and is often booked up for set lunches. Food is typically Canarian. Demonstrations of La Gomera's strange whistling language (*el silbo*, ► 150) draw the crowds.

184 D4 ✉ Carretera General
☎ 922/800-916 ⌚ Daily noon–3:30

HERMIGUA

Café Pedro €

This establishment long known as the "Casa Creativa" is located directly next to the main village street. From the terrace, you can look down on the banana plantations in the valley. It is a perfect place for a cup of coffee and some cake, or a few tapas.

185 D4 Carretera General 56
922/881-023 Daily 10–8

AGULO

El Tambor €

A handy choice beside the Garajonay National Park Visitor Centre near Agulo, this rustic bar/restaurant serves appetising Gomeran specialities like *sopa de berros* (watercress soup). Combine a snack with a visit to the centre, with its folk museum and the small botanical garden.

185 D4 Agulo 922/800-709
Mon–Sat 11–6

VALLE GRAN REY

Restaurante Abraxas €/€€

Run by Germans, Restaurante Abraxas adds a touch of Far Eastern flair to traditional Gomeran cuisine. Thus, the meat dishes are prepared in a wok for example, and there are delicious curries, tofu and goat cheese specialities for the vegetarians. Fine liqueurs and brandies made of fruits such as mango and passion fruit come from the restaurant's own distillery. The cakes and even the ice cream are also made on location.

184 B3 La Puntilla (near the waterfront and Hotel Gran Rey)
922/805-982; www.abraxas-la-gomera.com
Thu–Tue 1–11

El Baifo €€

Indonesian cuisine with wonderfully light meals from the wok. Besides classics such as Bami Goreng, the restaurant also serves a special duck dish done to perfection. Reservation is recommended.

184 B3
Valle Gran Rey, La Playa, Edificio Normara
922/605-775
Sat–Thu 7pm–11pm

Where to... Shop

Crafts and food specialities are the main things to buy. Craft centres and workshops are scattered around the island in rural locations as well as the main resorts. The daily market in San Sebastián (Avenida de Colón; Mon–Sat morning) is worth a visit for crafts and fruit and vegetables, honey, wine and the Gomeran cream cheese Almogrote.

CRAFTS

For an overview of La Gomera's traditional wares, call in at the **Parque Nacional de Garajonay Visitor Centre** (Juego de Bolas, near Agulo, tel: 922/800-993), where textiles, musical instruments (tambourines and castanets), baskets made from banana leaves and woodwork are on display.

A craft workshop in Hermigua, **Los Telares** (tel: 922/880-781), specialises in local woven goods, especially hand-made rugs.

The villages of **Chipude** and **El Cercado** to the west of the Parque Nacional de Garajonay are well known for **pottery**, made in the traditional Guanche style without a wheel and fired with a coating of red clay. You can watch it being made in roadside potteries.

Valle Gran Rey has for a long time been an attractive base for expatriate New Age settlers in search of alternative lifestyles. Some make a living from jewellery, painting and other souvenirs.

There are many small boutiques in La Playa, Borbalán and Vueltas; a colourful market takes place at the La Calera bus station on Sundays (9–2).

MILK AND HONEY

A Gomeran speciality is ***queso de cabra*** (goat's cheese). Different varieties of it are sold at the supermarkets. Depending on its maturity, it can be a cream cheese, a lightly smoked cheese or a hard parmesan-like cheese. Generally, the 1–3kg (2–6lb) rounds of cheese are rolled in paprika or *gofio* flour, which also adds to the range of different flavours.

To go with the cheese, you can buy whole-grain bread in Valle Gran Rey at the German bakery (Borbalán, Calle El Llano s/n; www.pandevueltas.com). While not typical for Gomera, the combination still tastes delicious.

Another island product is ***miel de palma*** (palm honey), the sweet, sticky sap tapped from local date-palms. It can be spread on bread like ordinary honey, or used as a topping for pancakes and ice-cream.

Some of the fertile terraces of Valle Gran Rey are planted with **fruits** such as avocados, mangos and pawpaws. Interesting **wines** are produced on La Gomera too, especially around Agulo and Vallehermoso.

Where to... Go Out

Gomera is Tenerife's quiet neighbour and offers a stark contrast to the bustling resorts on the sister island. There are a couple of trendy bars in Valle Gran Rey, but don't expect an extravagant nightlife venue.

WALKING

For more information on walking in the Parque Nacional de Garajonay, call in at the **Visitor Centre** (at Juego de Bolas near Agulo off the north coast road, tel: 922/ 800-993; daily 9:30–4:30). Trails through the laurel forest start at La Laguna Grande and El Cedro, and free guided walks are organised once a week. Maps can be bought at the visitor centre or in San Sebastián and Valle Gran Rey.

LA GOMERA'S WHISTLING

Demonstrations of the strange whistling language known as *el silbo* (► 150) are laid on for visitors in popular tourist haunts such as Las Rosas near Vallehermoso (► 152).

BEACH LIFE

All La Gomeran **beaches** are black sand and most are stony, but at intervals around the main northern circuit route, steep tracks trickle down to pretty bays and fishing villages where you can while away a peaceful hour or two.

The beaches at **Valle Gran Rey** (► 150) and **Playa de Santiago** (► 158) are the most developed for tourism.

Playa de la Calera by Hermigua and the small **Playa de Alojera** on the west coast are more secluded.

BOAT TRIPS

From various points, excursion boats depart to inspect the closely packed basalt columns of **Los Órganos** off the north coast, named for their resemblance to organ pipes. These slender hexagonal formations are only visible from the sea. Regular trips are offered from Valle Gran Rey and Playa de Santiago; whale and dolphin watching is also available from the Harbour of Vueltas in Valle Gran Rey.

Walks & Tours

1 FORTALEZA

Walk

DISTANCE approx 12km/7.5mi (return) **TIME** 3.5 hours, plus time for small breaks and to look round **START/END POINT** Centro de Visitantes El Portillo on the north border of the Teide National Park 190 A4

You do not have to climb straight up the Pico del Teide; in the national park bearing the name of Spain's highest mountain, there are plenty of less strenuous tours. A fairly easy trail, for instance, goes from the El Portillo Visitor Centre to a rocky ridge called Fortaleza. With the exception of a short ascent to the Degollado del Cedro (Cedar Pass), the path undulates gently. At the same time you have an almost uninterrupted view of the Teide – provided that it is not hidden under the cloud. For that reason, try and choose a sunny day for this walk.

1–2

The path begins directly next to the entrance to the **El Portillo** Visitor Centre (➤ 126). There is a large board showing *Senderos* (hiking trails) no. 1 and no. 6; you need the no. 6. Follow the path through the botanical garden, which is initially paved and has metal railings. Depending on the time of year, you may see the viper's bugloss, giant fennel, and gorse in bloom.

2–3

You leave the botanical garden after some 100m through a turnstile. The well-beaten path initially leads

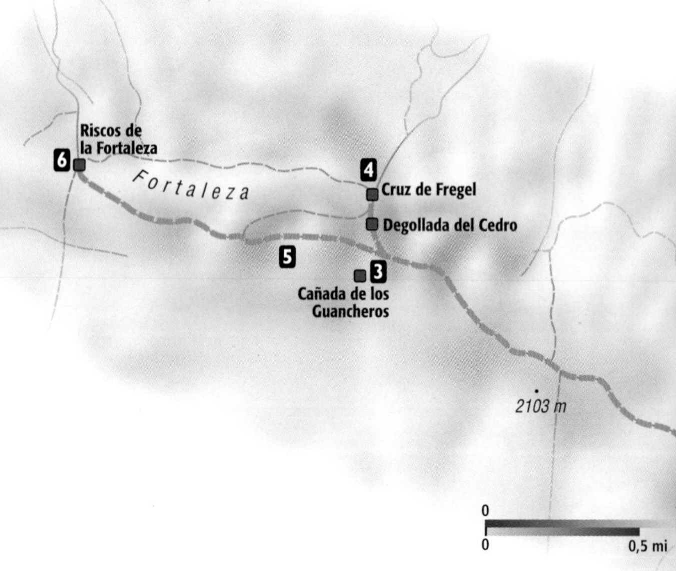

A pleasure at any time of years, hiking in Teide National Park

directly towards the **Pico del Teide** (➤ 126), and the conspicuous, pyramid-like form dominates the landscape. By a stone bench, you turn right still towards Teide. After about 10 minutes, the Sendero 6 branches off to the left. You however continue straight on through the landscape carpeted in Teide gorse. At the next crossroads, you also stay on Sendero 1, until after a good hour you reach the **Cañada de los Guancheros**, a distinct sandy plain.

3–4

You are now nearing the **Fortaleza**. In order to ascend the rocky mountain ridge, leave Sendero 1 on the right and walk up a sandy path to Degollada del Cedro. It takes about ten minutes to reach the top of the pass (2,100m/6,890ft), on which you will see the small chapel **Cruz de Fregel**. Here you can rest in the shade of two large "cedars" (actually pines) and enjoy the, hopefully cloudless, view of the Teide and of the north coast far below you.

4–5

Descend from the chapel again to Cañada de los Guancheros.

5–6

If you keep right, you can follow Sendero 1 to its bitter end at the foot of the Fortaleza, which will take you about half an hour. Should you do the walk at the beginning of July, you will pass a broad expanse of **Teide Viper's Bugloss**. The cone-shaped plants grows up to two metres tall and the red blossoms have become one of Tenerife's botanical emblems. From the end of the path, take the same way back to El Portillo.

PRACTICALITIES

Although you can do the walk easily enough in a pair of trainers, it is better to wear sturdy hiking boots. Bring drinking water and perhaps a little food. There are no restaurants along this route. You should remember to take sun protection and rainwear. The weather can change quickly in the mountains.

2 THE NORTH EAST & ANAGA MOUNTAINS

Tour

DISTANCE 93km/57.5mi
TIME A day trip including 2–3 hours' driving time
START/END POINT La Laguna 181 D4

La Laguna makes a perfect starting point for exploring the wild range of the Anaga Mountains to the north east. You can complete it in various ways, and the following circuit could just as easily start at Santa Cruz de Tenerife or San Andrés, which lie along the initial stage (the Chinamada option is a three-hour walk). Be prepared for spectacular scenery, some rural backwaters, and changeable weather.

1–2

From **La Laguna** (➤ 74) take the TF5 motorway to Santa Cruz de Tenerife and then continue towards San Andrés (➤ 54). You might want to start your day with a swim at the lovely **Playa de las Teresitas** (➤ 56). Otherwise, plunge straight in by taking the TF12 mountain road that winds north away from San Andrés.

2–3

In the space of just 9km (5.5mi) you climb about 600m (1,968ft) along this twisting road. As you snake through the mountain contours, sweeping vistas of the coast come repeatedly into view. Take the turn-off to **Taganana** (➤ 77) – the TF134 road. Just before the Túnel del Bailadero is a parking area to the right, and a lookout point. On emerging from the tunnel the magnificent sight of the Atlantic is below.

On your way down to Taganana there's a good viewpoint on the first hairpin bend. North east of Taganana rises the rock formation of the **Roque de las Ánimas**. It is worth stopping in Taganana, the Anaga range's main town, for a look around.

3–4

From Taganana the TF134 slips down to the coast and around the base of the Roque de las Ánimas (photo below). The first beach you reach is

A village nestles above the Roque de las Ánimas along the rugged Anaga coast

Playa de San Roque, popular with surfers and lined with several restaurants. This is the obvious place to stop for lunch, especially as in many of the small towns and villages you'd be hard pressed to find more than a (probably closed) bar.

5–6
From the coast, you drive the same way back into the mountains. On reaching the TF12 you proceed a short way west and then turn east (following the signs for Chamorga). You shortly reach the **Mirador del Bailadero**. If there is no mist, you

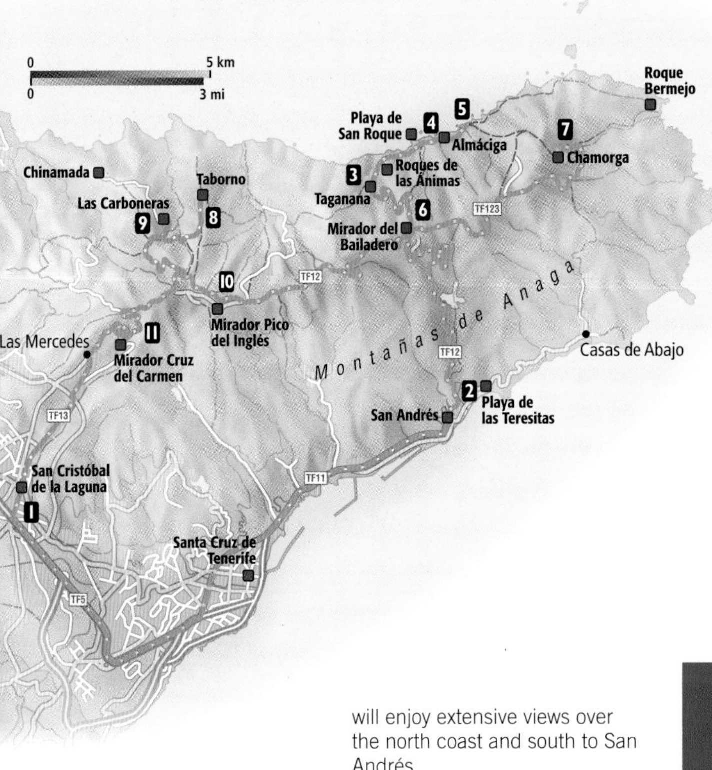

will enjoy extensive views over the north coast and south to San Andrés.

4–5
A side road cuts back half a kilometre (0.3mi) to **Almáciga**, a hamlet that does offer good views. The road ends at Bencijo, which really feels like the end of the road. From here, you could walk along the north-east coast as far as the **Roque Bermejo** (➤ 79), a tiny hamlet on the coast with a lighthouse nearby, about three hours away.

6–7
From the *mirador* the narrow TF123 road twists and turns, in part through thick woods, to the isolated settlement of **Chamorga** (➤ 77). Sunk deep in its rural torpor, Chamorga consists of a chapel, a spattering of houses and a strong population of dragon trees. A walking trail winds down the gorge, the **Barranco de Roque Bermejo**.

Magnificent vistas are repeated over and over while exploring the Anaga heights

7–8

Drive back along the TF 123 the 12km (7.5mi) to the crossroads with the TF12, turn onto it and continue west. About 7km (4.5mi) west of the junction is the turn (the TF145) for Taborno and Las Carboneras. Make for **Taborno** (➤ 78), where the houses seem to be doing a balancing act on the back of a north–south ridge. From the northern half of the town are wonderful views of the mighty Anaga coast.

8–9

Backtracking from Taborno, you can turn right after 3km (2mi) for **Las Carboneras** and then proceed from there on foot to **Chinamada** (➤ 78), or instead head about half a kilometre (0.3mi) back for the 5km (3-mile) walking trail to Chinamada, which, if you have the time, is more satisfying. Chinamada is curious, above all, for its houses built, in part, out of caves.

9–10

When you return to your car (if you decide to do one of the walks to Chinamada), head back to the TF12 and restart the westward journey. After about 2km (1mi) the **Mirador Pico del Inglés** is signposted south off the main road. From the lookout you have magnificent views over the south side of the Anaga mountain range and down to the coast around Santa Cruz de Tenerife.

10–11

A couple of kilometres further west you reach another fine lookout point on the south side of the main road, the **Mirador Cruz del Carmen**. Apart from the views, there is a visitor centre for the Anaga natural reserve (daily 9:30–4). From the *mirador* you soon start to lose altitude as you exit the western extremity of the Anaga. The trip south west along the TF12, and then the TF13 back to La Laguna via Las Mercedes is a brisker 9km (5.5mi).

3 THE NORTH WEST & TENO MASSIF

Tour

DISTANCE 77km/48mi
TIME A day trip including about 1.5–2 hours' driving time
START/END POINT Garachico 189 D5

Garachico, a charming coastal village with a handful of equally charming hotel options that are a far cry from the mass tourist ones to the south, makes a fine base for a driving tour. In the course of a day you can take in ocean views and wander to a mountain village, see an ancient dragon tree and staggering cliff faces and finish off with seafood at sunset. Forest fires in July 2007 have temporarily scarred some of the mountainsides around Masca. Although nature is in the process of recovering much of the lost terrain, blackened palm trees still bear witness to the devastating blaze.

1–2

It's a good idea to arrive in **Garachico** (► 105) the night before undertaking this excursion to give yourself time to relax. The natural rock pools, Castillo de San Miguel and especially the former Convento de San Francisco are all well worth some of your time. The following day, set off after an early breakfast for the 5km (3-mile) trip east to **Icod de los Vinos** (► 92). Here you can see the Drago Milenario, the

Garachico is nestled at the bottom of the mountains in a picturesque location overlooking the sea

oldest dragon tree on the island, estimated to be 500 years old. The old town is worth a wander and you should consider a visit to the San Marcos parish church, in which a precious silver cross is exhibited.

2–3

From Icod take the TF820 road which heads west and rises slowly to **El Tanque** (9km/5.5mi). As the road veers south it rises still more steeply, passing through Erjos and then reaching the **Puerto de Erjos pass** (1,117m/ 3,664ft), 8km (5mi) further on. You are now in the Teno Massif, which will remain a companion throughout the day. From the pass the road drops down for 4km (2.5mi) to **Santiago del Teide**, a laid-back town.

3–4

A side road exits west from Santiago and quickly winds its way up into the massif to about 1,000m (3,280ft). You soon reach a *mirador* with magnificent vistas out to sea. From this spectacular vantage point you drop into a series of tight, narrow switchbacks on the way to the delightful village of **Masca** (➤94), 5km (3mi) from Santiago. You could spend an hour or so just wandering around the palm-filled village and any one of its restaurants make wonderful lunch stops. Perhaps try **Chez Arlette** (➤114). Virtually all of them have remarkable views.

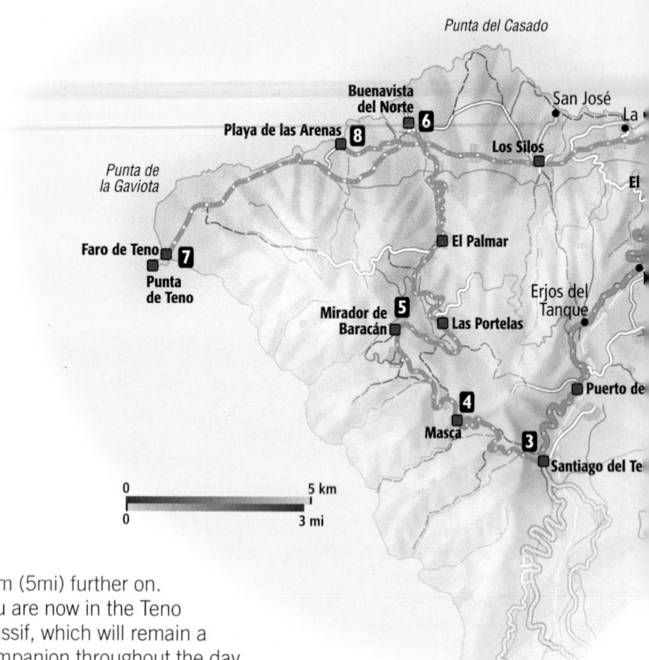

4–5

From Masca go north. On the right you will pass a waterfall that is particularly impressive in winter and another huddle of houses belonging to the same municipality. Over the next 5km (3mi) the road rises and dips, then rises again to reach the exposed **Mirador de Baracán**. On a windy day it feels as though your car might take flight, so powerful are the ocean gusts.

5–6

Beyond the *mirador* the road winds north for 12km (7.5mi) to **Buenavista del Norte** at the far north west of the island. Beautiful

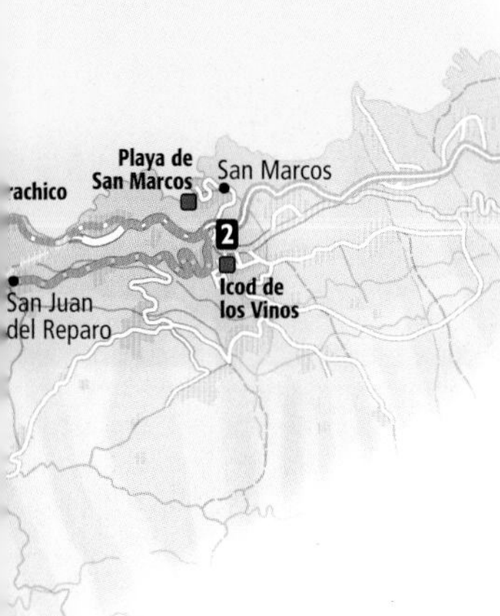

17th and 18th-century houses surround the plaza there with the Iglesia de Nuestra Señora de los Remedios. The original church is more than 500 years old. After a fire left only the tower standing, it was rebuilt according to the old plans. In the high country here the land is largely barren except for hordes of cacti. Then come a couple of *pueblos*, like **Las Portelas** and **El Palmar**, which has given its name to a local wine, and scattered houses and small farm holdings. In the distance many of the farming terraces have become overgrown.

6–7

Proceed 9km (5.5mi) west from Buenavista to the impressive **Punta de Teno** (➤ 110), along the TF445 road. Keep your eyes open for a turn-off right to **Playa de las Arenas** at the town exit. Veer left for Punta de Teno, but keep this fork in mind for the return trip.

Huge notices warn of rock falls and the danger of mudslides on this road – enter at your own risk. On a wet or very windy day you might think twice about proceeding, but otherwise plenty of people do it and the road itself is fine.

It gradually rises on an ever-higher shelf gouged out of the ominous dark volcanic cliff side. At the first tunnel there is a lookout point, although nowhere much to park.

The most breathtaking moment arrives when you exit the second tunnel at the 5km (3-mile) mark. The sight of the sheer cliffs dropping, all jagged edges and deep shadows, into the ocean below, is humbling.

For the next 4km (2.5mi) the road slowly descends to line up with the low coast plain that opens up to your right. There six windmills stand still, generating nothing but curiosity. Along with the hill to your left, it is covered with the peculiar shapes of the indigenous candelabra spurge bushes.

At the 9km (5.5-mile) mark, just short of the lighthouse, you reach the end of the road. Get out of the car to soak in the views of the majestic Teno coast to the south. From the lighthouse you can make out the islands of La Palma and La Gomera on a good day.

7–8

You now retrace your path towards **Buenavista**. Before you enter the town, look out for the Playa de las Arenas sign. Turn left and follow the signs for 2km (1mi). You pass another fork with two other beaches

The rugged country of the North West is one of the island's most beautiful attractions

signposted, Playa de las Mujeres (Women's Beach) and Playa del Fraile (Friar's Beach). Ignore them and keep on for **Playa de las Arenas**.

If the swell is up you won't see any sand, but if you have timed things right, you can sit down for a sunset drink at **Restaurante Burgado** (tel: 922/127-831) and perhaps stay for dinner. This simple place seems to have been carved from the coastal rock and a little cascade of water runs right through it.

8–10

Return to **Buenavista del Norte** and go east. The low-key urban spread means it is hard to know when Buenavista del Norte finishes and Los Silos, 4km (2.5mi) on, begins. You will notice that you are in serious banana country.

At **Los Silos** there is a modest black beach, which might be handy if you pass through earlier in the day. Otherwise continue on the 3km (2-mile) stretch to **Garachico**. Just before you reach the town you pass the **Mirador del Emigrante**. Presumably it was so named because people could watch their emigrant friends and relatives sailing off to America.

The Punta de Teno lighthouse is the end of the road

Practicalities

Practicalities

BEFORE YOU GO

WHAT YOU NEED

● Required
○ Suggested
▲ Not required

Some countries require a passport to remain valid for a minimum period (usually at least six months) beyond the date of entry – check beforehand.

	UK	USA	Canada	Australia	Ireland	Netherlands	Germany
Passport/National Identity Card	●	●	●	●	●	●	●
Visa (regulations can change – check before booking)	▲	▲	▲	▲	▲	▲	▲
Onward or Return Ticket	●	●	●	●	●	●	●
Health Inoculations (tetanus and polio)	▲	▲	▲	▲	▲	▲	▲
Health Documentation (➤ 178, Health)	●	▲	▲	▲	●	●	●
Travel Insurance	●	●	●	●	●	●	●
Driving Licence (national)	●	●	●	●	●	●	●
Car Insurance Certificate	●	●	●	●	●	●	●
Car Registration Document	●	●	●	●	●	●	●

WHEN TO GO

Santa Cruz

High season   Low season

JAN	FEB	MAR	APRIL	MAY	JUNE	JULY	AUG	SEP	OCT	NOV	DEC
20°C	21°C	23°C	24°C	25°C	27°C	28°C	29°C	28°C	26°C	23°C	20°C
68°F	70°F	73°F	75°F	77°F	80°F	82°F	84°F	82°F	79°F	73°F	68°F

Sun   Wet   Cloud

The temperatures above are the **average daily maximum** for each month. Although the Atlantic can be chilly, Tenerife is a year-round seaside destination. But the island's weather isn't uniform. The north coast and mountain areas are subtropical, while the south is arid and dry. Rainfall is at its highest in the north, where it can reach 750mm (30 inches) a year (but less than 20mm/0.75 inches in the south west). Most rain falls from November to February. The upper reaches of Mount Teide are generally snow-capped in winter and well into spring. Even at the height of summer it can be very cold. In winter it can get cold elsewhere in the evening. High season for northern Europeans escaping winter is December to March, but Spaniards crowd in during summer. A beautiful time to come is in spring when the air is crisp and the flowers in full bloom.

GETTING ADVANCE INFORMATION

Websites

- **Spanish Tourist Board:** **www.spain.info**
- **Tenerife Tourist Board:** **www.todotenerife.es**
- **Canary Islands Tourist Board:** **www.turismodecanarias.com**
www.etenerife.com is a useful unofficial website

GETTING THERE

By Air Tenerife absorbs a good percentage of the air traffic arriving in the Canary Islands. Most international and charter flights arrive in the modern **Tenerife Sur (Reina Sofía)** Airport in the south. Some international flights, along with a large share of Spanish mainland and inter-island flights, arrive at **Tenerife Norte (Los Rodeos)** Airport.
From the Islands Binter Canarias airlines runs daily flights from the Canary Islands, almost all of them to Tenerife Norte (Los Rodeos) Airport.
From the UK Iberia flies scheduled services from London to Tenerife via Madrid. However, there's a vast choice of direct flights through low-cost airlines including **Easyjet** and **Jet 2** plus hundreds of flights through holiday company airlines.
From the Rest of Europe Iberia flies to Tenerife from most European capitals via Barcelona or Madrid. Charter flights also operate from numerous cities across the continent.
From North America There are no direct flights from the USA or Canada, although you can fly with **Iberia** from New York, Los Angeles, Montreal and several other centres via Madrid. Iberia offers code-share with British Airways and American Airlines.
From Australia and New Zealand There are no direct flights to Spain but British Airways, Qantas and Cathy Pacific are One World alliance partners with Iberia for flights.
By Boat Regular inter-island car ferries and fast boats connect Santa Cruz with Las Palmas on Gran Canaria and Los Cristianos in southern Tenerife with the western islands (La Gomera, El Hierro and La Palma). A weekly ferry runs from Cádiz (on the Spanish mainland) to Tenerife – it takes almost two days.

TIME

Unlike the rest of Spain, the Canary Islands observe Greenwich Mean Time (GMT). Summer time (GMT+1) operates from the last Sunday in March to the last Sunday in October.

CURRENCY & FOREIGN EXCHANGE

The euro (€) is the official currency of Spain. Euro notes are in denominations of 5, 10, 20, 50, 100, 200 and 500; coins come in denominations of 1, 2 and 5 bronze-coloured euro cents and 10, 20 and 50 gold-coloured euro cents. In addition there is a 1 euro coin with a silver centre and gold surround and a 2 euro coin with a gold centre and silver surround.
Credit and debit cards are widely accepted for purchases. **Traveller's cheques** are not very common on the Canary Islands.
Exchange Banks generally offer the best rates for changing foreign currency and travellers' cheques. Commissions and exchange rates can vary wildly. You will need to present your passport when changing cash or travellers' cheques. You can also use credit and debit cards (Visa and Mastercard are the most widely accepted) for cash advance in banks and from cash machines (ATMs). You will usually be charged by your bank for the service.

TOURIST OFFICES OF SPAIN ➤ WWW.SPAIN.INFO

In the UK
PO Box 4009
London W1A 6NB
☎ 020 7486 8077
www.tourspain.co.uk

In the USA
☎ 212/265-8822
www.okspain.org

In Canada
2 Bloor Street West
Toronto, Ontario M4W 3E2
☎ (416) 961-3131
toronto@tourspain.es

WHEN YOU ARE THERE

NATIONAL HOLIDAYS

1 Jan	New Year's Day
6 Jan	Epiphany
Feb/Mar	Carnival Tuesday
Mar/Apr	Good Friday, Easter Monday
1 May	Labour Day
30 May	Canary Islands' Day
15 Aug	Feast of the Assumption
12 Oct	Spanish National Day
1 Nov	All Saints' Day
6 Dec	Constitution Day
8 Dec	Feast of the Immaculate Conception
25 Dec	Christmas Day

ELECTRICITY

The power supply is 220–225 volts. Sockets take standard continental-style plugs with two round pins.
Visitors from the UK require an adaptor (often available at the airport).
Visitors from the USA will require a voltage transformer.

OPENING HOURS

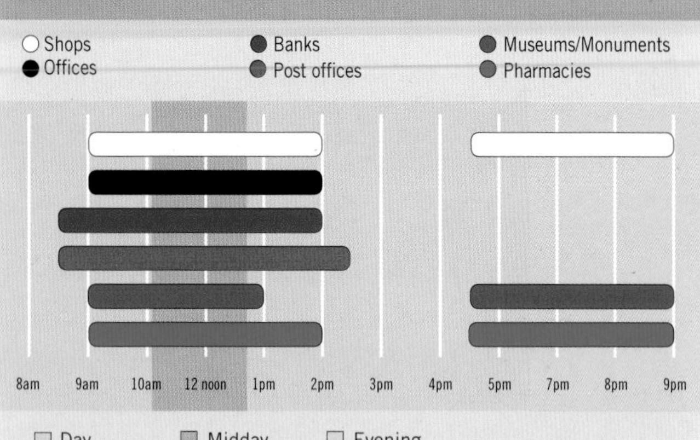

Offices Most government offices open Mon–Fri 9–2.
Shops Shops are generally open Mon–Fri 9–2 and 4:30/5–8. Many shops, travel agents and other businesses open on Saturday. Big department stores such as the El Corte Inglés chain tend to open Mon–Sat 9–9.
Banks Banks are usually open Mon–Fri 8:30–2. Some open on Saturday morning.
Post Offices Most post offices open Mon–Fri 8:30–2:30 and Sat 9:30–1. The main branch in Santa Cruz de Tenerife is open longer hours (► 171).
Museums Museums are sometimes closed for a period during lunch.

TIME DIFFERENCES

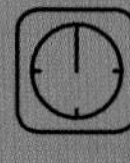

Tenerife
12 noon

London (GMT)
12 noon

Mainland Spain (CET)
1pm

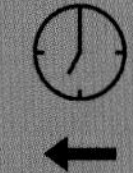

New York (EST)
7am

Sydney (AEST)
10pm

STAYING IN TOUCH

Post boxes are yellow. The **post office** in Santa Cruz de Tenerife is at Plaza de España, open Mon–Fri 8:30am– 8:30pm, Sat 9:30am–1pm. Stamps *(sellos)* are available from post offices, hotels, news kiosks and tobacconists. It will take about a week for a postcard to get to the UK.

The blue and green **public telephones** take coins and phonecards (*tarjetas telefónicas*), which are available from post offices and *estancos* (tobacconists).

International Dialling Codes:
Dial 00 followed by

UK:	44
USA/Canada:	1
Ireland:	353
Australia:	61
Spain:	34

Mobile providers and services: Mobile phones automatically tune in to the partner network. Purchasing a local prepaid card can be less expensive. The Spanish word for mobile phone is *móvil.*

WiFi and internet: WiFi hotspots are generally only available in the more expensive hotels. In Caribe, Alondras Park, Varadero, Marino, Oro Blanco, Westhaven Bay, Florasol and Panoramica Garden you can use the WiFi service provided by Wavenet Canarias (www.wavenetcanarias.com).
There are internet cafés in La Orotava (Cibernet, Calle Salazar 27), Santa Cruz de Tenerife (Cyberdream, Calle Iriarte 16, www.cyberdream.es), Playa de las Américas (Informática el Camisón, Calle Antonio Domínguez 47), Puerto de la Cruz (PL@ZAnet, Plaza del Charco, C.C. Olimpia), and in Los Cristianos (Office Point, Bulevar Chajofe 10)

PERSONAL SAFETY

Violence against tourists is unusual. Theft from cars is the most common form of crime. To help prevent crime:

- Do not leave valuables on the beach or poolside.
- Always lock valuables in hotel safety deposit boxes.
- Never leave anything inside your car.
- Avoid walking alone at night.
- Do not carry around more cash than you need.

Police assistance:
☎ 112 from any phone

TIPS/GRATUITIES

Tipping is not expected for all services.
As a general guide:
Restaurants: up to 10%
Tour guides, Porters and Chambermaids: €1
Cafés/bars, Taxis, Toilets, Hairdressers: Small change

POLICE (POLICÍA NACIONAL)	**112**
FIRE (BOMBEROS)	**112**
AMBULANCE (AMBULANCIA)	**112**

Practicalities

HEALTH

Insurance EU nationals can get free or reduced-rate emergency medical treatment with the relevant documentation (European Health Insurance Card for UK nationals) although private medical insurance is strongly recommended and is essential for all other visitors.

Dental Services Dentists operate privately (see the Yellow Pages/*Páginas Amarillas*). Treatment may be covered by your insurance.

Weather Visitors from cooler countries are especially vulnerable to the effects of the sun. You should cover up with a high-factor sunblock and drink plenty. Children need to be well protected, especially when playing near the sea, as water and sand reflect the sun's rays.

Drugs Prescription and non-prescription drugs and medicines are available from pharmacies, usually distinguished by a large green cross. Outside normal hours, a notice on the door of each pharmacy should give the address of the nearest duty chemist.

Safe Water Tap water is generally safe to drink. Mineral water *(agua mineral)* is widely available and inexpensive. If you see a sign *agua no potable* at a fountain, don't drink from it.

CONCESSIONS

Students Tenerife and the other Canary Islands do not attract backpacking youngsters in any great way. There are few concessions for students and holders of an International Student Identity Card aren't going to get much mileage out of it. Museums are generally free and it is not recognised for much else.
Senior Citizens Tenerife, which is geared up for tourists and has a benign climate, is a popular destination for older travellers. You can travel independently with ease or organise a package through tour operators specialising in holidays for senior citizens.

TRAVELLING WITH A DISABILITY

Although things are improving, many public buildings, hotels and restaurants remain inaccessible to wheelchair users. Some buses and axis in Santa Cruz have been adapted for wheelchair access. For more information on what has been done to help visitors with disabilities see the **Tourism for All** website at www.tourismforall.org.uk.

SCHILDREN

Hotels and restaurants are generally very child friendly, and many hotels have playgrounds, parks, mini-golf and children's pools. Special attractions for kids are marked out with the logo shown above.

RESTROOMS

There are few public toilets so it's a good idea to make the most of visits to hotels, museums, restaurants, cafés, bars and shops.

CUSTOMS

The export of souvenirs made of endangered animals or plants is strictly forbidden.

EMBASSIES AND CONSULATES

UK
☎ 922/286-863

USA
☎ 91/587-2200
(Madrid)

Ireland
☎ 928/297-728
(Gran Canaria)

Australia
☎ C91/353-6600
(Madrid)

Canada
☎ 91/423-3250
(Madrid)

Useful Words and Phrases

Spanish **(español)**, also known as Castilian **(castellano)** to distinguish it from other tongues spoken in Spain, is the language of the Canary Islands. The islanders' version has a sing-song quality more reminiscent of the Spanish spoken in Latin America than the mainland.

GREETINGS AND COMMON WORDS

Do you speak English? **¿Habla inglés?**
I don't understand **No entiendo**
I don't speak Spanish **No hablo español**
Yes/No **Sí/no**
OK **Vale/de acuerdo**
Please **Por favor**
Thank you (very much) **(Muchas) gracias**
You're welcome **De nada**
Hello/Goodbye **Hola/adiós**
Good morning **Buenos días**
Good afternoon/evening **Buenas tardes**
Good night **Buenas noches**
How are you? **¿Qué tal?**
Excuse me **Perdón**
How much is this? **¿Cuánto vale?**
I'd like... **Quisiera/me gustaría**

EMERGENCY!

Help! **¡Socorro!/¡Ayuda!**
Could you help me please? **¿Podría ayudarme por favor?**
Could you call a doctor please? **¿Podría llamar a un médico por favor?**

DIRECTIONS AND TRAVELLING

Aeroplane **Avión**
Airport **Aeropuerto**
Car **Coche**
Boat **Barco**
Bus **Autobús/guagua**
Bus stop **Parada de autobús**
Station **Estación**
Ticket (single/return)
Billete (de ida/de ida y vuelta)
I'm lost **Me he perdido**
Where is...? **¿Dónde está...?**
How do I get to...? **¿Cómo llego a...?**
the beach **la playa**
the telephone **el teléfono**
the toilets **los servicios**
Left/right **Izquierda/derecha**
Straight on **Todo recto**

ACCOMMODATION

Do you have a single/double room available?
¿Tiene una habitación individual/doble?
with/without bath/toilet/shower
con/sin baño/lavabo/ducha
Does that include breakfast?
¿Incluye el desayuno?
Could I see the room?
¿Puedo ver la habitación?
I'll take this room **Cojo esta habitación**
One night **Una noche**
Key/Lift **Llave/Ascensor**
Sea views **Vistas al mar**

DAYS

Today	**Hoy**
Tomorrow	**Mañana**
Yesterday	**Ayer**
Later	**Más tarde**
This week	**Esta semana**
Monday	**Lunes**
Tuesday	**Martes**
Wednesday	**Miércoles**
Thursday	**Jueves**
Friday	**Viernes**
Saturday	**Sábado**
Sunday	**Domingo**

NUMBERS

1	**uno**	11	**once**	21	**veintiuno**	200	**doscientos**
2	**dos**	12	**doce**	22	**veintidós**	300	**trescientos**
3	**tres**	13	**trece**	30	**treinta**	400	**cuatrocientos**
4	**cuatro**	14	**catorce**	40	**cuarenta**	500	**quinientos**
5	**cinco**	15	**quince**	50	**cincuenta**	600	**seiscientos**
6	**seis**	16	**dieciséis**	60	**sesenta**	700	**setecientos**
7	**siete**	17	**diecisiete**	70	**setenta**	800	**ochocientos**
8	**ocho**	18	**dieciocho**	80	**ochenta**	900	**novecientos**
9	**nueve**	19	**diecinueve**	90	**noventa**	1000	**mil**
10	**diez**	20	**veinte**	100	**cien**		

Useful Words and Phrases

RESTAURANT

I'd like to book a table
Quisiera reservar una mesa
A table for two please
Una mesa para dos, por favor
Could we see the menu, please?
¿Nos trae la carta, por favor?
What's this? **¿Qué es esto?**
A bottle/glass of... **Una botella/copa de...**

Could I have the bill please?
¿La cuenta, por favor?
Service charge included **Servicio incluido**
Waiter/waitress **Camarero/a**
Breakfast **Desayuno**
Lunch **Almuerzo**
Dinner **Cena**
Menu **La carta**

MENU READER

a la plancha grilled
aceite oil
aceituna olive
agua water
ajo garlic
almendra almond
anchoas anchovies
arroz rice
atún tuna

bacalao cod
berenjena aubergines
bistec steak
bocadillo sandwich

café coffee
calamares squid
cangrejo crab
carne meat
cebolla onion
cerdo pork
cerezas cherries
cerveza beer
champiñones mushrooms
chocolate chocolate
chorizo spicy sausage
chuleta chop
conejo rabbit
cordero lamb
crema cream
crudo raw
cubierto(s) cover (cutlery)
cuchara spoon
cuchillo knife

embutidos sausages
ensalada salad
entrante starter
espárragos asparagus

filete fillet
flan crème caramel
frambuesa raspberry
fresa strawberry
frito fried
fruta fruit

galleta biscuit
gambas prawns
gazpacho andaluz gazpacho (cold soup)
guisantes peas

habas broad beans
helado ice cream
hígado liver
huevos fritos/ revueltos fried/ scrambled eggs

jamón serrano ham (cured)
jamón York ham (cooked)
judías beans
judías verdes French beans
jugo fruit juice

langosta lobster
leche milk
lechuga lettuce
legumbres pulses
lengua tongue
lenguado sole
limón lemon
lomo de cerdo pork tenderloin

mantequilla butter
manzana apple
mariscos seafood
mejillones mussels
melocotón peach
melón melon
merluza hake
mero sea bass
miel honey

naranja orange

ostra oyster

pan bread
papas arrugadas Canarian-style boiled potatoes
patata potato
patatas fritas chips
pato duck
pepinillo gherkin
pepino cucumber
pera pear
perejil parsley
pescado fish
pez espada swordfish
picante hot/spicy
pimientos red/green peppers
piña pineapple
plátano banana
pollo chicken
postre dessert
primer plato first course
pulpo octopus
queso cheese

rape monkfish
relleno filled/stuffed
riñones kidneys

salchicha sausage
salchichón salami
salmón salmon
salmonete red mullet
salsa sauce
seco dry
segundo plato main course
solomillo de ternera fillet of beef
sopa soup

té tea
tenedor fork
ternera beef
tocino bacon
tortilla española Spanish omelette
tortilla francesa plain omelette
trucha trout

uva grape

verduras green vegetables
vino blanco white wine
vino rosado rosé wine
vino tinto red wine zanahorias carrots

Road Atlas

For chapters: see inside front cover

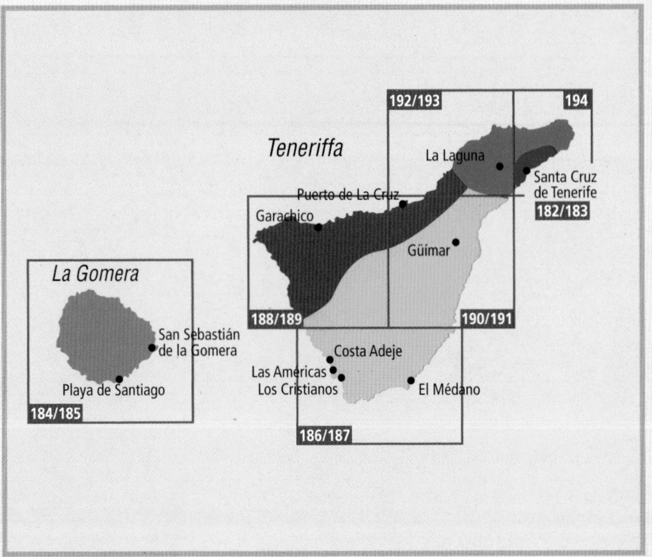

Key to Road Atlas

TF-1 Motorway

Dual carriage-way

TF-28 Trunk road

TF-24 Main Road

Secondary road

Dirt road

Lane

Footpath

Airport / Ferry port

Marina / Place of interest

Castle, Fortress / Ruin

Church, chapel / Cave

Museum / Radio or TV tower

Lighthouse / Windmill

Golf course / Campground

Monument / (Swimming) beach

Diving / Windsurfing

1 TOP 10

26 Don't Miss

22 At Your Leisure

1 : 180.000

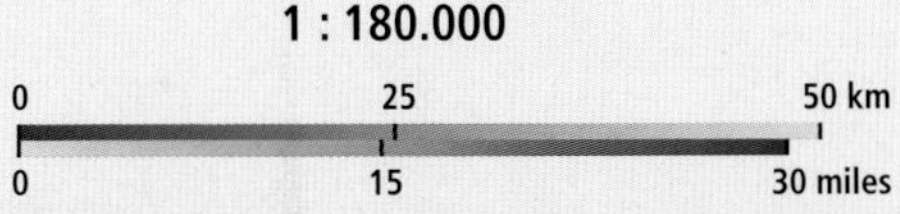

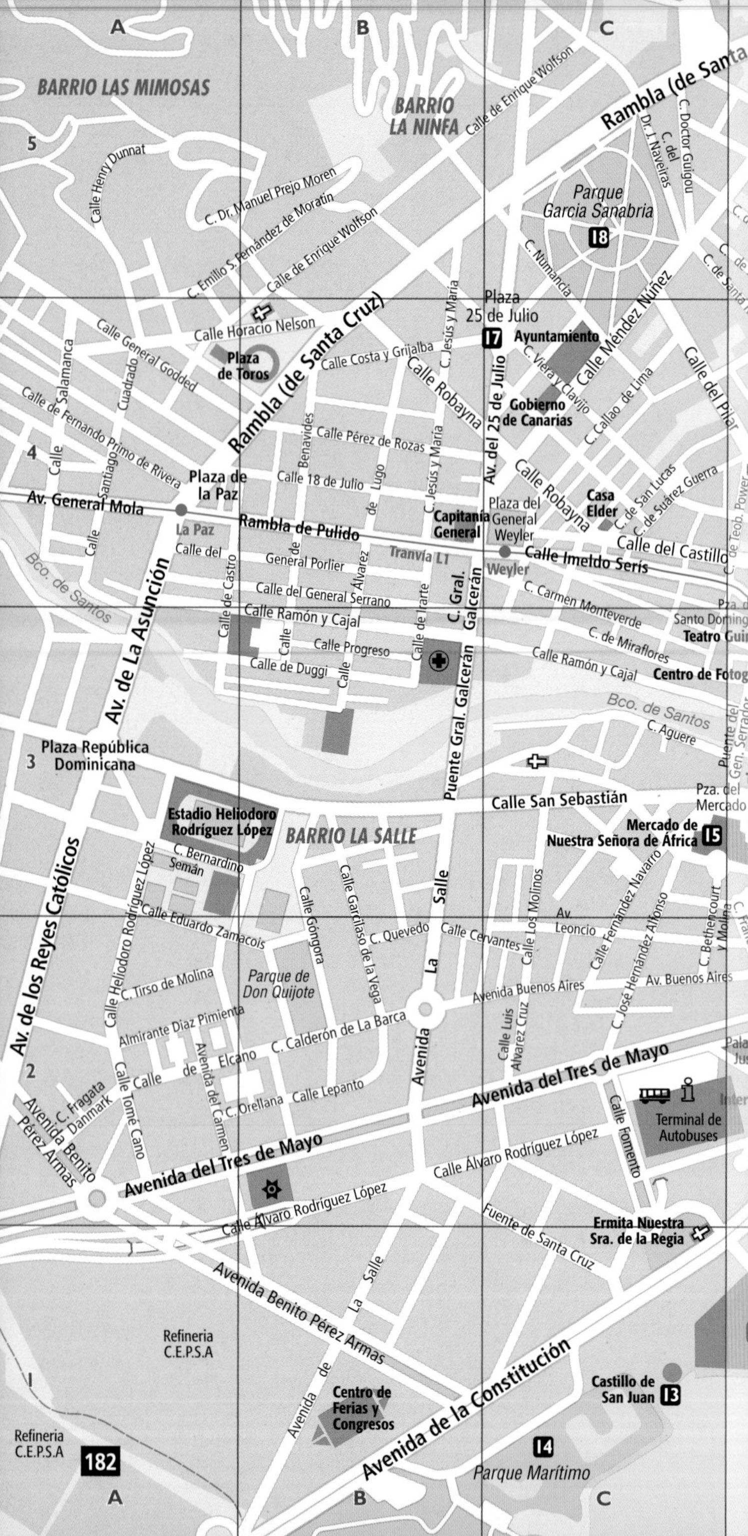
A
B
C
BARRIO LAS MIMOSAS
BARRIO LA NINFA
Rambla (de Santa
Calle de Enrique Wolfson
Calle Henry Dunnat
C. Dr. Manuel Prejo Moren
C. Emilio S. Fernández de Moratín
Calle de Enrique Wolfson
C. Doctor Guigou
Dr. J. Naveiras
C. del
Parque García Sanabria
18
C. Numancia
Plaza 25 de Julio
17
Ayuntamiento
Calle Horacio Nelson
Plaza de Toros
Rambla (de Santa Cruz)
Calle Costa y Grijalba
C. Jesús y María
Calle Robayna
Av. del 25 de Julio
C. Viera y Clavijo
Calle Méndez Núñez
Calle del Pilar
Gobierno de Canarias
C. Callao de Lima
Calle General Godded
Calle Salamanca
Cuadrado
Calle de Fernando Primo de Rivera
Calle Santiago
Calle Pérez de Rozas
Benavides
Calle 18 de Julio
Lugo
C. Jesús y María
Calle Robayna
Casa Elder
C. de San Lucas
C. de Suárez Guerra
C. de Teob. Power
Av. General Mola
Plaza de la Paz
La Paz
Rambla de Pulido
Capitanía General
Plaza del General Weyler
Weyler
Calle Imeldo Serís
Calle del Castillo
Calle del
General Porlier
de Álvarez
Tranvía L1
C. Gral. Galcerán
Bco. de Santos
Calle de Castro
Calle del General Serrano
C. Carmen Monteverde
Pza. de Santo Domingo
Av. de La Asunción
Calle Ramón y Cajal
Calle Progreso
Calle de Irarte
C. de Miraflores
Teatro Guim
Calle de Duggi
Calle Ramón y Cajal
Centro de Fotog
Bco. de Santos
C. Aguere
Puente del Gen. Serrador
Plaza República Dominicana
Puente Gral. Galcerán
Calle San Sebastián
Pza. del Mercado
Estadio Heliodoro Rodríguez López
BARRIO LA SALLE
Mercado de Nuestra Señora de África
15
Av. de los Reyes Católicos
C. Bernardino Semán
Calle Heliodoro Rodríguez López
Calle Góngora
Calle Garcilaso de la Vega
Avenida La Salle
Calle Los Molinos
Calle Fernández Navarro
Calle Eduardo Zamacois
C. Quevedo
Calle Cervantes
Av. Leoncio
C. Bethencourt y Molina
C. José Hernández Alfonso
C. Tirso de Molina
Parque de Don Quijote
Avenida Buenos Aires
Av. Buenos Aires
Almirante Díaz Pimienta
C. Calderón de La Barca
Calle Luis Álvarez Cruz
Calle de Elcano
Avenida del Carmen
C. Orellana
Calle Lepanto
Avenida del Tres de Mayo
C. Fragata Danmark
Calle Tomé Cano
Calle Fomento
Terminal de Autobuses
Avenida Benito Pérez Armas
Avenida del Tres de Mayo
Calle Álvaro Rodríguez López
Calle Álvaro Rodríguez López
Fuente de Santa Cruz
Ermita Nuestra Sra. de la Regia
Avenida Benito Pérez Armas
La Salle
Refineria C.E.P.S.A
Avenida de
Centro de Ferias y Congresos
Avenida de la Constitución
Castillo de San Juan
13
14
Parque Marítimo
Refineria C.E.P.S.A
5
4
3
2
1

Santa Cruz)
D
E
F
Museo Militar
19
EL TOSCAL
5
C. de San Miguel
C. de San Martín
Santiago
C. de
Calle de la Rosa
C. de San Francisco Javier
C. de San Vincente Ferrer
C. de Santa Rosalía
Avenida de Anaga
Puerto
C. de San Juan Bautista
C. San Francisco
Avenida Cuba Marina
Estación Marítima
Pza. del Patriotismo
C. de E. Calzadilla
4
Pza. del Príncipe de Asturias
C. Ruiz de Padrón
Iglesia de San Francisco
Muelle Sur
12
C. de Villalba Hervás
C. de Teob. Power
C. de Bethencourt Alfonso
Casino
Pza. de la Candelaria
10
Plaza de España
Guimerá
Monumento a los Caídos
C. del Doctor Allart
C. del General Gutiérrez
Calle Imeldo Serís
Palacio Insular
Pza. de la Madera
de Fotografía
C. de Candelaria
Pza. de la Iglesia
C. de Domínguez Alfonso
11
Fundación
Dársena Sur
Puente del Gen. Serrador
Iglesia Nuestra Señora de la Concepción
16
Tenerife Espacio de las Artes
3
Pza. del Mercado
15
Av. de Bravo Murillo
Av. Marítima
Calle de San Manuel Guimerá
C. Francisco Bonnín
Tranvía L1
Vía de Servicio Muelle de Enlace
Avenida de la Constitución
Dársena de Los Llanos
Palacio de Justicia
2
Intercambiador
Oceano Atlántico
13 Auditorio
0
400 m
0
400 yd
1
Santa Cruz de Tenerife
D
E
F

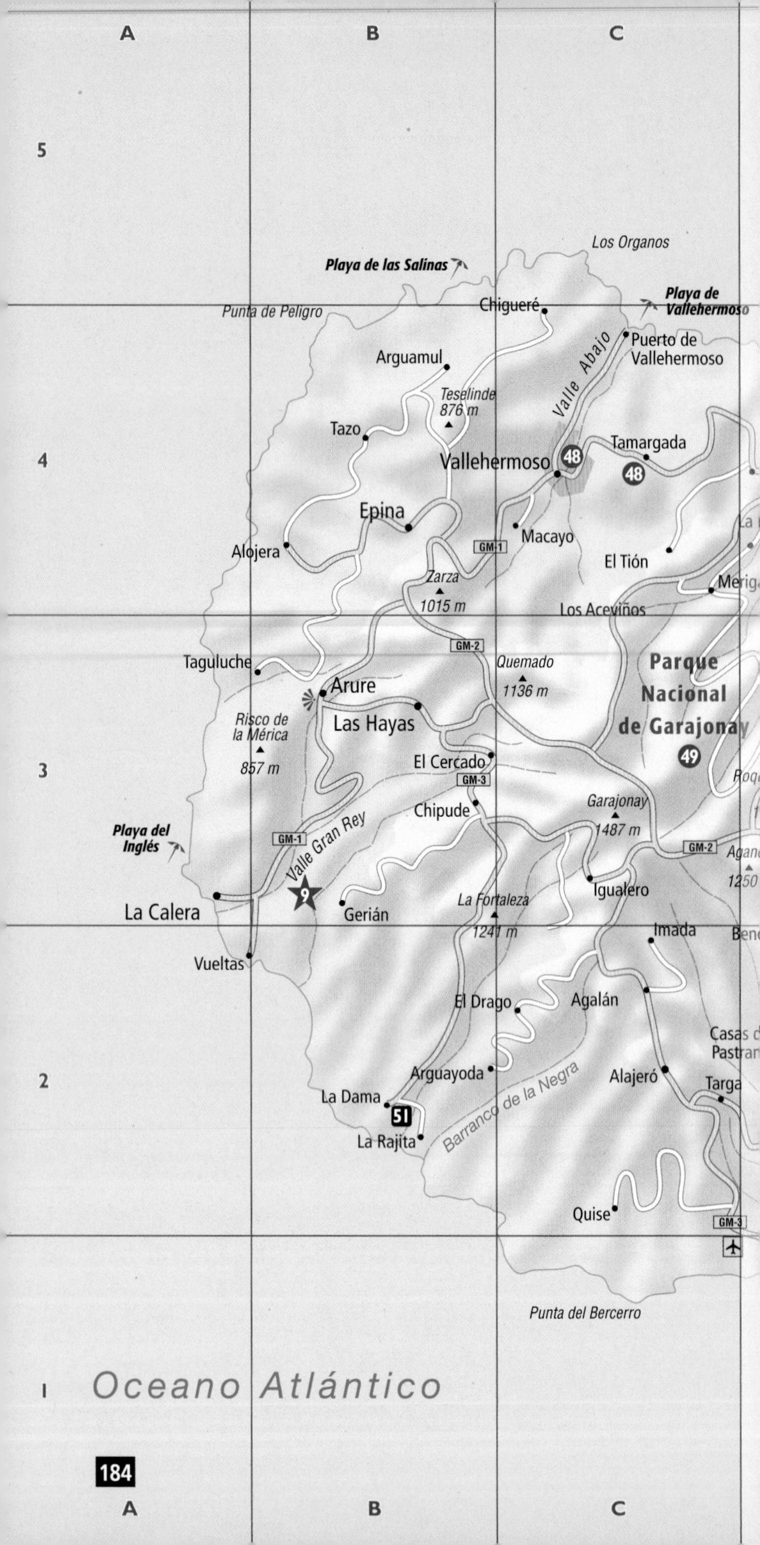
A
B
C
5
Los Organos
Playa de las Salinas
Playa de Vallehermoso
Punta de Peligro
Chigueré
Puerto de Vallehermoso
Arguamul
Valle Abajo
Teselinde 876 m
Tazo
Tamargada
4
Vallehermoso
48
48
Epina
Macayo
Alojera
GM-1
El Tión
Zarza 1015 m
Los Aceviños
GM-2
Taguluche
Quemado 1136 m
Parque Nacional de Garajonay
Arure
Las Hayas
Risco de la Mérica 857 m
El Cercado
49
3
GM-3
Chipude
Garajonay 1487 m
Playa del Inglés
GM-1
Valle Gran Rey
GM-2
Igualero
9
La Calera
Gerián
La Fortaleza 1241 m
Imada
Vueltas
El Drago
Agalán
Arguayoda
Alajeró
2
La Dama
51
La Rajita
Barranco de la Negra
Quise
GM-3
Punta del Bercerro
1
Oceano Atlántico
A
B
C

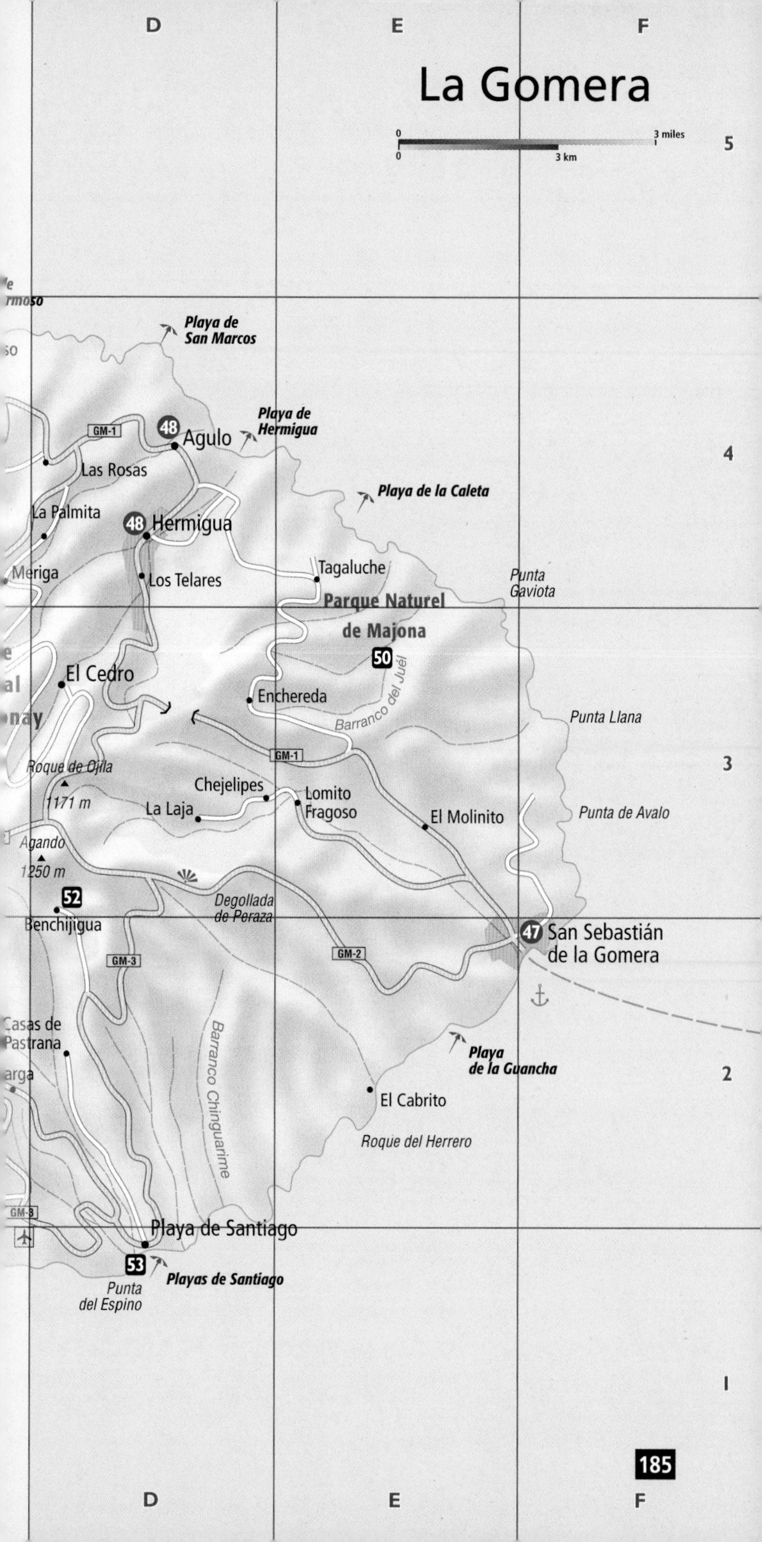

D
E
F
La Gomera
0
3 miles
0
3 km
5
4
3
2
1
Playa de San Marcos
Playa de Hermigua
48
Agulo
GM-1
Las Rosas
Playa de la Caleta
La Palmita
48
Hermigua
Meriga
Los Telares
Tagaluche
Punta Gaviota
Parque Naturel de Majona
50
El Cedro
Enchereda
Barranco del Juel
Punta Llana
GM-1
Roque de Ojila
1171 m
Chejelipes
La Laja
Lomito Fragoso
El Molinito
Punta de Avalo
Agando
1250 m
52
Benchijigua
Degollada de Peraza
47
San Sebastián de la Gomera
GM-3
GM-2
Casas de Pastrana
Barranco Chinguarime
Playa de la Guancha
El Cabrito
Roque del Herrero
GM-3
Playa de Santiago
53
Playas de Santiago
Punta del Espino

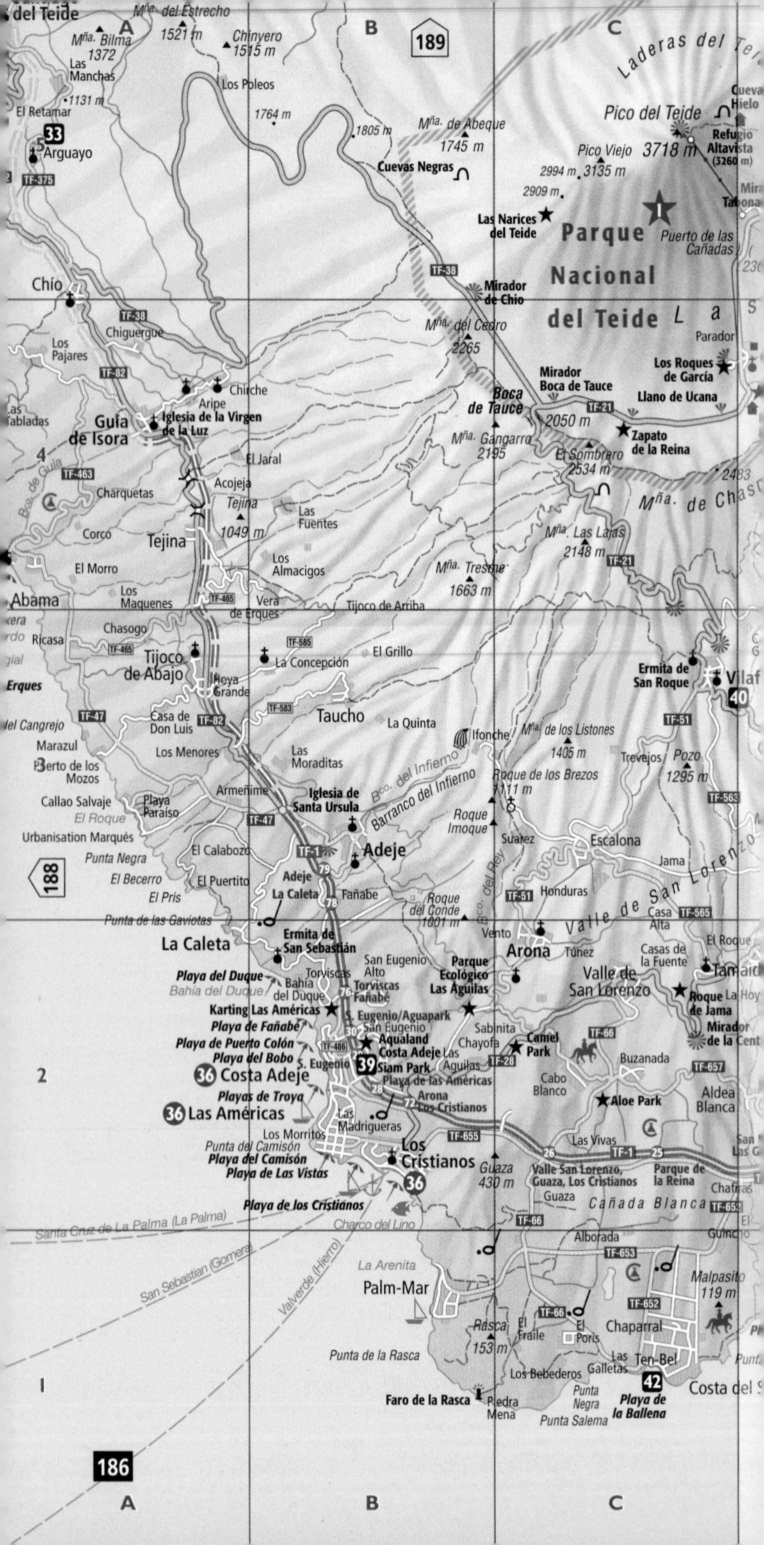

del Teide
Mña. del Estrecho
1521 m
A
B
189
C
Mña. Bilma
1372
Chinyero
1515 m
Laderas del Te
Las Manchas
Los Poleos
1131 m
El Retamar
1764 m
1805 m
Mña. de Abeque
1745 m
Pico del Teide
3718 m
Refugio Altavista (3260 m)
33
Arguayo
TF-375
Pico Viejo
2994 m
3135 m
2909 m
Cuevas Negras
Las Narices del Teide
Parque Nacional del Teide
Puerto de las Cañadas
TF-38
Chío
Mirador de Chio
TF-38
Mña. del Cedro
2265
Chiguergue
Los Pajares
TF-82
Parador
Los Roques de García
Mirador Boca de Tauce
Boca de Tauce
Llano de Ucana
Aripe
Chirche
TF-21
2050 m
Las Tabladas
Guía de Isora
Iglesia de la Virgen de la Luz
Zapato de la Reina
Mña. Gangarro
2195
El Sombrero
2534 m
4
El Jaral
TF-463
Bco. de Guía
Acojeja
2483
Mña. de Chasna
Charquetas
Tejina
1049 m
Las Fuentes
Corco
Tejina
Mña. Las Lajas
2148 m
TF-21
El Morro
Los Almacigos
Mña. Tresme
1663 m
Abama
Los Maquenes
TF-465
Vera de Erques
Tijoco de Arriba
Chasogo
Ricasa
TF-465
TF-585
Tijoco de Abajo
La Concepción
El Grillo
Erques
Hoya Grande
Ermita de San Roque
Vilaflor
40
TF-47
TF-583
Taucho
La Quinta
del Cangrejo
Casa de Don Luis
TF-82
TF-51
Ifonche
Mña. de los Listones
1405 m
Marazul
3
Puerto de los Mozos
Los Menores
Las Moraditas
Bco. del Infierno
Barranco del Infierno
Trevejos
Pozo
1295 m
Roque de los Brezos
1111 m
Armeñime
TF-563
Callao Salvaje
Playa Paraíso
El Roque
Iglesia de Santa Ursula
Roque Imoque
Urbanisation Marqués
TF-47
Adeje
Suarez
Escalona
Punta Negra
188
El Calabozo
TF-1
79
Jama
El Becerro
El Puertito
Adeje
Valle de San Lorenzo
El Pris
La Caleta
Fañabe
78
Roque del Conde
1001 m
Bco. del Rey
TF-51
Honduras
Punta de las Gaviotas
Casa Alta
TF-565
La Caleta
Ermita de San Sebastián
Vento
Arona
El Roque
Túnez
Casas de la Fuente
Tamaide
Playa del Duque
Bahía del Duque
San Eugenio Alto
Torviscas
Bahía del Duque
Torviscas Fañabe
Parque Ecológico Las Aguilas
Valle de San Lorenzo
Roque de Jama
La Hoya
Karting Las Américas
76
Playa de Fañabe
S. Eugenio/Aguapark
San Eugenio
Sabinita
Mirador de la Centinela
Playa de Puerto Colón
30
Aqualand Costa Adeje
Chayofa
Camel Park
TF-66
TF-486
Las Aguilas
Playa del Bobo
S. Eugenio
39
Siam Park
TF-28
Buzanada
2
36
Costa Adeje
Playa de las Américas
TF-657
Playas de Troya
28
Arona
Cabo Blanco
Aloe Park
Aldea Blanca
36
Las Américas
72
Los Cristianos
Las Madrigueras
Los Morritos
TF-655
Las Vivas
San Isidro
Las G
Punta del Camisón
Los Cristianos
Guaza
430 m
26
TF-1
25
Playa del Camisón
Valle San Lorenzo, Guaza, Los Cristianos
Parque de la Reina
Playa de Las Vistas
36
Chafiras
Guaza
Cañada Blanca
Playa de los Cristianos
TF-652
Santa Cruz de La Palma (La Palma)
Charco del Lino
TF-66
El Guincho
Alborada
TF-653
San Sebastian (Gomera)
Valverde (Hierro)
La Arenita
Malpasito
119 m
Palm-Mar
TF-652
TF-66
Rasca
153 m
El Fraile
El Porís
Chaparral
Punta de la Rasca
Las Galletas
Ten-Bel
1
Los Bebederos
42
Costa del S
Faro de la Rasca
Piedra Mena
Punta Negra
Punta Salema
Playa de la Ballena
A
B
C

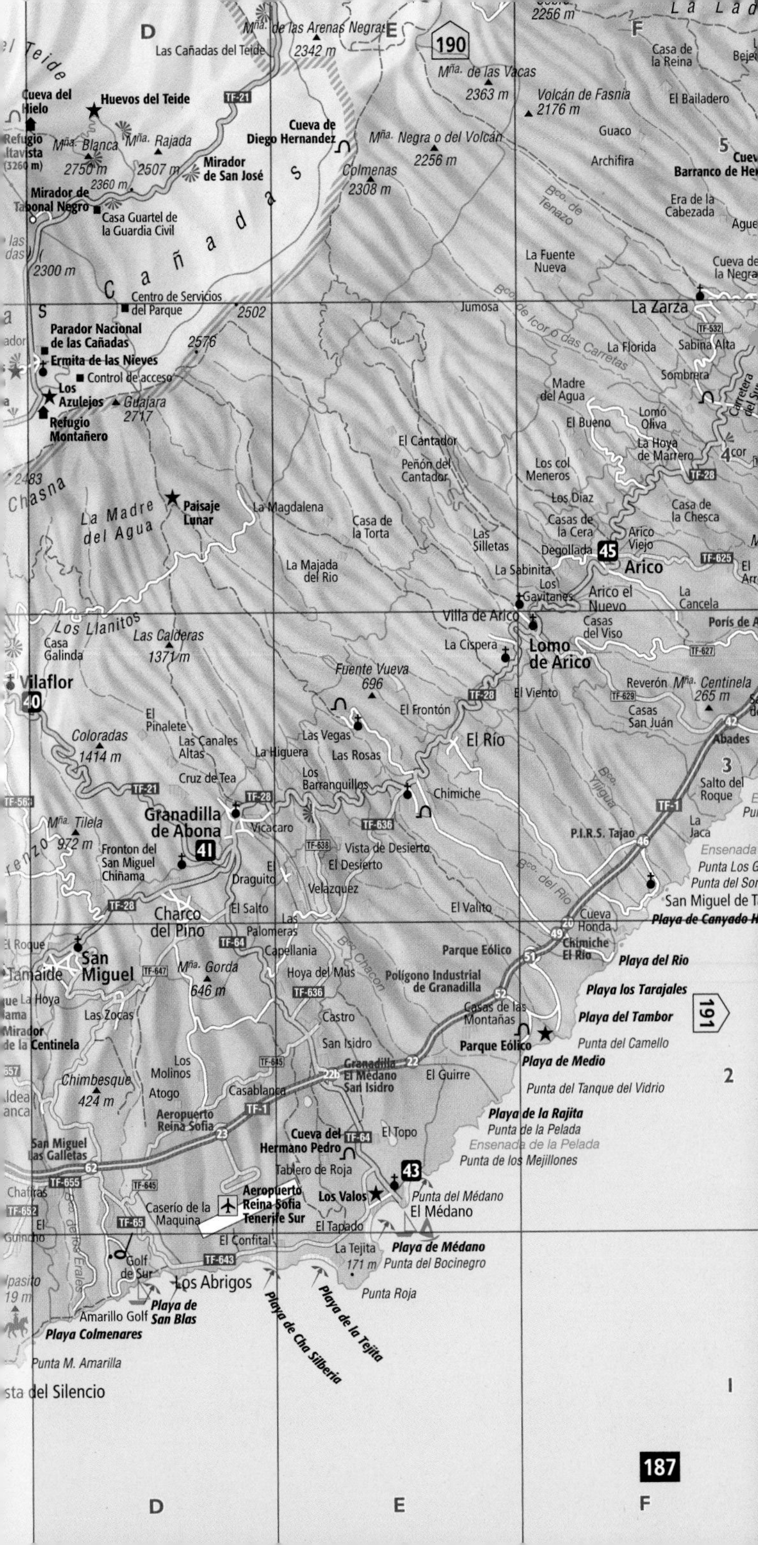
D
E
F
190
Las Cañadas del Teide
Mña. de las Arenas Negras
2342 m
Mña. de las Vacas
2363 m
Volcán de Fasnia
2176 m
Casa de la Reina
El Bailadero
Cueva del Hielo
Huevos del Teide
Refugio Altavista (3260 m)
Mña. Blanca
2750 m
Mña. Rajada
2507 m
Mirador de San José
Cueva de Diego Hernandez
Mña. Negra o del Volcán
2256 m
Guaco
Archifira
Colmenas
2308 m
Mirador de Tabonal Negro
Casa Guartel de la Guardia Civil
2300 m
Cañadas
Centro de Servicios del Parque
2502
La Fuente Nueva
Jumosa
La Zarza
Parador Nacional de las Cañadas
Ermita de las Nieves
Control de acceso
Los Azulejos
Guajara
2717
Refugio Montañero
2576
La Florida
Sabina Alta
Sombrera
Madre del Agua
El Bueno
Lomo Oliva
La Hoya de Marrero
El Cantador
Peñon del Cantador
Los col Meneros
Los Diaz
Casa de la Chesca
Chasna
La Madre del Agua
Paisaje Lunar
La Magdalena
Casa de la Torta
Casas de la Cera
Las Silletas
Arico Viejo
Degollada
45
Arico
La Majada del Rio
La Sabinita
Los Gavitanes
Arico el Nuevo
La Cancela
Villa de Arico
Casas del Viso
Poris de A
Los Llanitos
Las Calderas
1371 m
Casa Galinda
La Cispera
Lomo de Arico
Vilaflor
40
Fuente Vueva
696
Reverón
Mña. Centinela
265 m
El Viento
El Frontón
Casas San Juán
Abades
El Pinalete
Coloradas
1414 m
Las Canales Altas
La Higuera
Las Vegas
Las Rosas
El Río
Cruz de Tea
Los Barranquillos
Chimiche
Salto del Roque
La Jaca
Granadilla de Abona
Vicacaro
Mña. Tilela
972 m
Fronton del San Miguel Chiñama
41
Vista de Desierto
El Desierto
P.I.R.S. Tajao
Ensenada
Punta Los
Punta del Sor
San Miguel de T
El Draguito
Velazquez
El Salto
El Valito
Charco del Pino
Las Palomeras
Cueva Honda
Playa de Canyado H
San Miguel
Capellania
Mña. Gorda
646 m
Parque Eólico
Chimiche
El Rio
Playa del Rio
Hoya del Mus
Poligono Industrial de Granadilla
Playa los Tarajales
La Hoya
Las Zocas
Mirador de la Centinela
Casas de las Montañas
Playa del Tambor
191
Castro
San Isidro
Parque Eólico
Punta del Camello
Playa de Medio
Los Molinos
Atogo
Chimbesque
424 m
Granadilla El Médano San Isidro
El Guirre
Punta del Tanque del Vidrio
Casablanca
Aeropuerto Reina Sofia
Playa de la Rajita
Punta de la Pelada
Ensenada de la Pelada
Punta de los Mejillones
San Miguel Las Galletas
Cueva del Hermano Pedro
El Topo
Tablero de Roja
43
Los Valos
Punta del Médano
El Médano
Caserío de la Maquina
Aeropuerto Reina Sofia Tenerife Sur
El Tapado
El Confital
La Tejita
171 m
Playa de Médano
Punta del Bocinegro
Golf de Sur
Los Abrigos
Punta Roja
Playa de San Blas
Amarillo Golf
Playa Colmenares
Playa de Cha Silberia
Playa de la Tejita
Punta M. Amarilla
Costa del Silencio
TF-21
TF-28
TF-532
TF-625
TF-627
TF-629
TF-1
TF-636
TF-638
TF-64
TF-647
TF-645
TF-655
TF-652
TF-65
TF-643
1
2
3
4
5

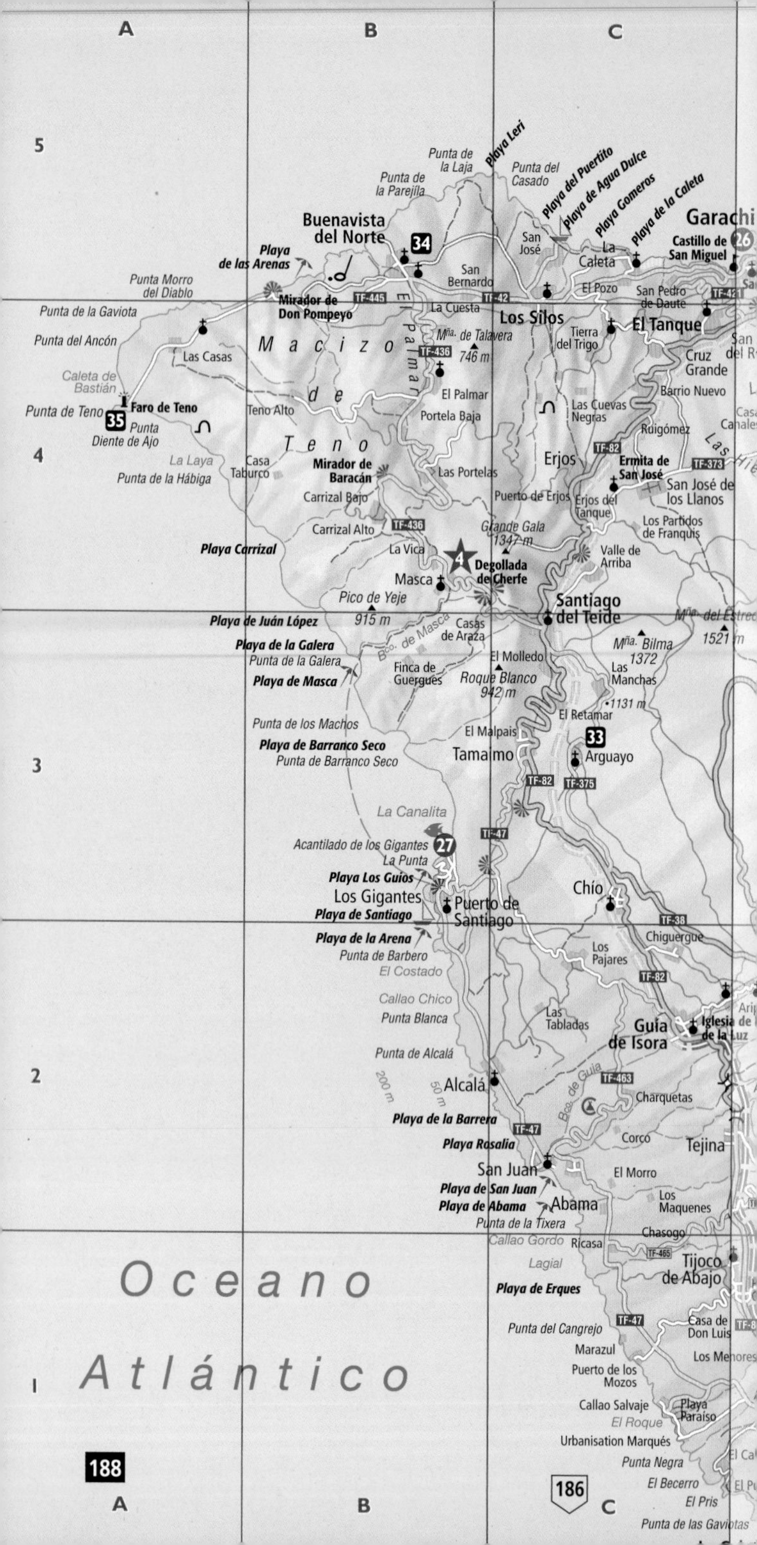
A
B
C
5
4
3
2
1
Punta de la Laja
Playa Leri
Punta de la Parejila
Punta del Casado
Playa del Puertito
Playa de Agua Dulce
Playa Gomeros
Playa de la Caleta
Garachi
Buenavista del Norte
34
Playa de las Arenas
San José
La Caleta
Castillo de San Miguel
26
San Bernardo
Punta Morro del Diablo
Mirador de Don Pompeyo
TF-445
TF-42
El Pozo
San Pedro de Daute
TF-421
Punta de la Gaviota
La Cuesta
Los Silos
El Tanque
Punta del Ancón
Las Casas
Macizo de Teno
El Palmar
Mña. de Talavera
746 m
TF-436
Tierra del Trigo
Cruz Grande
Caleta de Bastián
El Palmar
Barrio Nuevo
Punta de Teno
Faro de Teno
35
Teno Alto
Portela Baja
Las Cuevas Negras
Punta Diente de Ajo
Ruigómez
La Laya
Casa Taburco
Erjos
TF-82
Ermita de San José
TF-373
Punta de la Hábiga
Mirador de Baracán
Las Portelas
San José de los Llanos
Carrizal Bajo
Puerto de Erjos
Erjos del Tanque
Carrizal Alto
TF-436
Grande Gala
1347 m
Los Partidos de Franquis
Playa Carrizal
La Vica
4
Degollada de Cherfe
Valle de Arriba
Masca
Pico de Yeje
915 m
Santiago del Teide
Playa de Juán López
Casas de Araza
1521 m
Playa de la Galera
Bco. de Masca
Mña. Bilma
1372
Punta de la Galera
El Molledo
Playa de Masca
Finca de Guergues
Roque Blanco
942 m
Las Manchas
1131 m
El Retamar
Punta de los Machos
El Malpais
33
Playa de Barranco Seco
Tamaimo
Arguayo
Punta de Barranco Seco
TF-82
TF-375
La Canalita
TF-47
Acantilado de los Gigantes
27
La Punta
Playa Los Guíos
Chío
Los Gigantes
Puerto de Santiago
Playa de Santiago
TF-38
Playa de la Arena
Chiguergue
Punta de Barbero
Los Pajares
El Costado
TF-82
Callao Chico
Punta Blanca
Las Tabladas
Guía de Isora
Iglesia de la Luz
Punta de Alcalá
Alcalá
200 m
50 m
Bco. de Guía
TF-463
Charquetas
Playa de la Barrera
TF-47
Corco
Playa Rosalía
Tejina
San Juan
El Morro
Playa de San Juan
Playa de Abama
Abama
Los Maquenes
Punta de la Tixera
Callao Gordo
Ricasa
Chasogo
TF-465
Lagial
Tijoco de Abajo
Oceano
Playa de Erques
Punta del Cangrejo
TF-47
Casa de Don Luis
Marazul
Los Menores
Atlántico
Puerto de los Mozos
Callao Salvaje
Playa Paraíso
El Roque
Urbanisation Marqués
Punta Negra
El Becerro
El Pris
Punta de las Gaviotas
186

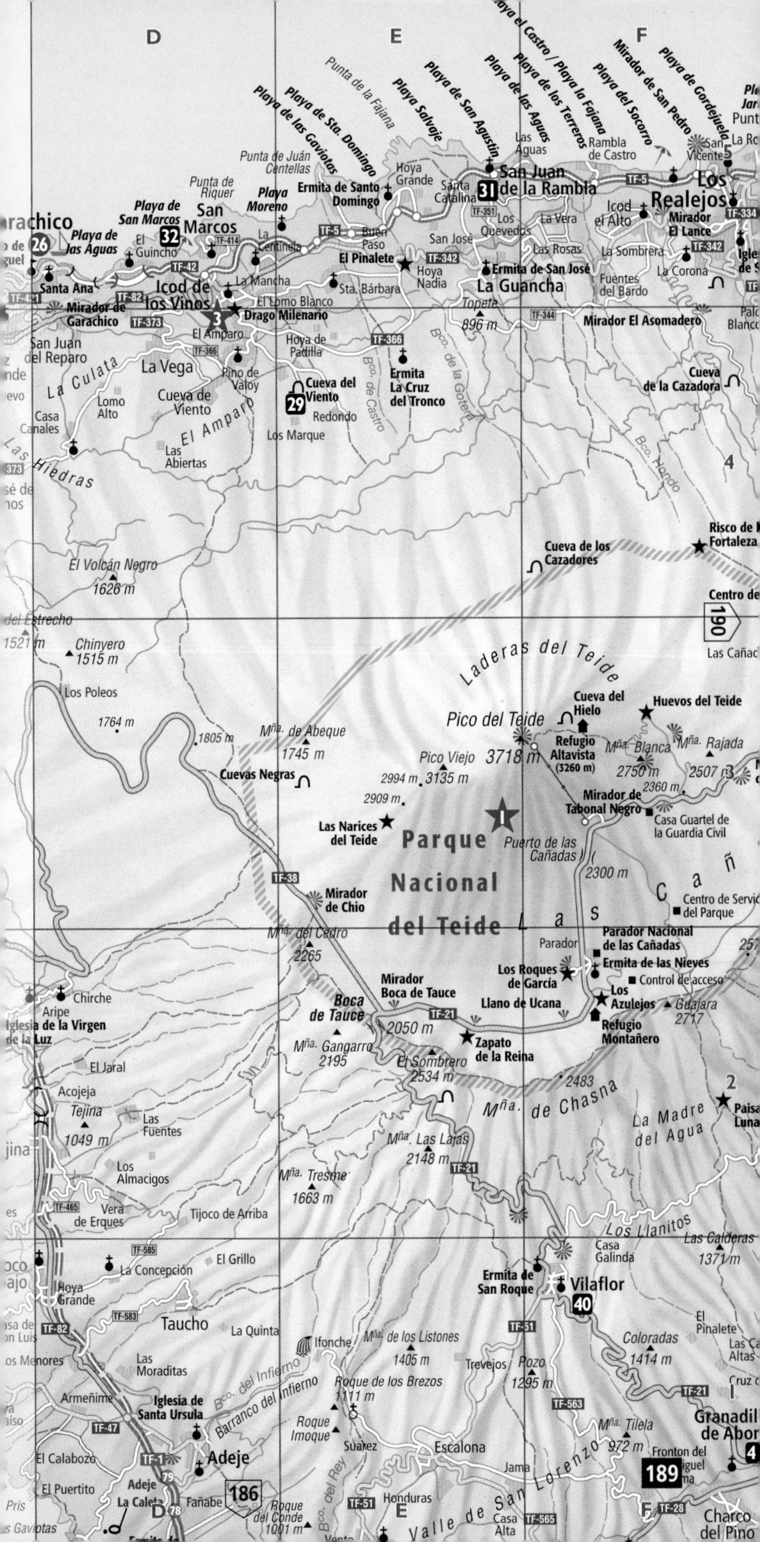

D
E
F
Playa de las Gaviotas
Playa de Sta. Domingo
Playa Salvaje
Playa de San Agustín
Playa de las Aguas
Playa de los Terreros
Playa el Castro / Playa la Fajana
Playa del Socorro
Mirador de San Pedro
Playa de Gordejuela
Punta de la Fajana
Punta de Juán Centellas
Punta de Riquer
Playa Moreno
Playa de San Marcos
San Marcos
Garachico
Playa de las Aguas
Santa Ana
Mirador de Garachico
Icod de los Vinos
Drago Milenario
El Amparo
San Juan del Reparo
La Vega
La Culata
Lomo Alto
Casa Canales
Cueva de Viento
El Amparo
Las Abiertas
Las Hiedras
Pino de Valoy
Hoya de Padilla
Cueva del Viento
Redondo
Los Marque
Ermita La Cruz del Tronco
Ermita de Santo Domingo
Hoya Grande
Santa Catalina
San Juan de la Rambla
Las Aguas
Rambla de Castro
San Vicente
Los Realejos
Icod el Alto
Mirador El Lance
La Corona
La Sombrera
Fuentes del Bardo
La Guancha
Ermita de San José
Las Rosas
La Vera
Los Quevedos
San José
Hoya Nadia
El Pinalete
Buen Paso
La Centinela
La Mancha
Sta. Bárbara
El Lomo Blanco
Topete 896 m
Mirador El Asomadero
Cueva de la Cazadora
Bco. Hondo
Bco. de la Gotera
Bco. de Castro
El Guincho
Risco de la Fortaleza
Cueva de los Cazadores
El Volcán Negro 1626 m
del Estrecho 1521 m
Chinyero 1515 m
Los Poleos
1764 m
1805 m
Mña. de Abeque 1745 m
Cuevas Negras
Laderas del Teide
Centro de
190
Las Cañad
Pico del Teide 3718 m
Cueva del Hielo
Huevos del Teide
Refugio Altavista (3260 m)
Mña. Blanca 2750 m
Mña. Rajada 2507 m
2360 m
Pico Viejo 3135 m
2994 m
2909 m
Mirador de Tabonal Negro
Casa Guartel de la Guardia Civil
Las Narices del Teide
Parque Nacional del Teide
Puerto de las Cañadas
2300 m
Las Cañ
Mirador de Chio
Centro de Servic del Parque
Mña. del Cedro 2265
Parador
Parador Nacional de las Cañadas
Ermita de las Nieves
Control de acceso
Los Roques de García
Los Azulejos
Refugio Montañero
Guajara 2717
Mirador Boca de Tauce
Boca de Tauce
Llano de Ucana
2050 m
Zapato de la Reina
Mña. Gangarro 2195
El Sombrero 2534 m
2483
Mña. de Chasna
La Madre del Agua
Paisa Luna
Chirche
Aripe
Iglesia de la Virgen de la Luz
El Jaral
Acojeja
Tejina 1049 m
Las Fuentes
Los Almacigos
Mña. Las Lajas 2148 m
Mña. Tresme 1663 m
Vera de Erques
Tijoco de Arriba
Los Llanitos
Las Calderas 1371 m
Casa Galinda
El Grillo
La Concepción
Hoya Grande
Ermita de San Roque
Vilaflor
Taucho
La Quinta
El Pinalete
Las Moraditas
Ifonche
Mña. de los Listones 1405 m
Trevejos
Pozo 1295 m
Coloradas 1414 m
Armeñime
Iglesia de Santa Ursula
Bco. del Infierno
Barranco del Infierno
Roque de los Brezos 1111 m
Roque Imoque
Suarez
Escalona
Mña. Tilela 972 m
Granadilla de Abona
Frontón del
El Calabozo
Adeje
El Puertito
La Caleta
Fañabe
186
Roque del Conde 1001 m
Bco. del Rey
Honduras
Valle de San Lorenzo
Jama
Casa Alta
Charco del Pino
189
Los Menores
TF-5
TF-42
TF-82
TF-373
TF-366
TF-414
TF-342
TF-344
TF-351
TF-334
TF-38
TF-21
TF-465
TF-585
TF-583
TF-51
TF-563
TF-47
TF-1
TF-565
TF-28

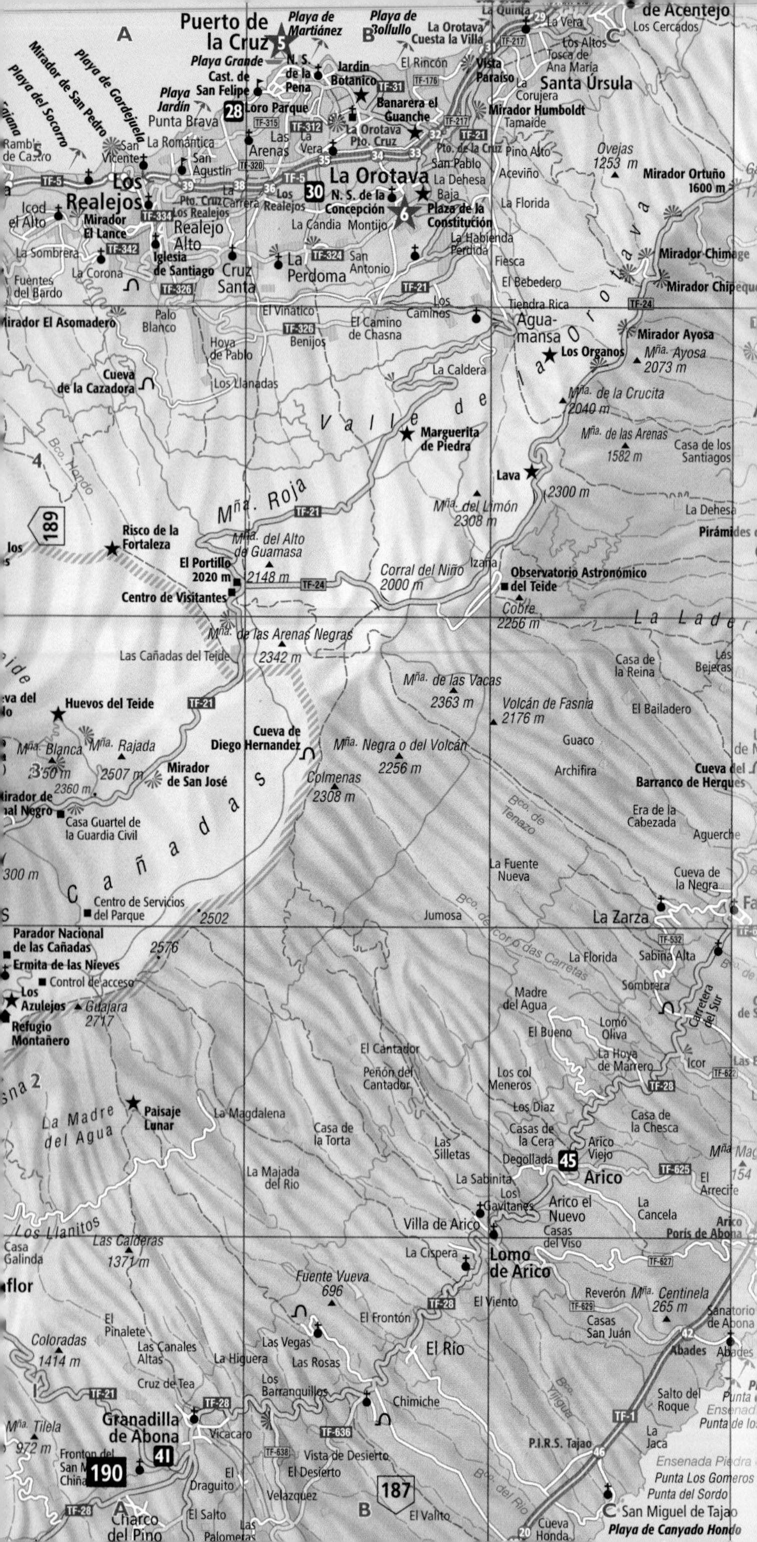

A
B
C
Puerto de la Cruz
Playa de Martiánez
Playa de Bollullo
La Orotava Cuesta la Villa
La Quinta
La Vera
de Acentejo
Los Cercados
Los Altos
Tosca de Ana María
Santa Úrsula
Playa de Gordejuela
Mirador de San Pedro
Playa del Socorro
Playa Grande
N. S. de la Pena
Jardín Botanico
El Rincón
Vista Paraíso
La Corujera
Cast. de San Felipe
Playa Jardín
Loro Parque
Banarera el Guanche
Mirador Humboldt
Tamaide
Punta Brava
La Romántica
San Vicente
Las Arenas
La Vera
La Orotava Pto. Cruz
Pto. de la Cruz
Pino Alto
Rambla de Castro
San Agustín
San Pablo
Ovejas 1253 m
Mirador Ortuño 1600 m
Los Realejos
La Orotava
La Dehesa
Aceviño
Icod el Alto
Pto. Cruz Los Realejos
La Carrera
Los Realejos
N. S. de la Concepción
Baja
Plaza de la Constitución
La Florida
Mirador El Lance
Realejo Alto
La Candia
Montijo
La Habienda Perdida
La Sombrera
Iglesia de Santiago
Cruz Santa
La Perdoma
San Antonio
Fiesca
Mirador Chimague
La Corona
Fuentes del Bardo
El Bebedero
Mirador Chipeque
Tiendra Rica
Palo Blanco
El Vinatico
Los Caminos
Mirador El Asomadero
Benijos
El Camino de Chasna
Aguamansa
Mirador Ayosa
Hoya de Pablo
Los Organos
Mña. Ayosa 2073 m
Cueva de la Cazadora
Los Llanadas
La Caldera
Mña. de la Crucita 2040 m
Valle de la Orotava
Marguerita de Piedra
Mña. de las Arenas 1582 m
Casa de los Santiagos
Bco. Hondo
Lava
2300 m
Mña. Roja
Mña. del Limón 2308 m
La Dehesa
Pirámides
189
Risco de la Fortaleza
Mña. del Alto de Guamasa
El Portillo 2020 m
2148 m
Corral del Niño 2000 m
Izaña
Observatorio Astronómico del Teide
Centro de Visitantes
Cobre 2256 m
La Ladera
Mña. de las Arenas Negras
Las Cañadas del Teide
2342 m
Casa de la Reina
Las Bejeras
Mña. de las Vacas 2363 m
Huevos del Teide
Volcán de Fasnia 2176 m
El Bailadero
Cueva de Diego Hernandez
Mña. Blanca
Mña. Rajada
Mña. Negra o del Volcán 2256 m
Guaco
2750 m
2507 m
Mirador de San José
Archifira
Cueva del Barranco de Herques
2360 m
Colmenas 2308 m
Casa Guartel de la Guardia Civil
Bco. de Tenazo
Era de la Cabezada
Aguerche
Cañadas
300 m
La Fuente Nueva
Cueva de la Negra
Centro de Servicios del Parque
2502
Jumosa
La Zarza
Parador Nacional de las Cañadas
2576
Bco. de Coro das Carretas
La Florida
Sabina Alta
Ermita de las Nieves
Control de acceso
Madre del Agua
Sombrera
Los Azulejos
Guajara 2717
Carretera del Sur
Refugio Montañero
El Bueno
Lomo Oliva
El Cantador
La Hoya de Marrero
Peñón del Cantador
Los col Meneros
Icor
Los Diaz
Paisaje Lunar
La Madre del Agua
La Magdalena
Casa de la Torta
Casas de la Cera
Arico Viejo
Casa de la Chesca
Las Silletas
Degollada
45
Arico
Mña.
154
La Majada del Rio
La Sabinita
Los Gavitanes
Arico el Nuevo
El Arrecife
La Cancela
Los Llanitos
Las Calderas 1371 m
Villa de Arico
Casas del Viso
Arico
Porís de Abona
Casa Galinda
La Cispera
Lomo de Arico
Fuente Vueva 696
El Viento
Reverón
Mña. Centinela 265 m
Sanatorio de Abona
El Pinalete
El Frontón
Casas San Juán
Coloradas 1414 m
Las Canales Altas
Las Vegas
El Río
42
Abades
La Higuera
Las Rosas
Cruz de Tea
Los Barranquillos
Chimiche
Salto del Roque
Bco. Yfigue
Granadilla de Abona
Vicacaro
Mña. Tilela 972 m
P.I.R.S. Tajao
La Jaca
41
Vista de Desierto
El Desierto
Ensenada Piedra
Punta Los Gomeros
Punta del Sordo
190
El Draguito
Velazquez
187
Bco. del Rio
San Miguel de Tajao
Playa de Canyado Hondo
Charco del Pino
El Salto
Las Palomeras
El Valito
Cueva Honda

Montaña Grande
1120 m
Mña Cabeza de Toro
1500 m
Las Raíces
Las Lagunetas
193
Casas Las Señas
Las Barreras
Tablero
Santa María del Mar
Azabe
Playa del Muerto
Punta de la Encedida
Santa María del Mar
El Pilar
Machado
La Suerte del Espino
San Isidro
Nuestra Señora del Rosario
Playa Berruguete
Radazul
194
Tabaiba
Playa de la Nea
Bosque de la Esperanza
Bco. Hondo
582 m
Lomo Chupadero
Barranco Hondo
Urban. Radazul
Punta de Guadamojete
Barranco Hondo
Gaitero
1747 m
Bco. de Araca
Punta del Morro
Igueste
Las Caletillas
Las Caletillas
Playa de las Caletas
Guaya
Araya
Las Arenitas
Club Nautico
El Charcito
Punta Larga
Playa de las Arenas
Los Loros
Las Cuevecitas
Candelaria
Carretera del Sur
Basilica de la Virgen
Candelaria
38
Playa de Samanrines
Malpaís
Arafo
Playa de la Viuda
Lomo del Caballo
Poligono Industrial
Chogo
Topo Negro
La Hidalga
El Socorro
Playa de la Entrada
Medio Camino
Arafo
Icoro
Chacaica
Las Cañadas
Playa de Lima
La Planta
Punta de la Entrada
Pirámides de Güímar
37
Güímar
Volcan de Güímar
276 m
Malpais
Salamanca
El Riego
Punta de la Cruz
Puerto de Güímar
Las Rosas
Bco. Fregenal
Las Guirres
46
Anocheza
Alta Vista
Mirador de Don Martín
Puerto de Güímar
Morra de los Bosios
Pájara
Hoya del Pozo
La Medida
Playa de Arriba o las Bajas
El Pelao
La Tosea
Punta Gache
Lomo de Mena
Punta Prieta
La Caleta
Playa de la Caleta
La Caleta
El Escobonal
Playa Barranco Arriba
La Corujera
Cano
Playa de la Margallera
El Escobonal
El Tablado
Playa de Chimaje
Punta del Porís
El Tablado
Bco. de Herques
Fasnia
Fasnia
Los Roques
Playa de Toquerque
Punta del Abrigo
Bco. de San Joaquín
Los Roques
Cambio de Sentido
Playa del Abrigo
Punta la Canal
Las Eras
Punta de Honduras
Las Eras
Playa Honda
Cuevas de las Ricas
Playa las Carretas
Oceano
Mña Magua
154
Playa de las Ceras
Punta del Rineón
Atlántico
El Arrecife
Playa de la Caleta
Arico
Abona
44
Punta la Ternera
Porís de Abona
Puerto de Abona
Playa Grande
Punta de los Requetés
Sanatorio de Abona
Faro de Abona
Casas El Faro
Punta de Cueva Nueva
Abades
Playa de los Abrigos
Playa del Ganado
Punta de Abades
Ensenada de Abades
Punta de los Jureles
D
E
F
5
4
3
2
1

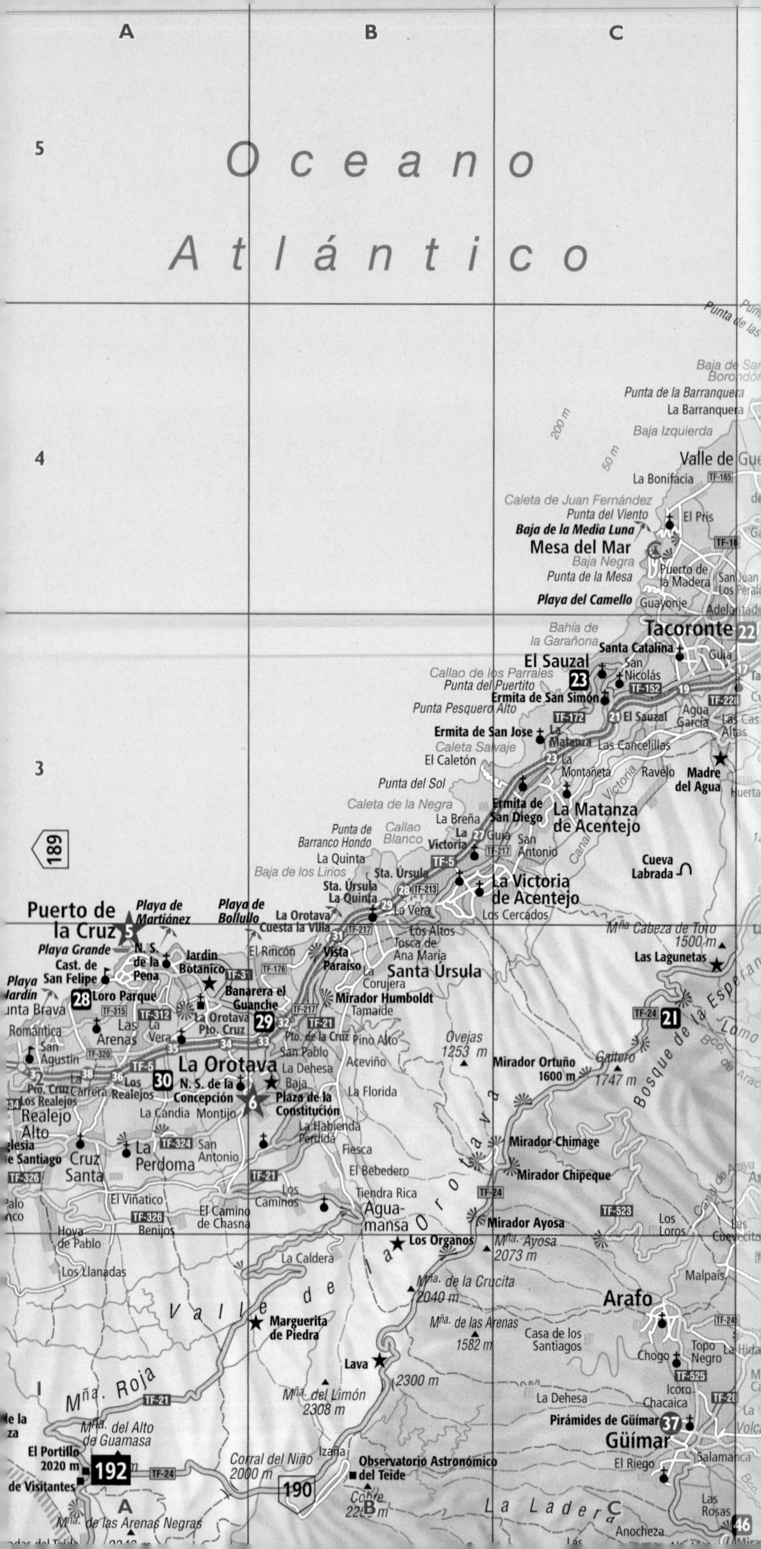

A
B
C
5
4
3
Oceano
Atlántico
Punta de la Barranquera
La Barranquera
Baja Izquierda
200 m
50 m
Valle de Gue
La Bonifacia
TF-165
Caleta de Juan Fernández
Punta del Viento
El Pris
Baja de la Media Luna
Mesa del Mar
TF-16
Baja Negra
Punta de la Mesa
Puerto de la Madera
San Juan
Playa del Camello
Guayonje
Bahía de la Garañona
Tacoronte
22
Santa Catalina
El Sauzal
San Nicolás
23
Guía
Callao de los Parrales
Punta del Puertito
TF-152
19
Ermita de San Simón
TF-228
Punta Pesquero Alto
TF-172
21
El Sauzal
Agua García
Las Cas Altas
Ermita de San Jose
La Matanza
Caleta Salvaje
Las Cancelillas
El Caletón
23
La Montañeta
Ravelo
Madre del Agua
Punta del Sol
Huerta
Caleta de la Negra
Ermita de San Diego
La Matanza de Acentejo
Punta de Barranco Hondo
Callao Blanco
La Breña
La Victoria
27
Guía
San Antonio
TF-217
Canal de la Victoria
189
La Quinta
TF-5
Cueva Labrada
Baja de los Lirios
Sta. Úrsula
Sta. Úrsula La Quinta
28
TF-213
La Victoria de Acentejo
Puerto de la Cruz
5
Playa de Martiánez
Playa de Bollullo
La Orotava Cuesta la Villa
29
La Vera
Los Cercados
Mña Cabeza de Toro 1500 m
Playa Grande
N. S. de la Pena
Jardin Botanico
TF-31
El Rincón
TF-176
TF-217
31
Vista Paraíso
Los Altos
Tosca de Ana María
Santa Úrsula
Las Lagunetas
Cast. de San Felipe
La Corujera
Playa Jardín
28
Loro Parque
Banarera el Guanche
Mirador Humboldt
Tamaide
TF-24
21
Punta Brava
TF-315
TF-312
La Orotava Pto. Cruz
29
32
TF-217
TF-21
Romántica
Las Arenas
La Vera
34
33
Pto. de la Cruz
Pino Alto
Ovejas 1253 m
San Agustín
TF-320
35
San Pablo
Aceviño
Mirador Ortuño 1600 m
Gaitero 1747 m
Bosque de la Esperanza
Lomo
Bco. de Araca
32
38
TF-5
36
La Orotava
La Dehesa
Pto. Cruz
La Carrera
Los Realejos
30
N. S. de la Concepción
6
Baja
La Florida
Plaza de la Constitución
Los Realejos
Realejo Alto
La Candia
Montijo
La Habienda Perdida
Iglesia de Santiago
Cruz Santa
La Perdoma
TF-324
San Antonio
Fiesca
Mirador Chimage
TF-326
TF-21
El Bebedero
Mirador Chipeque
El Viñatico
Los Caminos
Tiendra Rica
TF-24
TF-326
El Camino de Chasna
Benijos
Agua-mansa
TF-523
Mirador Ayosa
Los Loros
Las Cuevecitas
Hoya de Pablo
Los Organos
Mña. Ayosa 2073 m
La Caldera
Los Llanadas
Mña. de la Crucita 2040 m
Malpaís
Valle de la Orotava
Arafo
Marguerita de Piedra
Mña. de las Arenas 1582 m
Casa de los Santiagos
TF-245
Topo Negro
Chogo
La Hidalga
Lava
2300 m
TF-525
Mña. Roja
Mña. del Limón 2308 m
Icoro
Chacaica
TF-21
La Dehesa
Mña. del Alto de Guamasa
Pirámides de Güímar
37
Güímar
El Portillo 2020 m
192
TF-24
Corral del Niño 2000 m
Izaña
Observatorio Astronómico del Teide
El Riego
Salamanca
de Visitantes
190
Cobre 2200 m
La Ladera
Las Rosas
Mña. de las Arenas Negras
Anocheza
46

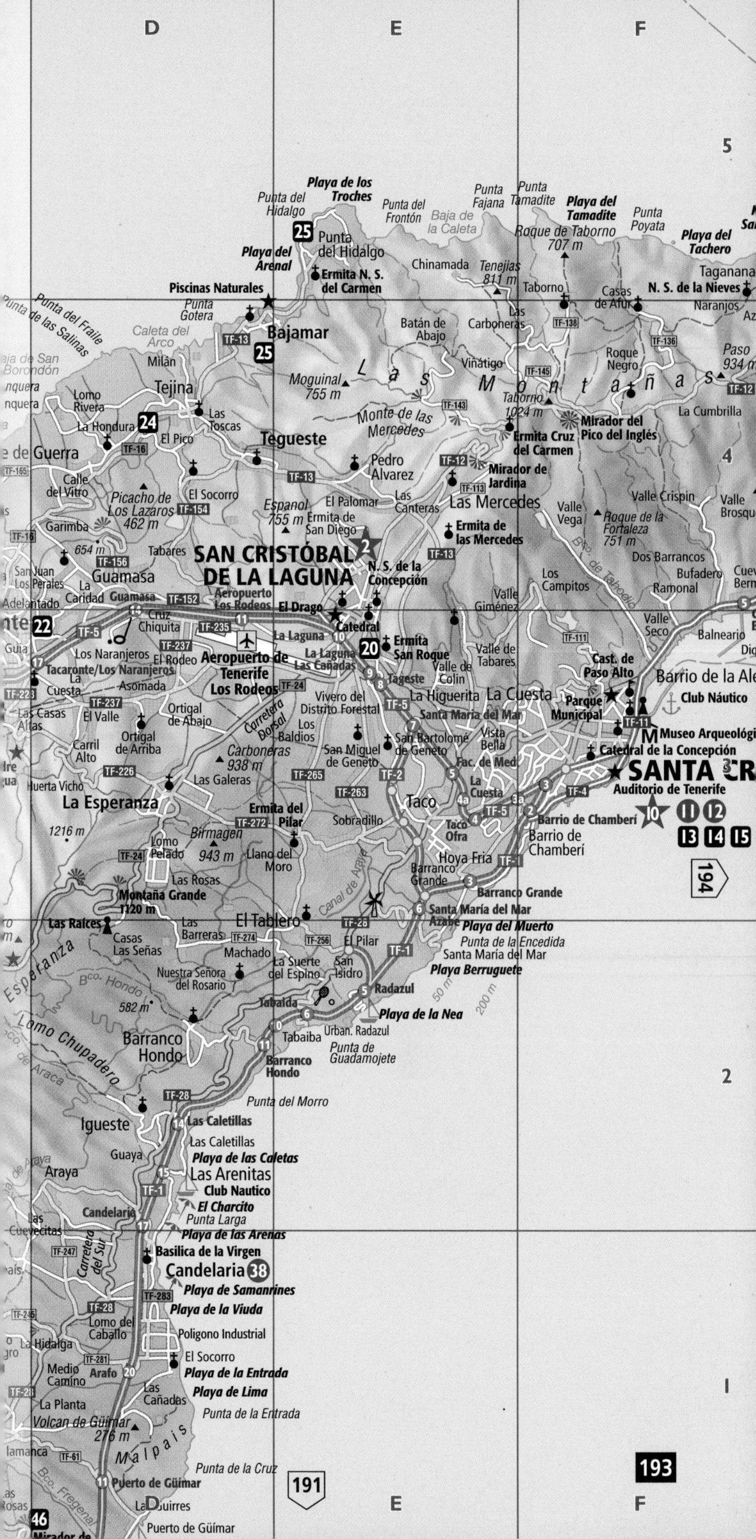

D
E
F
5
4
2
1
Playa de los Troches
Punta del Hidalgo
Punta del Frontón
Baja de la Caleta
Punta Fajana
Punta Tamadite
Playa del Tamadite
Punta Poyata
Playa del Tachero
Roque de Taborno 707 m
Playa del Arenal
Ermita N. S. del Carmen
Chinamada
Tenejías 811 m
Taborno
Casas de Afur
Taganana
N. S. de la Nieves
Naranjos
Piscinas Naturales
Punta Gotera
Bajamar
Punta del Fraile
Punta de las Salinas
Caleta del Arco
Batán de Abajo
Las Carboneras
Roque Negro
Paso 934 m
Milán
Moguinal 755 m
Las Montañas
Vinátigo
Taborno 1024 m
Tejina
Lomo Rivera
Las Toscas
La Hondura
El Pico
Tegueste
Monte de las Mercedes
Mirador del Pico del Inglés
Ermita Cruz del Carmen
La Cumbrilla
de Guerra
Pedro Alvarez
Mirador de Jardina
Calle del Vitro
Picacho de Los Lazaros 462 m
El Socorro
Espanol 755 m
El Palomar
Las Canteras
Las Mercedes
Valle Crispín
Valle Vega
Roque de la Fortaleza 751 m
Garimba
Ermita de San Diego
Ermita de las Mercedes
654 m
Tabares
SAN CRISTÓBAL DE LA LAGUNA
N. S. de la Concepción
Dos Barrancos
San Juan
Los Perales
Guamasa
La Caridad
Los Campitos
Bufadero
Ramonal
Adelantado
Aeropuerto Los Rodeos
El Drago
Valle Giménez
Cruz Chiquita
Catedral
La Laguna
Ermita San Roque
Valle Seco
Balneario
Guia
Los Naranjeros
El Rodeo
Aeropuerto de Tenerife Los Rodeos
La Laguna Las Cañadas
Valle de Tabares
Valle de Colín
Cast. de Paso Alto
Barrio de la Al
Tacaronte/Los Naranjeros
La Cuesta
Asomada
Tageste
La Higuerita
La Cuesta
Parque Municipal
Club Náutico
Las Casas Altas
El Valle
Ortigal de Abajo
Carretera Dorsal
Vivero del Distrito Forestal
Santa María del Mar
Ortigal de Arriba
Los Baldíos
San Bartolomé de Geneto
Vista Bella
Museo Arqueológi
Carril Alto
Carboneras 938 m
San Miguel de Geneto
Fac. de Med.
Catedral de la Concepción
SANTA CR
Huerta Vicho
Las Galeras
La Cuesta
Auditorio de Tenerife
La Esperanza
Taco
Barrio de Chamberí
Ermita del Pilar
Sobradillo
Taco Ofra
1216 m
Lomo Pelado
Birmagen 943 m
Llano del Moro
Hoya Fría
Barrio de Chamberí
194
Barranco Grande
Las Rosas
Montaña Grande 1120 m
Barranco Grande
Canal de Araya
Santa María del Mar
Azabe
Playa del Muerto
Las Raíces
Las Barreras
El Tablero
Punta de la Encedida
Casas Las Señas
Machado
El Pilar
Santa María del Mar
Esperanza
Nuestra Señora del Rosario
La Suerte del Espino
San Isidro
Playa Berruguete
Bco. Hondo
Radazul
582 m
Tabaida
50 m
200 m
Playa de la Nea
Lomo Chupadero
Tabaiba
Urban. Radazul
Barranco Hondo
Barranco Hondo
Punta de Guadamojete
Bco. de Araca
Punta del Morro
Igueste
Las Caletillas
Las Caletillas
Guaya
Playa de las Caletas
Araya
Las Arenitas
Club Nautico
El Charcito
Candelaria
Punta Larga
Las Cuevecitas
Playa de las Arenas
Carretera del Sur
Basilica de la Virgen
Candelaria
Playa de Samanrines
Playa de la Viuda
Lomo del Caballo
Poligono Industrial
La Hidalga
El Socorro
Medio Camino
Arafo
Playa de la Entrada
Playa de Lima
Las Cañadas
La Planta
Punta de la Entrada
Volcan de Güímar 276 m
Malpaís
Punta de la Cruz
Puerto de Güímar
Bco. Fregenal
La Guirres
Puerto de Güímar
Mirador de
191

A
B
C
5
Roque de Fuera
179 m
Roque de Tierra
Punto Bajo Las Palmas
Playa de El Draguillo
Faro de Anaga
Las Palmas
Roque Bermejo
Casas Blancas
Punta El Jurado
Punta Fajana
Punta Tamadite
Playa del Tamadite
Punta Poyata
Playa de San Roque
Playa de Benijo
Benijo
El Draguillo
Roque de Taborno
707 m
Playa del Tachero
Chamorga
Punta del Drago
Tenejias
811 m
Taganana
Almaciga
Lomo de las Bodegas
Playa de Anosmo
Taborno
Casas de Afur
N. S. de la Nieves
Roque de las Bodegas
Chinobre
910 m
Bco. de Anosma
Las Carboneras
Naranjos
Azanos
El Bailadero
Punta de Anaga
Roque Negro
Paso
934 m
Mña. de las Toscas
365 m
Playa de Ijuana
Vinátigo
Pico de Limante
798 m
Montañas de Anaga
Lomo Bermejo
Taborno
1024 m
Embalse de Acaimo
Punta de Antequera
Mirador del Pico del Inglés
La Cumbrilla
Semaforo
427 m
Playa de Antequera
Ermita Cruz del Carmen
563 m
Punta de Antequera
Tierras
Ensenada de Zapata
Mirador de Jardina
Roque Chiguel
695 m
Bco. de las Huertas
Igueste
El Roquete
Playa del Llano
Las Mercedes
Valle Crispin
Valle Brosque
Los Órganos
Playa del Burro
Playa Cueva de Agua
Ermita de las Mercedes
Valle Vega
Roque de la Fortaleza
751 m
El Roque
318
Playa de las Gaviotas
Punta de los Organos
Playa de las Teresitas
Cádiz
Dos Barrancos
Bufadero
Cueva Bermeja
San Andrés
Los Campitos
Bco. de Tahodio
Ramonal
Ist. Español de Oceanográfico
Punta del Valle de San Andrés
Valle Giménez
Las Palmas (Gran Canaria)
Valle Seco
Cueva Bermeja
Dársena Pesquera
Balneario
Valle de Tabares
Dique del Este
Cast. de Paso Alto
Barrio de la Alegría
Agaete (Gran Canaria)
La Cuesta
Parque Municipal
Club Náutico
Vista Bella
Museo Arqueológico
Catedral de la Concepción
SANTA CRUZ DE TENERIFE
La Cuesta
Auditorio de Tenerife
Barrio de Chamberí
Barrio de Chamberí
Barranco Grande
María del Mar
Playa del Muerto
Punta de la Encedida
Berruguete
200 m
193
2
Oceano
Atlántico
1
A
B
C

Index

Index

Index / Picture Credits

Picture Credits

AA/C. Jones: 26/27, 51, 52, 56, 57 (top), 59, 70, 71 (top), 71 (bottom), 73, 74, 75, 79, 80, 82, 88, 91 (top), 97, 105, 106, 120, 126/127, 130, 132, 133, 138, 146, 147 (top), 150, 153, 157, 166, 168, 172 (bottom), 177 (top)

AA/R. Moore: 14, 55 (bottom), 62 (bottom), 107, 122/123, 127, 131, 135, 169

AA/K. Paterson: 90

AA/C. Sawyer: 22, 60, 63, 78, 128, 134, 137, 147 (bottom), 148, 151, 152, 154, 155, 156, 172 (top)

AA/J. Tims: 55 (top), 61, 62 (top), 72, 77, 81, 104, 119 (bottom), 177 (bottom left), 177 (bottom right)

AFP/Getty: 13, 16

akg-images: 21

akg-images/Nimatallah: 20

Birgit Borowski: 165

DuMont Bildarchiv/Martin Sasse: 7, 8, 10/11, 15, 19, 28, 29, 48, 53, 54, 57 (bottom), 58, 76, 89, 96, 98, 99, 102, 103, 110, 119 (top), 125, 129, 130, 136, 149, 158

Rolf Goetz: 30/31

laif/Bernd Jonkmanns: 93

laif/Gerhard Westrich: 100/101

LOOK-foto/age fotostock: 17, 23, 108

LOOK-foto/Reinhard Dirscherl: 24, 25

LOOK-foto/Jürgen Richter: 4, 18, 32, 95

On the cover: huber images: Rainer Mirau (top), mauritius images/Imagebroker/ Stella (bottom), getty images (background)

1st Edition 2015

Worldwide Distribution: Marco Polo Travel Publishing Ltd
Pinewood, Chineham Business Park
Crockford Lane, Chineham
Basingstoke, Hampshire RG24 8AL, United Kingdom.

Authors: Damien Simonis, Lindsay Hunt ("Where to..."),
Lindsay Bennett, Rolf Goetz
Editor: Robert Fischer (www.vrb-muenchen.de)
Revised editing and translation: Sarah Trenker, Munich
Program supervisor: Birgit Borowski
Chief editor: Rainer Eisenschmid

Cartography: © MAIRDUMONT GmbH & Co. KG, Ostfildern
3D-illustrations: jangled nerves, Stuttgart

Printed in China

Despite all of our authors' thorough research, errors can creep in. The publishers do not accept any liability for this. Whether you want to praise, alert us to errors or give us a personal tip – please don't hesitate to email or post:

MARCO POLO Travel Publishing Ltd
Pinewood, Chineham Business Park
Crockford Lane, Chineham
Basingstoke, Hampshire RG24 8AL
United Kingdom
Email: sales@marcopolouk.com

10 REASONS
TO COME BACK AGAIN

1. The **best climate in the world** is worth a trip at any time of the year.
2. Tenerife's **volcanic legacy** is a constant source of inspiration.
3. The **excellent network of hiking trails** offers no end of attractive possibilities.
4. **Canarian flora** holds wonderful surprises in store all year round.
5. Time and again, the **Loro Parque** awaits you with stunning new attractions.
6. You will never get tired of watching the **sun set over the Masca Gorge**.
7. You won't find anywhere else where the *papas arrugadas con mojo verde* taste better.
8. The **traditional fish restaurants** on the waterfront beg to be visited time and again.
9. There is also a lot to explore on Tenerife's **neighbouring islands**.
10. **Canarian Carnival**: Once is never enough.